SOPHIA

John Pordage

Library of Congress Cataloging-in-Publication Data

Names: Pordage, John, 1607-1681, author.
Title: Sophia / by John Pordage ; translated by Alan G. Paddle.
Description: 1st [edition]. | Minneapolis, MN : Grailstone Press, 2017. |
  Series: The works of John Pordage ; Volume 1 | Translated into English from a German translation of an original English manuscript, written about 1675 and now lost.
Identifiers: LCCN 2016000211 | ISBN 9781596500204
Subjects: LCSH: Spiritual life. | Contemplation. | Mysticism. | Wisdom.
Classification: LCC BL624 .P647 2016 | DDC 248.2/2--dc23
LC record available at https://lccn.loc.gov/2016000211

Copyright © 2018 Grailstone Press / Versluis Media

All rights reserved. No part of this publication may be reproduced or transmitted in any form or by any means, electronic or mechanical, including photocopying, recording, or any information storage and retrieval system now known or to be invented, without permission in writing from the publisher, except by a reviewer who wishes to quote brief passages in a review.

The paper used in this publication meets the minimum requirements of ANSI/NISO Z39.48-1992 (R 1997) (Permanence of Paper).

Designed by Katie Grimes

A Grailstone Press Book
New Cultures Press
Minneapolis, Minnesota

Visit us at
www.newcultures.org

Printed and bound in the United States of America

20 19 18   1 2 3 4 5 6 7 8 9 10

CONTENTS

Introduction 1

Sophia.. 7

   General Contents of this Treatise 9

   General Contents of the Chapters 17

   The Treatise... 33

      Chapter 1.. 35

      Chapter 2 37

      Chapter 3 53

      Chapter 4 61

      Chapter 5.. 65

      Chapter 6 69

      Chapter 7..73

      Chapter 8 79

      Chapter 9 87

      Chapter 10..91

      Chapter 11 97

      Chapter 12 101

      Chapter 13 109

Chapter 14	139
Chapter 15	143
Chapter 16	157
Chapter 17	169
Chapter 18	179
Chapter 19	193
Chapter 20	215
Chapter 21	231
Chapter 22	253
Register of Words and Concepts	307
Register of Scriptural Passages	379

INTRODUCTION

It is with great pleasure that we introduce this first volume in a monumental translation project that will make available for the very first time in English previously untranslated works of John Pordage (1607–1681). Pordage wrote in the tradition of Jacob Boehme, the great German mystic (1575–1624), but Pordage's work is very clear, and reflects his own direct spiritual experiences and life. Pordage was a mystic in his own right, arguably the most important English mystic of the past few centuries. In what follows, I will briefly recount Pordage's life and work, and then introduce this particular volume, *Sophia*.

Pordage was born in 1607, the son of a London merchant family, entered Pembroke College, Oxford, in 1623, and may have received an M.D. at Oxford in 1640.[1] It is the case that Pordage practiced medicine,

---

[1] Works that refer to Pordage include Brian Gibbons, *Gender in Mystical and Occult Thought: Behmenism and its Development in England* (Cambridge: Cambridge University Press, 1996); Bernard Gorceix, *Flambée et Agonie, Mystiques du XVII siècle allemand* (Sisteron: Présence, 1977); Gorceix,*Johann Georg Gichtel, Théosophe D'Amsterdam* (Paris: L'Age d'Homme, 1975); Serge Hutin, *Les Disciples anglais de Jacob Boehme aux XVIIe et XVIIIe siécles* (Paris: Editions Denoël, 1960); Rufus Jones, *Studies in Mystical Religion* (London: Macmillan, 1909); Jones, *Spiritual Reformers in the Sixteenth and Seventeenth Centuries*

but primarily he was a mystic and spiritual guide as well as an author. Pordage entered into the holy orders of the Anglican Church and was made vicar of the parish of St Lawrence's at Reading in 1644, and under the sponsorship of Elias Ashmole, he was made rector of the well-to-do parish at Bradfield, a position he held until 1654.

During their time at Bradfield, Pordage, his wife Mary, and their children experienced an exceptional series of visions or apparitions. Pordage and his family were said to have seen angels and experienced demonic phenomena, and during the same period gathered a small group of theosophical practitioners. This group eventually included Thomas Bromley and Edmund Brice (Oxford-educated authors of significant theosophical works), and women like Anne Bathurst and Mrs. Joanna Oxenbridge, both upper-class women who wrote down their experiences in spiritual journals.

After a short time at Bradfield, Pordage was brought up on a collection of spurious charges that he disproved and from which he was exonerated. However, a few years later, he was brought up again

---

(London: Macmillan, 1914); Nils Thune, *The Behmenists and the Philadelphians: A Contribution to the Study of English Mysticism in the 17th and 18th Centuries* (Uppsala: Almquist and Wiksells, 1948); Arthur Versluis, *Theosophia: Hidden Dimensions of Christianity* (Hudson: Lindisfarne, 1994); Versluis, *Wisdom's Children: A Christian Esoteric Tradition* (Albany: SUNY, 1999); Versluis, ed., *Wisdom's Book: The Sophia Anthology* (St. Paul: Paragon House, 2000); and Versluis, ed., *The Wisdom of John Pordage* (St. Paul: New Grail, 2004).

INTRODUCTION

on similar charges and this time he was removed from his pastorate. For the remainder of his life, Pordage and his small group remained a private, almost monastic circle. Late in life, from the early 1670s until his death in 1681, Pordage wrote most of his books, which were based entirely on his own spiritual experience. Exemplary of these is the treatise *Sophia*, probably written in 1675, published here for the first time in English, as the original English manuscript was lost, and only a German translation has been available until the publication of this book you have in your hands.

In *Sophia*, Pordage presents his understanding of Sophanic visionary practice through twenty-two journal entries dated 21 June to 10 July. Pordage begins by explaining the nature of Sophia, or Divine Wisdom, as well as of the Light World, and the soul's hunger and thirst for spiritual truth. He discusses the meaning of the biblical references to the creation of a "new heaven and a new earth"; of the harmony of this world below and that above; of the Paradisical Eden in the Soul; and of the Quintessence or Elixir of Life. Pordage explains that the Holy Virgin reveals the New Jerusalem in the heart and soul of the newly reborn man, and discusses in detail the way that the contemplative process unfolds inwardly as a Sophianic revelation and creation in this life of the "magical earth" one can inhabit posthumously.

Sophia presents Pordage's keys to contemplative practice and the inner life. Not far into the treatise, Pordage observes that the contemplative may be inclined to hunt for the Wisdom of God and divine revelation somewhere else, and may be caught up in various belief structures. However, in due course, the wise realize that they don't need to seek to ascend, but rather only need to let themselves settle into their own inner Ground. If one relaxes inwardly, it is possible for the hidden door of Sophia to open, so one can then meet the Virgin Sophia directly and experience peace. They may also experience the *Abgrund* or *Chaos* in and of which Sophia creates the "new paradise" of a new inner earth. Much of the book centers on the nature of the hidden new inner eternal earth that is generated by and through the power of Sophia.

The inner "magical earth" is not a copy of the physical earth, but rather is a paradisal world of a different kind of materiality, which he calls a "principium" whose limits only God knows. The independent magical earth can be accessed anywhere on our earth, but it is hidden because it is not comprehensible by "stumplike" or truncated reason. Discursive reason alone cannot reach it, and Pordage even observes that it's better not to even mention it to those who belong to the schools or academies of the modern world, because they cannot comprehend it. Only the inner eye of the contemplative can see it.

The inner paradisal world comes into being, Pordage says, via the Trinity and the power of Sophia, which is like a mirror of the divine. What is more, this Sophianic world that he terms a magical earth existed before the Fall of man, before evil; it belongs more to eternity than to our mutable world. We could almost term it a paradisal "interworld." Pordage then discusses how our posthumous destiny should not be understood as a choice between only heaven and hell as two possibilities, because those who enter heaven must be spotless, and who fits that description in this world? Not so many. However, by explicating the verse that "in my Father's house are many dwellings," Pordage holds that the magical earth presents many possibilities for one's afterlife, and indeed, for posthumous spiritual growth therein.

However, there is also what Pordage terms a "dark magical fire" that came into being with the Fall, and in particular with the Fall of the angels. Those who dwell in this dark fire do suffer, but that is because they drew the dark principle into themselves and made themselves fit into that dark and wrathful world of suffering. For Pordage, our posthumous destiny is determined not by an outside judge but by we ourselves. We have the choice to enter a paradisal realm with which we are already familiar during life—or we can fill our earthly lives with wrath, evil, anxiety, and suffering, which then is what will greet us in eternity after death.

What Pordage is offering in *Sophia* is a kind of roadmap as to how, in this short human life, we might open our eye that sees into eternity. If we open this eye, we can experience for ourselves the paradisal earth after death, wherein after death we can continue to spiritually develop. Obviously, however, what Pordage presents is for many people a new kind of Christianity, not one based in confessional affirmations, but rather one based in the inner life. It is mysticism of a rare kind in the Western Christian world, one that is perhaps closer to Tibetan Buddhism or to the kind of imaginal religion described by Henry Corbin.

SOPHIA

In *Sophia*, Pordage shows how, by engaging in contemplative practice, one begins to develop while on earth, the light-body and "magical earth" in which one lives posthumously in bliss. Sophia is central to these inner processes as described by Pordage; this makes sense because just as creation came about through Sophia, so too inward contemplative praxis in Pordage's work has a Sophianic dimension because it is a symmetrical kind of new creation.

One comes to know Sophia through contemplative "sinking" of the consciousness, quieting and opening oneself to her; but one is also, in knowing Sophia, as Pordage makes clear, enabling the revelation of a new inner creative activity that has all manner of implications for one's afterlife. The Sophianic contemplative process awakens the eye that sees in eternity, and it allows one to generate the light-body that exists beyond time and space as we understand them in the physical cosmos. Sophia, for Pordage, is key to awakening to eternal life, that is, put another away, to life in timelessness.

I do not know any parallel to Pordage's *Sophia* in the Western religious tradition as a whole; it is a rare and profound work that now, for the first time since it was written in the 1670s, is again seeing the light of day in Pordage's native tongue. This is an important milestone. We hope this book will be of assistance to all those who wish to understand new and deeper aspects of the Christian mystical tradition.

—Arthur Versluis

SOPHIA

The Lovely Eternal Virgin of Divine Wisdom

OR

Wondrous Spiritual Discoveries and Revelations which Precious Wisdom has granted to a Holy Soul

Wherein Wisdom opens to the soul how it comes to perfectly discern its regeneration, enjoys essential communion with Wisdom, becomes capable of manifesting Wisdom's secrets, and finally attains to the wedding of the Lamb. Wisdom tells the soul what grave temptations it will experience at the hands of evil spirits if it does not remain watchful and awake against its enemies in the inner struggle. The soul is taught how it must endure Wisdom's smelting and purifying fire that tills out all astrayness and unpureness within it. It learns what soul and spirit are, how they are differentiated from one another, and what heaven and earth are within man. It learns what is involved in being a true philosopher. It comes to know what God, Wisdom and Wisdom's depths and keys are within the soul itself; also what Wisdom is and how it is differentiated from the Holy Trinity and is yet one with the Trinity.

In addition, how Man comes to understand that the outer Visible-world is a figure and Ur-Image for the invisible world within him; how heaven and earth must stand in a relationship of sweet harmony with each other if our inward vegetable, animal and mineral life is to be fruitful; how the Temple of the Lord, along with the Holy of Holies and its Holy Place in the soul and spirit have been overcome, devastated and destroyed by evil and unpure spirits; how the soul and spirit must be smelted around, purified and renewed before the upper Zion and the New Jerusalem can be revealed anew within them.

And finally, how those souls who die in the struggle before they have fully overcome their enemies are saved from the Dragon's anguish and hellish kingdom through the office of the Father and the Son. Although they are not able to immediately enter into illumination, they nevertheless enter the Father's house, the Light-world, in which there are many dwellings prepared for departed souls; what the primordial cause of evil is and what the significance is of the weighty soul-struggles of many mortals.

Written by John Pordage, M.D. in 1675

Translated from the manuscript and Published in Amsterdam in the Blessed Salvation Year of Our Lord 1699

GENERAL CONTENTS OF THIS TREATISE

Every soul that hopes to attain to divine Wisdom must possess an intense longing for it and pray to her unceasingly to receive it. The soul is both drawn and impelled to Wisdom by her great excellence and wondrous beauty, and particularly by the remembrance that she is an intimate connoisseur of the mysteries of the knowledge of God, both within and beyond nature, as well as a lover of all God's works.[2] This remembrance evokes a vehement, sharp desire in the ground of the soul to investigate this Spirit of Wisdom with great earnestness and to seek after her. It is God who brings this to pass, and who, although He is but One, can yet do all things and can make anew everything that is old.

This intensity and sharpness of spiritual desire in the soul's fiery ground is called a hunger and thirst in this treatise. Blessed are they who, like the author, are awakened and driven to love and seek Wisdom by this hunger and thirst, seeing that they long to slake and satisfy their anxious hunger and thirsty desire for the Divine Principle and the Light-World whose promise has been proclaimed here. However, it can take a very long time, sometimes more than twenty years for some persons, until the heavenly Virgin

---

[2] *Wisdom of Solomon* 8:4

of Divine Wisdom truly appears and reveals herself to the Soul-Spirit, in order to refresh, console and strengthen it in quiet and rest, as well as to assuage the strong impulse and intense drive of the soul-spirit's consuming hunger.

For after the soul has investigated many paths in the attempt to find Wisdom and, notwithstanding its keen searching and violent pursuit of her, has utterly failed and lost hope of finding her, it becomes weary and discouraged. When neither earnest prayer nor spiritual meditation has the slightest effect upon Wisdom—no pleading or desire seems to move Wisdom to descend and take up her abode in the heart of man—then the soul becomes utterly convinced that, by the power of its active or effectual spirit, or through the acts or impact of faith and hope (after it has spent a long time in the attempt), it possesses no ability to break down the wall that separates it from the Divine Principle. In addition, because the soul-spirit realizes that it has consistently been misled in its attempts to rise up out of itself, and has always missed its goal, it concludes that this cannot be the proper path, even though it has been deemed worthy to receive divine visions, revelations and ecstasies in the meanwhile. It comes to the conclusion that there can be no other way to attain to the Wisdom of God and its Principle than to descend and to sink down into its own inward ground and no longer to look outside itself.

When the soul-spirit finally sinks down into itself the gate of the Depth of Wisdom is immediately thrown open to it and it is led into the holy eternal Principle of the Light-World, into the wine cellar of the New Lebanon, into the magical earth in which the virgin Sophia, the virgin of the Wisdom of God appears to it. After the soul-spirit has discovered a little of the beauty of Sophia, she announces her message. This is the content of the next chapter, which conveys the deepest teaching concerning passive or patient stillness or calm of the soul. This chapter concludes with a hymn, wherein Wisdom teaches her disciples to sing praise for the great revelation of the New Creation and the planting of the New Paradise.

Perhaps the soul is not mindful and courageous enough always to return to its natural center, to allow itself, through this passive and patient stillness, to sink down and enter into the Abyss and Chaos from which this New Paradise has been created and formed, so that it does not rise up and fly away into the heights. If this self-elevation occurs, the soul is in danger of being fearfully tempted by an innumerable host of evil spirits from the dark world as well as from the elemental and astral principles. The Divine Protectress, however, appears again to the soul in its greatest extremity, and when that soul, with weakening power and sinking spirit, is struggling with the evil spirits and messengers of hell, she refreshes anew the exhausted, discouraged soul-spirit and reminds it of the lesson that she had given it to learn. She makes new promises to the soul and gives to the apprentice of her divine art and science a new teaching in which earth and heaven, or the lower and upper portions of the New Creation, are linked in a sweet harmony. This will be explained in the third chapter.

The third lesson deals with the true inward and

essential purification and also with the secret fire and oven of the wisdom of true disciples. This will be treated in the fourth chapter.

After this has taken place the spiritual artist or adept must trace and follow the entire process of the divine mystery and wait upon it. The first thing that he discovers and realizes after the creation and bringing forth of his new magical earth is the living, vital effect of this secret fire and hidden oven of the wise in the multifarious energies of vegetation or the vegetable life. On this account this process can be referred to as the planting of the inward Garden of Eden. In this Paradise the soul-spirit receives the chalice of Wisdom, which is its elixir of life and its vegetable quintessence. This is the content of the fifth chapter.

After this first formation and implantation of the paradisal earth in the mystical ground of the soul has taken place, something new is immediately discovered and revealed, namely the melting away and dissolution of the prior heaven in order that it might be renewed. This will be the material of the sixth chapter.

These then are the prerequisites and necessities that are required of a true philosopher. If he possesses these, Wisdom continues to instruct him in the following marvelous, strange circumstances. She does this by teaching him that a philosopher or lover of Divine Wisdom: 1) must come to know his own nature, which consists of heaven and earth; 2) must come to recognize God and Wisdom within himself; 3) must come to know the great depths or Abyss of Wisdom; and 4) must come to recognize the keys that give him the ability to open and close the great depths of Wisdom as well as all the secrets and wonders that lie hidden in her fiery regions. The seventh chapter treats of this.

Afterwards the soul-spirit is encouraged and impelled to a more exact contemplation of self-knowledge. Then Wisdom is presented to him in the form of a sphere. The harmony of the microcosm, or his small world, with the macrocosm, the large world, is demonstrated to him. This occurs in the eighth chapter. This is explained in more detail in chapter nine with regard to the visible heaven and its lights, and in chapter ten with regard to the visible earth. In chapter eleven a fore-image of this process is presented in 1) the vegetable realm and 2) the animal realm, while a fore-image in the mineral realm is presented in chapter twelve. These things are curious indeed!

In chapter thirteen there follows a rather extensive description of the small human globe and its fallen, broken condition. First we will look at the terrestrial globe and then, in chapter fourteen, the celestial sphere. Here we will cite and explain many passages from the biblical prophets, particularly from the *Revelation* of Saint John the Divine.

Further, we will describe the state of their renewal in a most particular, precise way. We will examine the celestial sphere in chapter fifteen and the terrestrial globe in chapter sixteen. This examination will occur largely in terms of revealing the secret meanings of Holy Scripture.

In the following chapters the Spirit of Wisdom guides its apprentice to the various gates, displays them to him and hands him the keys with which he may open those gates.

The first gate to which she brings him is called the Gate of Conviction. This gate is different from the previous convictions that had taken place during the dispensations or service of the Father and the Son. This gate is opened up in the seventeenth chapter. During this discussion we will also show what the state and habitation is of those souls who have departed this life during the dispensations and service of the Father and the Son and have, therefore, not attained the third and final service.

In the eighteenth chapter Wisdom opens to him the next gate, which is called the Gate of Destruction or Purification. It is also the first gate of renewal, through which Wisdom teaches him wherein the service of John the Baptist and Elijah consists.

The third gate of Wisdom is the Gate of Dissolution. Here the hieroglyphics or secret meanings, or fore-images and sayings of the ancient sages, all of which refer to this magical gate, are explained. The teachings of the ancient biblical prophets referring to this gate are explained in the nineteenth chapter, and the words of Christ and His apostles are interpreted in the twentieth chapter.

In the twenty-first chapter the apprentice of Wisdom is guided to her fourth gate, called the Gate of New Creation. This is, at the same time, her second gate of renewal. In chapter twenty-two, the final chapter, we will examine the varying states of the new magical heaven and new magical earth in man. We will provide numerous examples and clear explanations of the various properties in this final

GENERAL CONTENTS

chapter. Finally, we will thoroughly investigate and clearly discuss the origin of evil. We will also speak about how absolutely necessary it is to pass through this gate and enter into the realm of Wisdom.

*Content of the Chapters of this Treatise,
which is called*

SOPHIA

OR

The Virgin of Wisdom

CHAPTER 1

Instructs us how Sophia, or the virgin of Wisdom, descends with her divine Principle or Light-World into a soul which hungers and thirsts after her. After all of that soul's own energies have been exhausted, she appeases its anguished hunger and slakes its painful thirst.

CHAPTER 2

Teaches that passive or suffering patience, the Sabbath and the soul's rest are a necessary preparation for full completion of the regeneration or New Creation of the New Heaven and New Earth in the spirit and soul of man. Sophia, or the virgin of God's Wisdom, appears therein, reveals her beauty to the soul, and announces her message to it.

CHAPTER 3

Demonstrates how the darkness upon the Depths, according to *Genesis* 1:2, customarily reveals itself in the soul, unless that soul remains courageous and alert. It shows how it is through Wisdom that the first light is produced and made to shine. This light immediately reveals and makes known the true harmony that exists between lower and upper things, that is, between earth and heaven or the soul and the spirit.

CHAPTER 4

Instructs us how precious Sophia, or the heavenly virgin of Wisdom, comes with her true, essential purification-fire to reveal herself in the soul, to refine the old earth within it, to burn away and consume everything unpure from it, and to make it new. Hereby we come to understand the secret fire and the smelting oven of true philosophers.

CHAPTER 5

Instructs us further how eternal Wisdom, after she has thoroughly cleansed the earth with her refining-fire and has re-established the paradisal Eden in the soul by a new planting, causes everything therein to blossom forth and become delightfully verdant.

GENERAL CONTENTS

She causes such growth in the New Earth or soul by constantly nourishing and watering it with the vegetable quintessence or elixir of life.

CHAPTER 6

Teaches us that the purification-fire taking place in the earth or soul of man is the divine Day of Wisdom. On that day the old heavens within us, along with their lights and energies, must be smelted and pass away, before the New Heavens, together with their lights and energies, can be formed and revealed within man's spirit or intellect, will and senses.

CHAPTER 7

In this chapter Wisdom reveals to the author that she intends to make of him a true philosopher by teaching him about: 1) how he himself and his own eternal nature consist of heavens and earth; 2) God and Wisdom within him; 3) the great Depths of virginal Wisdom; and 4) how to recognize the secret keys whereby Wisdom's great Depths, as well as all the mysteries, secrets and wonders lying hidden in her fiery region, may be unlocked and locked again.

CHAPTER 8

Here eternal Wisdom further instructs her new

philosopher that the heavens within him are his own eternal spirit or his eternal intellect, will and senses. His earth, however, is his soul or heart, with their affections and passions or desires and cravings. She also teaches him how he may come to know what God, Wisdom and her Depths and, finally, what her keys are.

CHAPTER 9

Here Wisdom reveals and demonstrates to the author that, because his heavens and earth or spirit and soul are a microcosm within her globe, the outward heavens are a fore-image of the inward heavens. She also shows what the inward heavens actually are and how, in all things, the inward heavens harmonize with, and are in agreement with, the outward heavens.

CHAPTER 10

In this chapter the virgin of Wisdom discloses to the author the wondrous and delightful harmony of the outward earth with the inward earth of man, as well as what that inward earth actually is. She also tells him that the new, paradisal Garden of Eden shall blossom forth verdantly from that inward earth and must, therefore, exist within man himself. Then, with the blessing of God, the vegetable life in this inward earth shall produce from the seed of Wisdom different fruits than it did while it was under the Curse.

GENERAL CONTENTS

CHAPTER 11

Here Wisdom continues and shows the further harmony between the outward and inward earth, as well as how animal or bestial life shall arise in the renewed earth, in similarity to the outward creation in *Genesis* 1:24. She indicates what is meant to be understood by such living creatures, cattle and creeping worms within us. Finally, she discloses how the eternal spirit of man shall rule and have dominion in his earth over all these sorts of animals, according to *Genesis* 1:26.

CHAPTER 12

In this chapter Wisdom introduces the author to the mineral realm and life in his inward earth of the heart, according to the model and fore-image of the outward earth. She indicates to him what precious gold, silver, gems and pearls are wont to grow forth from this renewed earth, according to the mystical or secret interpretation of what is described in *Genesis* 2:12*ff*. Why has this gold-seed for the production of the stone of the wise been discovered by so few? What sort of furnace and fire pertain to it? How can it ultimately be produced! She says that the eternal spirit of man should be lord and king in this New World.

CHAPTER 13

Here Wisdom further discloses to the author that, although the eternal spirit in man is the king of the inward world, yet that spirit is still in a state of decay or in the process of arising again from the fall. Thus, his heavens and earth are in the same condition. Thereupon, Wisdom describes to him in detail from Scripture the fallen state of his microcosm. She begins with his spiritual heavenly sphere, whereby she clearly discloses and interprets the mystical and secret understandings of many passages of Scripture. She tells how numberless spirits are excluded from the New Jerusalem. In order to demonstrate the fallen, wretched state of man, and to redeem him from that state, Wisdom first reveals the Gate of Conviction to the author. He is convinced thereby of his abominable state of depravity, and realizes that he must seek after and grasp adequate means for his rescue.

CHAPTER 14

In this chapter Sophia, or the virgin of Wisdom, demonstrates further to the author that the holy place and the holy of holies within man has been devastated and has become the habitation of the unpure spirits. He is told that Wisdom must bring down the heart of God into the heart of man and God's spirit into the spirit of man, if the spirit of man is to become the holy of holies again, and the soul of man is to become the holy place. This must take place effectually and essentially, not in visions and revelations.

CHAPTER 15

Here Wisdom instructs the author and exhorts him to investigate what Holy Scripture says concerning the renewed state of man's heavens and earth or spirit and soul, and concerning all of their energies and capacities. The author does so and demonstrates how the entire man, in his intellect, will and sense, as well as in his heart, with its desires and cravings, is described and depicted in its renewed state by Scripture. Here we see that when sensual, sensory life is renewed, Paradise blossoms forth in the spirit of the intellect and is recognized, and Mount Zion and the New Jerusalem are perceived once more.

CHAPTER 16

In this chapter Wisdom further commands the author to investigate what Holy Scripture says concerning the renewed earth or soul and heart of man. What does it say about the animal or bestial life that has arisen therein in all of its different species? The author indicates this in great detail. He also shows how Paradise and the faded Garden of Eden, along with the Tree of Life, blossom forth, become verdant and manifest themselves within it, as does the mineral realm. He speaks of how God shall re-establish His tabernacle and temple, with its holy place and holy of holies, as well as Mount Zion and the New Jerusalem. He speaks of what sorts of ministering energies for man the various affections and passions shall be, after they are purified.

CHAPTER 17

Here Wisdom continues and promises the author to conduct him through all of her gates and into the New Jerusalem. The first of these she calls the Gate of Conviction. By this gate he will become inwardly convinced that his heavens and earth or his spirit and soul are still in a state of unpureness and thus in astrayness and selfness. Hence, he still lives separated from intimate fellowship with God. If, on the other hand, his heavens and earth were perfectly renewed, he would enjoy most intimate friendship and fellowship with God upon Mount Zion. Wisdom instructs the author further that he was, until then, effectually involved in the work of purification during the dispensations and offices of the Father and of the Son. Those two offices were, however, only a work of preparation for this Gate of Conviction. This purification had thus not yet been perfected and manifested. Rather, his heavens and earth were still mixed with unpureness and astrayness. In a similar way, the heathen had not been fully exterminated from Canaan until the time of Solomon, who was a figure of the day of the advent of Jesus in the spirit or of the dispensation of the Holy Spirit. On that day the victory over astrayness and selfness shall be fully obtained and all warfare and strife shall inwardly cease. Those who departed this outward body before their souls were fully purified, in struggle during the offices either of the Father or of the Son, were certainly freed from the realm of darkness or of the Dragon and from eternal anguish. They were brought to a dwelling place in the light-world but could not yet be fully transfigured or enter into Zion and the New Jerusalem until all astrayness and selfness was completely tilled out and all seven abominable nations were utterly overcome and exterminated.

CHAPTER 18

After the author has been led through the first gate, Wisdom here discloses to him her second gate, which she tells him is the Gate of Destruction or of Purification and Renewal. She calls it thus because, after his coming to the conviction that his old heavens and earth were still unpure, those heavens and earth must be purified and renewed by being smelted around. This destruction would not occur by water, as in earlier times, but by fire, according to *2 Peter* 3:7, 12. It would not occur by elemental fire or by hellish anger-fire, nor would it occur by fire from Mount Sinai in zeal and the rigor of divine justice. Rather, it would occur out of God's grace and mercy, by the fire of Mount Zion, by the fire of love, a fire which consumes nothing but earthiness, evil, astrayness and selfness. For in the days of the Father and of the Son all that astrayness and selfness was

SOPHIA

still too strong to be driven out and expelled. On this fiery, burning day, however, they shall be burned up and consumed, and the seven abominable nations in the heart shall be devoured. The smelter and regulator of this fire is neither the Father nor the Son; neither is it Jesus in the flesh nor Jesus in the spirit. Rather, this fire prepares the way for the birth of Jesus in the spirit and for the true Day of Pentecost of the Holy Spirit. Because it is an office of preparation, John the Baptist shall perform the same service as he did before the birth of Jesus in the flesh. He shall do this by the hand of an invisible spirit which did not consider it robbery to be equal in divinity with the Holy Trinity. This fiery, consuming day is not the Father's day of conviction by anguish and terror of conscience on account of sin. It is also not the day of the Son, upon which the heart is purified by faith. For these two days have already occurred and passed, and were not able to fully deliver the soul from all astrayness and selfness. For this the second advent of Jesus, in the spirit, and the day of the Holy Spirit are necessary. Before these can occur, a fiery office of preparation takes place, which is called the Day of Wisdom. On this day, Wisdom prepares her children, by her fiery smelting oven which she has erected in their souls and spirits, for the transfiguration of Mount Zion and the New Jerusalem. Here Wisdom shows how the author set aside her first calling, ate again from the forbidden Tree of Death, and thereby himself prevented the complete dissolution of his old heavens and earth. She exhorts him not to believe the quibbles of doubting reason but to endure her fire within him, until it has completely burned out all the evil seeds of astrayness, the Dragon and the Beast. She further instructs him that those who confuse her with the Father, the Son and the Holy Spirit are false philosophers. She is, to be sure, an energy and spirit that is distinguished from the Holy Trinity, but the Holy Trinity works within her.

CHAPTER 19

In this chapter Wisdom further instructs the author in the knowledge of true philosophy, after she has led him to her third gate, the Gate of Smelting-Around, Purification and Renewal. Here she teaches him how he can attain to the utter annihilation of his old, evil selfness. To this purpose, she explains and helps him to understand the *hieroglyphica* or fore-images, and also the metaphorically and allegorically allusive, obscure expressions and prophecies of the ancient wise men and prophets which pointed toward Wisdom's fiery day. These expressions and prophecies have been interpreted in an entirely different sense by reason. Sentence had already been passed during the two previous dispensations of the Father and of the Son that the old heavens and earth, together with all earthy and evil, wicked and dark spirits within man, should be smelted around by fire. Yet the execution of this sentence has not been fully accomplished, and such wicked spirits remain alive to this day. Now, however, on Wisdom's final Day of Judgment, their utter destruction by Wisdom's flames has been determined. At the same time, her fiery day is simply an office of preparation for the advent of Jesus in the spirit, and for making straight the way for the descent of the Holy Spirit into the spirit and soul of man. Wisdom does this because neither the kingdom of Mount Zion nor New Jerusalem may appear in the unpure heavens and earth of man.

CHAPTER 20

Here Wisdom continues to clearly explain how the teachings of Christ and the apostles pointed toward her fiery day, and to demonstrate to the author how, in this case, these teachings agreed with the prophecies of the wise men and prophets who preceded them. Such teachings and prophecies pointed toward the fact that everything was to pass away in fire upon her great day. In addition, Wisdom discloses to him the secret figures and fore-images in the Old and New Testaments which foresaw the same thing.

CHAPTER 21

At this point the virgin of Wisdom has also led the author through her third gate, namely the Gate of Smelting-Around, Purification and Renewal, as the first part of her fiery office, wherein all unpureness has been smelted away from his heavens and earth or spirit and soul, yet those heavens and earth still remain in their inherent essence. She now promises him to lead him through her fourth gate, which she calls her delightful, charming gate, and to effect a complete renewal within him. Here she commands him to pay great attention to: 1) the names of this renewal of his New Heavens and New Earth; 2) the place and location where they are to be renewed; 3) who it is that shall renew them, namely Wisdom; 4) what it is by which they shall be renewed, namely by love-fire; 5) what these New Heavens and New Earth within man actually are: namely, the New Heavens are his eternal spirit, with his intellect, will and senses, while the New Earth is his eternal soul or heart, with all of its desirous affections and passions; (6) what it means to create New Heavens and a New Earth within man; also when it shall be that this renewal is completed, so that he might know when this work has been accomplished and manifested; and finally (7) what the final purpose of this renewal of his heavens and earth or spirit and soul is, and why it was unavoidably necessary that they be renewed and that the eternal man be restored.

CHAPTER 22

After Wisdom has brought the author to her fourth gate, which is the second gate of renewal, or the lovely, charming and beautiful gate, she promises him that she wishes to begin the renewal of his earth, and afterward also his heavens, and finally to place the New Adam within them. After this, she presents those heavens and earth within him, effectual and essential, that is, renewed, for his contemplation. Here she particularly describes the properties of the new, magical earth in detail, as well as the purpose for which it was created. There follows a disclosure of the many and varied habitations in immeasurable eternity, as well as the fact that there are not just two, namely heaven and hell (as reason opines), but instead many, according to Christ's own testimony. This matter has seldom been taken into consideration by rational theologians; otherwise they could not have limited these habitations to merely two, that is, heaven and hell or the light-world and the world of darkness. They also would not have imagined that all eternal spirits which depart the body and this visible world and pass away necessarily had to enter either heaven or hell only. In this they act against their own principles, in that they confess that no one can be wholly without sin in this flesh-body, and thus must live in a mixed state consisting of good and evil, light and darkness, flesh and spirit. Consequently, man must die in that state of weakness, imperfection and unpureness. Holy Scripture states clearly and explicitly, however, that no unpure spirit, nor anything which is defiled, may enter into the Kingdom of Christ or the New Jerusalem, or may ascend directly into the state of glory. Only such spirits as have been thoroughly perfected, or are free from all astrayness and selfness, and are without blemish or taint may do this. Therefore, there must necessarily be many habitations. Hereafter follows the successive generation and creation of the worlds, as indicated in the figure of the author of the *Theologia Mystica*.[3] This chapter irrefutably maintains that the hellish, anguished Principle was not created by God but was

---

[3] John Pordage, *Mystic Divinitie* (London, 1683)

made by the spirit of error and his angels as a lake and pit. It is not of such a nature as is customarily taught, nor are Paradise and the outward world. Following *Genesis* 3:17*ff*, an explanation is given for how the Curse came upon the outward and the inward earth, as well as what that Curse actually is. It is made clear that this earth has become a dwelling place for all evil, unpure spirits, such that they are able to go in and out of the human spirit and bring about unspeakably great evil. From this it becomes completely clear who the author and origin of evil, astrayness and misery is. The statement is made that God sends no one to hell, but that all those who enter there have allowed themselves to be lured, tempted and drawn by the devils. Otherwise, the evil spirits would not be permitted to prowl around like roaring lions seeking whom they might devour, but would have to wait in their smoke hole until God sent the damned to them. The devils cannot be certain of their prey and booty until they possess it completely in their *centrum*, when it is fully of one will with them. We can see that this is true by the fact that few persons die without a mighty battle and struggle for the eternal spirit being evident.

SOPHIA

OR

*Spiritual Revelations of the blessed departed
Reverend John Pordage*

*Given by Divine Wisdom Herself and Recorded in
the Year of Our Lord Jesus Christ, 1675*

CHAPTER 1

June 21st

As I lay in great hunger and painful thirst in my spirit and found myself encompassed by grim, thorny anguish, I could find no peace in this condition. I was even pierced by despair and disbelief, mistrust and suspicious jealousy, and filled with hard, terrible thoughts toward Sophia, or essential Wisdom. At that moment she came to me and descended into my spirit with her healing energy. She soothed my bloody wounds, appeased my grim hunger, slaked my intense thirst and [2] anguished longing, and caused my spirit to dissolve into pure gentleness and serenity. She poured into me her healing oil, which calmed me inwardly and created a pleasing quiet stillness within me. By doing this she convinced my spirit that she had descended to me to heal my helpless, forlorn spirit and to alleviate and cure my painful wounds with her universal and highly effective balsam and medicine. I felt myself effectually anointed with her wonder-oil or balsam and it gave me immediate relief. Nevertheless, I still vacillated between hope and fear and knew neither the hand nor the medicine by which I had received such alleviation and refreshment.

CHAPTER 2

June 22nd

I felt and experienced this precious oil and balsam blend with my spirit, alleviate, quicken and soften it with stillness and rest. Moreover, she convinced my spirit that I was on the wrong path, that I had toiled day and night using my own capacities, that I had worn myself out and made myself anxious through my own energies, and had struggled earnestly, employing solely my own abilities. Yet, since I would never, in all eternity, be able to overcome and win the victory through my own efforts alone, She had come down to teach me that my own energies and abilities should keep still and wait in suffering patience.[4] It was for this reason that she had caused the divine oil and [3] balsam to flow into me, that it should alleviate and still the sharp, violent and hungry fire of my too greedily seeking and struggling spirit, since this was not the right path to the gate of her Depth. For my own efforts, my own seeking and my own running in the power of my own energies would not attain to

---

[4] *Romans* 9:16: "So, then, it is not of him that willeth, nor of him that runneth, but of God that showeth mercy."

SOPHIA

her *centrum*.[5] Although I had attempted many paths to reach her eternal Principle, and tried through hope, faith, patience, gentleness, all sorts of prayer and pleading, through loud cries, supplications and earnest entreaties to find her, yet none of these was the way to reach Wisdom herself or her Principle. I had sought for her entirely outside myself, had aspired to ascend high beyond myself, and had attempted to penetrate the separating wall of her heavenly Principle by the energy and capacity of my own active spirit. I did this in order to participate in Wisdom and partake of her. This could not be, since Wisdom and her Principle could only be sought and found within me, not outside.

This was a wholly new teaching and new instruction for me and, for that reason, was very difficult for my spirit to believe and accept. Although I had sunk down with my will-spirit into myself in softness, humbleness, patience and letting-go-ness toward the spirit of God the Father and the divine will of Wisdom, yet the eye of my will-spirit looked upwards away from me, thinking that the Principle of Wisdom must be partaken of outside of me, and that my will-spirit, with earnest longing, must struggle and labor upon the path of ascent in order to be accepted into that Principle. And yet, I could not attain it in this way. Then Wisdom herself condescended to enter my spirit and drew the eye of my spirit inward so that it could perceive itself and might discover Wisdom and her Principle through the path of descent. Thus I might be able to turn the eye of my understanding inwards,

---

[5] center

into myself, [4] and find Wisdom and her Principle for which my spirit so longed. After my eternal will-spirit and the eye of my intellect had been drawn inwards, I truly experienced an energy awakening within me that visited my spirit. For I felt a mighty, effectual energy that worked powerfully upon all of my active energies and properties, and impelled my spirit to seek earnestly. It placed words and material in my mouth and anointed all of my wheels or soul-energies with a precious oil that made them rejoice and feel serenity at the same time. I did not know, however, who it was who had visited me and did not understand who was impelling me. To be sure, I felt an unctuous energy, a through-penetrating energy, a circulating or upwards-and-downwards moving energy, a movement stirring in and through all the energies and properties in my inward and eternal man. The name and the nature of such energy were unknown to me, however. I did not know what name I should give to it, nor what I should call it. At the same time, I experienced it as a stirring movement. I felt it as a moving energy that worked within me gently and lovingly, appeasing the wrath of my hunger and slaking the fierceness of my thirst. It taught me to stand still and assured me that it would not fail to accomplish its own work and reveal its intentions with joy and gladness. My eternal spirit was astounded by this sudden alteration. I appeared to myself as one who is dreaming and tarried yet between hope and fear. I hoped inwardly that this work would proceed but also feared that my previous hunger and painful thirst would return, that my precious oil, which had anointed my inner wheels, would run out or dry out and that, as a result, the hungry, thirsty fear would return to my spirit.

June 23rd

[5] As I still trained the eye of my understanding upon this gentle-soothing-unctuous anointment that moved so gracefully in the properties or contours of my soul and spirit, it caused to flee from my spirit all disbelief, despair, distrust and all of the suspicious thoughts that I had previously entertained. It expelled from me all of the fearful spirits that cast down our courage and encouraged me to wait upon the spirit or energy that was awakening within me (which, because it was unknown and invisible to my Inward Man at that time, I felt moving as a fine, subtle, pure, penetrating, active and circulating, or upwards-and-downwards moving energy in and through all the sensual energies and capacities of my spirit, and through all the effective properties and contours of my soul. As I prayed, the invisible spirit said to me: "I have descended into you; I have entered into your nature; I have penetrated your bronze doors and have broken your iron bars. I have come with my power and with my healing oil, in order to pour it into your eternal sensual and rational energies or capacities, forms and properties and to mix it with them. I have come to establish my New Creation within you, to make a New Heaven and New Earth within you, in which nothing but righteousness, namely my own just nature, shall dwell. It was referring to the words of Saint Peter: "We look for new heavens and a new

earth, in which dwelleth righteousness."[6] The spirit continued and said: "I have come to establish these things in you and to raise up this new invisible creation in you inwardly, [6] not outside of you. I have come to make a philosopher of you, and to instruct you in the fundamentals and hidden principles of the divine and heavenly philosophy. You will hear from me and learn how I am going to form this New Creation within you. Your eternal spirit will abide with me, and you will see all of this with your own eyes. For I have come not merely to present you with this in a vision or to make it known to you by a revelation, but rather to bring it about actively by my creative, working word and to produce it essentially. For I have come to establish it effectively by my creative *Fiat*,[7] and you shall behold the way and fashion in which this will be accomplished and founded in you by my magical art. Your own eyes will see this performed in you." Upon this, that speaking energy began to form the New Creation within me in the following manner:

Firstly, it presented to my inward sight its divine Chaos, which was a round circle, a deep abyss like unto a sphere, in which nothing could be seen or heard, but which was rather a deep void without ground. It was immeasurable and, to the eye of my eternal spirit, contained nothing visible; and yet all things were invisibly hidden there. This divine Chaos revealed itself as a huge, immeasurable empty space or location that contained nothing other than a pure, active working energy. It revealed itself to the eye

---

[6] *2 Peter* 3:13
[7] Let there be

of my spirit as a formless clump and as a confused mass. It was a great formless depth devoid of all ideas. After I had contemplated this at length with the understanding-eye of my spirit, I saw that this was the foundation and ground of the New Creation which was to be formed within me.

Secondly, and following this, I was shown that in this deepest Un-ground there is a wise, prudent and understanding spirit [7] that lives and moves within and through it and is the working agent within it. And I saw that it was a quick, subtle and penetrating energy, a permeating energy, an impelling and compelling energy. Moreover, I was granted the realization that this mighty working spirit could be none other than the Spirit of Wisdom herself. Then, like an observer, my eternal spirit contemplated what the nature of the Spirit of Wisdom might be. For I saw that her spirit was an invisible energy, pure energy, yea nothing other than pure energy; a sheer, pure act or working, a weaving motion; a sharp, quick, penetrating, circulating, working energy; an active, efficacious and mighty energy. I saw her to be this in the divine Chaos; I felt her to be this in the sensual and rational energies and capacities of my eternal spirit and in the properties and contours of my eternal soul.

Thirdly, she showed and presented to me the four eternal elements from the deepest abyss of this deep Chaos. Through her divine art she brought them into being or unfolded them; She extracted them from that mixed mass and drove them upwards as ethereal mists; then she blended them with each other, and the four eternal elements became intermingled and coagulated; or, through Wisdom's art, they were immediately hardened and made substantial; brought to an equal temperature in number, weight and mass; freed from all excess and conflict, so that they were united in unanimous equality and harmony. Wisdom said to me that the process of blending and making substantial the four eternal elements (coagulation), which had been accomplished within me by her working energy, had transformed them into a single eternal element. This single element represented her New Earth, her dry land or *terra firma*, her holy and solid ground upon which she moved and lived. [8] She had planted this New Earth in my soul so that my spirit would be able to live, move and dwell upon this Earth that had been formed and planted in the midst or most inward *centrum*[8] of my heart. Thereupon Wisdom said to me: I wish to dwell with you upon this New Earth, to walk and talk with you here, and be found nowhere else but here.

The speaking Word added: Behold the *centrum* of nature, the *centrum* of your New Earth. Here in your heart, in the midst of this New Earth, Wisdom has planted a central fire, in order to ignite, to warm, to digest and to let spring forth that which her hand shall sow in this New Earth. Without this central fire the New Earth would prove to be barren, desolate, rough and primitive, an infertile ground and territory. Then I truly felt that she had planted this central fire, which by means of its gentle warmth was a digesting flame, in the midst of my New Earth for fruitfulness.

Further, I truly felt that she had poured out a precious moisture or sap, like a powerful life-oil, and

---

[8] center

had mixed it with the central fire, so that it would cause the fire to burn gently, brightly and sweetly, and would prevent it from going out. Otherwise, that fire might easily be curbed, smothered and finally extinguished. This oil, however, causes the central fire to burn sweetly and joyfully, and tends the flames of the central fire. At the same time, it is the food and nutrition by which the fire nourishes itself and is eternally maintained. Thus, there is no fear that the divine fire will go out, as long as it is nourished and maintained by this oil. By her magical art, divine Wisdom blended the oil and the fire in unity and harmony in the heart and the center of the New Earth, so that this newly formed and created earth might become fertile soil [9] and bring forth abundant fruits.

Fourthly, Wisdom fed this New Earth with the clear, crystalline Water of Life like a river. She surrounded the newly formed, created earth and nourished it with this water, so that it might be fruitful earth and ground. For this reason the New Earth was established by the water, because the water made it fertile. Without the Water of Life, which energetically penetrates the pores, veins and arteries of this New Earth, there could be no fertile soil. Lacking the living water of this river, there would be but an infertile desert and wilderness, covered only with weeds and thistles. This is the reason why Wisdom chose to surround this earth with the river of the Water of Life.

Afterward, Wisdom sowed this New Earth, this heavenly land, with eternal, immortal, incorruptible Seeds of Life—with living seeds by her own hand. In that same hour burst forth full growth and a rich

CHAPTER 2

harvest that filled the New Earth. All of the trees of life grew forth from this earth; their limbs and branches were so abundantly laden with fruit that they bent down towards the ground. All plants that appeal to the taste and the eye grew forth immediately, along with the herbs that the Seeds of Life contained. They grew there as nourishment and sustenance for the first Adam. In an instant Paradise burst forth from the heart and center of this New Earth, and the lost Garden of Eden, the pleasure garden, became verdant. Immediately it blossomed in full abundance with all trees, plants and herbs from the seed of life that they contained without the need for tilling, plowing or sowing the New Earth. It was Wisdom alone, with her tincturing oil, her powerful elixir and her penetrating energy, that caused this pleasure garden to green forth in all abundance [10] and joy without any labor. For she herself is the circulating oil, the penetrating tincture, the working energy, the vivacious life and the movement in and through everything in Paradise. Here I perceived the fruits and herbs of Paradise that my eternal man was now to eat, and from which he was to live. These fruits were peace, love, gentleness, humility, unity, harmony, patience, brotherly love, purity, innocence, uprightness, constancy, loyalty, hope, faith, heartiness and other such heavenly herbs that are filled with divine energy and oil. These herbs combine into a pleasurable, tasty dish when they partake of the marrow and fat of the pleasing oil that flows through them.

After this the speaking Word continued: Behold now your New Earth that has been formed within you and consider Paradise and the Garden of Eden. Look how they grow, burst forth and blossom without labor and toil in your new ground and formed earth by the power of my penetrating tincture and circulating oil, which is the elixir of their fertility. Examine your Paradise and your Garden of Eden, which have now been formed within you and planted, for which you so long have ardently desired and labored. There was no other way for the Paradise within you to green and for your Garden of Eden to be renewed than for them to be recreated within you by the creative energy and *Fiat* that I possess. I have made you a plant of my own planting, a garden of my pleasure and joy, a work of my own hands. Know, therefore, that I have entered my garden within you in order to mix my wine, my oil, my heavenly energy and liquor with the herbs, plants and fruits that bear the seeds of life within them, so that they might [11] grow, multiply and be abundant. Thus may you become as the Garden of God and form a fruitful and fertile field within yourself, so that neither barrenness nor infertility might be discovered within you. For the garden of all abundance and plenty has been planted in the midst of your New Earth. This New Earth is holy ground and it is your holy land, wherein nothing other than my pure virginity and just nature shall dwell. Only good seed shall grow in this New Earth; I have sown no evil seed therein, nothing other there than the seeds of eternal life: no evil seed of eternal death, no other seed than that of immortality and incorruptibility, no seed of mortality; my hand has sown no seed of corruptibility in this newly formed ground and earth: no foreign seed, no seed of any other nature or property than the seed of my own divine nature,

CHAPTER 2

the seed of my divinity and my eternity; no seed of the serpent, no poisonous seed has been sown in this your New Earth. My hand has sown no seed of enmity or contrariety: neither thistles nor thorns, no roots of bitterness, no herbs of fear, no wrath, no anger, no envy, no malice, no hatred, neither ill will nor jealousy. No strife grows in my paradisal garden; no weeds but rather herbs and plants that serve as food and are pleasant to eat. It is always summertime in the paradisal garden formed in the midst of your New Earth; it is even a constantly mild and gentle springtime. This garden brings forth and displays only pleasant-scented flowers that vaunt all sorts of lovely colors. It is a rich field of plenteousness, an abundant harvest. There is neither winter nor autumn within it; no infertility is ever found therein. Behold now your new-formed earth, which has been brought to life by my unctuous energy and liquor. Look how your newly regenerated paradise and your newly created garden [12] of Eden and of pleasure blossom as a result. It has been formed and planted in your heart by my creative energy and by the *Fiat* of omnipotence. Turn your eyes inward, therefore, and examine it, for I have entered my newly formed paradisal garden, which I planted in your heart and bosom. I will water it with my water of life. I will mix my oil and energy with my seeds, herbs, plants and flowers and cause my lilies to grow and my roses to blossom forth. In that garden I will walk and talk with you. There I will treat with you intimately and enjoy close fellowship. There I will spend time with you and be your dearest friend. There I will reveal myself to you and share my love with you. I will not allow myself to be found outside of this holy ground and my paradisal garden. You may try to find me outside of the garden, but you will not find me, for I desire to walk with you only within this your holy land. No forbidden fruit, no seed of mortality, grows in this paradisal ground of yours. Instead, there are trees, plants and herbs through which eternal life and immortality flow.

This power of Wisdom prophesied further concerning imminent and future things, in order to encourage me. She prophesied to me and predicted that, even as she had formed and created my New Earth within me and had planted the Garden of Eden and Paradise in my New Earth, she also desired to create a New Heaven for me, which she would plant in the spirit of my soul and in the sensual and rational energies and capacities of my inward eternal man. She wished to plant the same in my mind, will and senses. After she had accomplished her new creation (or regeneration) in me, her New Heaven and New Earth, and [13] had caused Paradise to blossom forth in both of them, she wished to create a New Adam, a Second Adam (she was referring to my own eternal spirit), whom she would establish therein as a lord and king to reign over it with power and dominion. I was to be tested, proved and tempted for this purpose. In addition, she warned me and counseled me to endure and resist my forty days of temptation uprightly, and not to fall in Paradise as the First Adam had done. Instead, she turned my eyes toward Jesus Christ, the Second Adam, Who successfully passed the test of temptation and gave true evidence of His faithfulness, constancy, love and faith, and Who, thereupon, was made steward over the treasury of God. She told me that He would be my pattern and fore-image and that I must follow after His example.

Hereupon I was granted a spirit of prayer that earnestly compelled me to pray that in such a day and hour of temptation the fear of the Lord would keep me safe, would be with me, and would cause me to remain constant and faithful, like a noble hero of Wisdom, so that I could fight Wisdom's fight. Empowered by the seed of virginal Wisdom, I could shatter the head of the serpent and be victorious over it.

After this I was given to understand that the power of Wisdom was able to bring forth her new creation in the twinkling of an eye and was able to create a New Heaven and a New Earth. However, for my sake she could only gradually bring forth her New Creation in me and by degrees, in order that my inward spirit could hear from her, see, recognize and learn how she created and brought forth into order and differentiation the New Heaven and Earth and her New Creation out of her own confused or unformed Chaos; how she produced order from disorder and differentiation out of confusion and disruption; how the New Heaven and Earth were produced from her eternal Chaos. In addition, how the subtle, [14] penetrating, working and permeating spirit of the Wisdom of God floated high over the deep, ungrounded Chaos, the four eternal elements, and how she, by the activity of her intermixing and blending, brought forth the New Earth and formed Paradise from that New Earth; how the spirit of Wisdom caused the plants, herbs, trees, fruits and flowers containing the seed of life within themselves

SOPHIA

to become verdant and blossom forth.

Now after this new-created earth and the Paradise planted within it as a true garden of pleasure and joy had been generated and made efficacious before the eyes of my understanding and had been planted in the midst of my heart and breast by the energy and ordering hand of Wisdom, She hid herself. She enclosed herself within her newly created earth or paradisal garden and granted to my eternal spirit time to meditate upon the wondrous forming of my New Earth and upon the ordered beauty of the flora that had been planted in the midst of my heart by her magical art and understanding. Thus ended the first lesson in divine philosophy imparted by divine Wisdom to the power of reason that belongs to the eternal spirit of my inward and eternal Man. After this, Wisdom placed a song of praise in my mouth to sing in her honor. With it I could praise her for forming the New Earth and regenerating Paradise, which were then effectually and inwardly born within me, and were planted by her creating energy.

> *Come, beautiful Love, eternal Bride of the soul, and bedew our roots,*
> *Let the beauty of your radiance gleam! And let your sweet light shine*
> *Upon the wild, primordial whirlwind and the pitch black darkness of night*
> *Let the Old Earth within me be regenerated and be renewed to its original purity*
> *Create anew my degenerated heart and let it rejoice in you [15]*
> *Smelt all selfness out of it and make it free of sin*

CHAPTER 2

That it might be eternally dedicated to you
I see you now truly bringing the seeds of heaven
From which a second Eden joyfully springs forth
The lovely rose of Sharon and the lily blossom there
In the midst of other blooms, truly a huge bouquet
Of the loveliest of flowers and of heavenly grace
For therein is no worm to cause decay or damage
To the least of them. In the center of that garden,
That Paradise, the energies of Wisdom ascend
Let my Love come into her garden, which has freshly blossomed.
Let all who venerate Wisdom come with her to taste of her fruit
(Which smells so sweetly) and sip the liquor of her nectar
Which flows so freely there / And those who imbibe of it
Are made drunk in spirit by its singular qualities
Let Wisdom remain here with her gleaming entourage
And let her banner, Love, wave above me forever!

CHAPTER 3

June 24th

After the beginning was made, I felt a numberless host of evil spirits, both from the dark world or the Principle of Darkness and from this earthy Principle surround the spirit of my intellect. They wished by sensible reasons to convince me that this New Earth would come to nothing and that my previous infecundity, as well as my painful hunger [16] and thirst, would return to devour my present fertility and joyfulness. And so I was surrounded and assailed day and night by the spirits of unbelief, fear and mistrust, and by a host of spirits that weakened my confidence and faith. They invaded my spirit by awakening a thousand thoughts within me and confusing me with their whisperings.

In the morning I felt the penetrating power of Wisdom again and perceived how she blazed up in my heart like a Central Flame through her viscous fire, which circulated and permeated all the energies of my intellect. It revealed to the spirit of my intellect that I had arrived at her Gate of Renewal and was now effectually entering that gate (which makes all things new) in my spirit. At this point she revealed to the spirit of my inward and eternal intellect the ensuing

Gate of Conviction, that is, that this work of renewal must be accomplished and made efficacious within my own self, and not outwardly. She showed me that I was mistaken if I thought that I could be received into her Principle, be transported and regenerated outwardly. Instead, Wisdom said that she must first descend into my spirit with her Principle and renew all things therein by her Principle before I would be able to ascend to her Principle. I myself, that is, my eternal spirit, intellect, will and senses, together with the essences of my soul, was the material that was to be renewed and regenerated. She declared that in no other way could the material of renewal be present within me, and that her Principle, which was to descend upon me, was the vehicle by which the material to be changed and transformed within me would make me into a new creation. She furthermore instructed me and caused me to realize that it had been [17] my greatest misunderstanding that I had intended to ascend into her heavenly Principle. Rather, it was she that must first descend into my spirit with her Principle and therewith, as a spirit, inwardly transform my spirit into a new creation. Now being convinced of this, I turned my eye inward to experience Wisdom as a penetrating energy and an efficacious circulating fire within me. I determined to attend upon the pleasant, stirring energy in her own Principle within me. It was given to me to see that I myself was the subject and the material of this renewal and that Wisdom, descending upon me in her own Principle to accomplish this renewing and regenerating work, was herself the efficacious material within me. This conviction allowed my

CHAPTER 3

reasoning property to awaken as from a dream in astonishment. It was a great pleasure to be subject to the persuasions and instruction of Wisdom.

After this she persuaded my spirit of another error: that I had striven to ascend to her Principle through my own energy and strength, and that I had striven to break open a gate into her Principle by my own power. I had attempted this through prayer, through loud cries, and through various forms of pleading and beseeching; even through long investigation and other types of activities; also through hope, faith, and trust. Thus I sought, knocked, cried out and struggled, yet none of these keys could open the gate of her Principle. All of these energies within me were far too weak to ever be able to open a gate into her eternal Principle unless she herself had already descended into me with her eternal Principle. The realization of this created the fearful hunger, the painful thirst and the desperation that overcame me. My own powers, [18] the capacities within me, could never have achieved anything unless she had previously, of her own free will, and with her Principle, condescended and come down to my eternal spirit with all its sensual and rational energies and capacities.

She further revealed to my intellect that, despite the work of renewal and restoration of all things, the work of justification, reconciliation, sanctification, transformation and glorification of the spirit itself would seem to be impossible because the rational spirit was in a degenerate condition, locked in a fleshly body and living in the earthy Principle. Yet, for Wisdom such things were not only possible but easy to accomplish. For her they were mere women's work and child's play to be brought about easily, accompanied by great pleasure and joy. Although it had been impossible for me to break through her gate into her Principle, yet it would be ridiculously easy for a sharp, subtle, penetrating spirit like hers to break through all the doors and gates of my Principle. Thus she might enter my spirit to accomplish all her works within me.

She showed me that my spirit must remain quiet and in repose; for she must be the chief agent in effecting the work of preparation for the renewal, justification, reconciliation, sanctification, glorification and redemption in my spirit. She demanded nothing further of me than that I should be like a tiny, innocent child, utterly passive or receptive; yes, that I should suffer her to accomplish her work within me. She desired to do this for me, seeing that she had descended for this purpose and had entered into my spirit with her fiery Love-Principle. To the end of renewing and purifying everything within me, she had erected her fiery oven in the midst of me, [19] in order to burn away, smelt, consume and till out all the chaff, astrayness and unpure earthiness that I harbored within. This pleasant, viscous fire-oven would effectually and perfectly accomplish the work within me as long as I remained and abided inwardly constant, for Wisdom required nothing less than a perfect agreement and unification of my will with her will, the complete cooperation of my will with hers, and the resting or repose of my will. She desired nothing more than the turning inward of my spirit and the participation of my spirit with her spirit. All that Wisdom desired was that my spirit should

CHAPTER 3

remain within me and with her in her fiery Ground and Principle, and that it should not depart again into the Principle of this world.

What gave my spirit pause was wondering how I could possibly do as Wisdom required, given that I am in this fallen state, in a body of sinful flesh, and in the earthy Principle of this world. At this she impelled me and moved me to beg her to bring about this work of New Creation in me. Just as Wisdom had formed my New Earth within me, she desired to proceed to create a New Heaven in my eternal spirit where she would shine like the Morning Star. She longed to order and place her divine and heavenly constellations or stars therein to rule over my New Earth. She also desired to place her seven fiery lamps, as her seven planets, in my confused, disordered heaven, as she had already promised. Here, in an instant, she revealed to me the connection or attachment and unification of the New Heaven and Earth for the sake of fecundity. She showed me how my inward New Earth depended upon the upper bodies and heavenly influences of my New Heaven within. In this sense, [20] the correlation was similar to that of the earth and heaven of this outward, visible creation. This outward earth would remain unfruitful and without growth, even though the hand of the sower had scattered seed upon it, unless it were watered by rain from the clouds and irradiated by the warm beams of the sun, notwithstanding the seed that had been sown upon it and the central fire contained within it. Even so with me. Notwithstanding that Wisdom had sown the eternal seed of life in the heart and center of my New Earth and had planted her Central Fire in the middle of my Heavenly Earth, yet the heavenly seed could not grow up in verdant energy, nor acquire a red fresh color, nor achieve a pleasant nutritional power and taste until it was moistened from the upper heaven by the water of life and refreshed by the bright warm beams radiating from the bosom of Wisdom. Wisdom would have to let fall the dripping dews of her honey, lying upon the branches of her tree, down upon the New Earth and the New Heaven. By this, their blessed interrelation and dependence one upon the other, the earth would become fruitful and abundant, free from all barrenness. She referred me to the words of the prophet Hosea, and moved me to beg her that my New Earth would cry out to her New Heaven, and that my New Heaven might hear the crying out and entreaties of my New Earth, and that Wisdom might immediately hear the cries and prayers of my New Heaven. Thus might Wisdom, by her innate harmony, rain down grain, wine and oil in abundance upon my earth. In this way, it might become an immensely fruitful earth, no longer unfruitful and sterile. May she hear the prayers of Jezreel, that is, my eternal spirit, and may I be heard by my heaven and earth, and answered when I call to them.[9] [21]

This lack of single-hearted harmony between my heaven and earth and Wisdom was the true sole deep cause of the inner aridity, barrenness, infertility and constant hunger that lay upon my spirit. Now as I turned my eye inward, I came to realize and to confess that I had begun to sense and experience

---

[9] *Hosea* 2:21-22

CHAPTER 3

that Wisdom had become my motivator, my guide, my inner impulse, my penetrator, my life, my energy and my effectuator. I am nothing. I can do nothing. She is my driving, efficacious, circulating energy. She is efficacious and I am passive. She is everything, I am nothing. She is my oil, my energy, my elixir, my gentleness, my joy and pleasure, my fecundity, my everything. I myself am a mere shadow; She is my divine, eternal, essential autonomy. She is the wheel within my wheel; her oil lubricates the wheels of my spirit. She lightens all of my burdens. She makes all to blossom and become verdant, to laugh and rejoice, without causing any uproar, loud laughter or noise to be heard in the pathways of our properties and forms. O blessed Sophia! I confess that you are the most inward, hidden and invisible of spirits; that you are the quickest, finest, sharpest virtue and piercing energy, which penetrates my spirit and sensual and rational energies and capacities. You pass through all of my doors and gates, although they are locked fast. You enter in and depart hence and waft incomprehensibly through them when it pleases you so to do. O divine Sophia, foster and perfect your work eternally! Work and weave inwardly in my wheels with your wine and oil, until you have utterly accomplished your work to your praise and glory! [22]

CHAPTER 4

June 25th

When I turned my eye inward to my New Earth and thought to observe how the work of renewal was proceeding, Sophia passed me quickly by and revealed herself to me with these words: "I have come to my Earth with my purifying- and refining-fire. This have I done to cleanse your Earth of all unpureness, dross and tin, and to free it of all its tares and chaff." In that same instant I felt her purifying- and refining-fire penetrate all my inward parts, piercing all and every property and form in a circulating or ascending and descending motion. Then she said within me: "This is your true, inward and essential purifying-fire. It is nothing other than my purifying-refining and consuming fire that you are now feeling and experiencing within you. No renewal of your earth can take place until it has been tested, refined and purified. For the renewal of your Earth can only occur through my refining and purifying flames." And I felt this true purifying-fire and the flames that effectually devoured my tares and chaff. Then she revealed herself in words foreshadowed in *Malachi* 4:1 and said: "See, my day is coming, which will burn like a smelting oven." I felt this burning day within me like a fire-oven and like a flaming furnace. All pride and evil, as she said, would be burned like chaff and stubble, so that neither root [23] nor branch would remain. If I were able to persist in the purifying- and refining-fire, this eternal flame—which I truly felt— would sweep clean and utterly purify my threshing floor and Earth from all tares, dross and vain desires. Then I cried out and said: "Who shall abide the fiery day of your coming? What flesh or spirit can stand when you appear in your melting- and refining-fire? And when you sit as a smelter, refiner and purifier of silver in your fiery flames?[10] Yet I saw truly that it was unavoidable that my spirit should undergo this fiery test and should have to endure this naturized and substantial purifications-fire. Without the incineration of all the earthy vain tares that had grown in such profusion in this earthy Principle, no renewal could take place, for very many thickets and coils had woven and wound themselves around my spirit. It was necessary that they be rooted out and removed from my spirit and from my New Earth by this purifying and refining fire. Accordingly, in order that I achieve a thorough and perfect purification from all tares and earthiness (for this is the initial step in a thoroughgoing renewal of the New Heaven and Earth), I consigned my will completely to her fiery smelting oven. My will had there to endure as in a fire of purification until all of my vain desires, like chaff, and the tares of earthy-mindedness should be consumed in the flames, and all my iron, tin and dross be utterly smelted away. Thus might I appear

---

[10] *Malachi* 3:1-3

CHAPTER 4

in my spirit as pure gold, and might see created and formed within me the New Heaven and New Earth. [24]

CHAPTER 5

June 26th

After this I looked inwards to see how my garden flourished and blossomed, what sorts of buds and blossoms my New Earth was bringing forth, and what sorts of fruits, herbs and seeds were emerging from this cleansing and purification by fire. The eye of my spirit saw the garden produce plants, rooted vegetables, herbs and seeds, all of which had their life within them: living fruits that grew spontaneously without toil or labor. A sandy, infertile desert had become a fruitful garden that resembled the Garden of God in its beauty and charm. I was absolutely amazed by this. My lilies and rosebuds—namely hope, faith, peace, joy, love, gentleness, humility, patience, brotherly love, trust and confidence in God, courage, nobility, bravery, submission, letting-go-ness—offered themselves willingly to me. These sorts of herbs, plants and trees, namely such virtues and graces, sprouted forth from my New Earth and made it not only fertile soil but also a lovely and joyful terrain because of its beauty, pleasantness and charm.

As I further contemplated my Garden of Eden and saw that the roots of my bitterness, namely disbelief,

SOPHIA

doubt, anxiety, slavish fear, mistrust, malevolence, envy, wrath, anger and many other such tares, were separated out from my graces and either pulled out root and branch [25] or consumed by the fire, Sophia herself appeared to me and said: "I have come into my garden to mix my wine and pour it out." I felt that she had mixed it and poured it out into the innermost recesses of my heart and into the center of my New Earth. This wine was indeed a new wine for me, a truly delicious wine; such a life-giving, invigorating refreshment in my heart that I turned the mouth of my spirit toward it to taste it and drink from it. It was a most pleasant, delicious potion upon my tongue, as if it had been drawn out from the most powerful extract of wine and from the juice of the most delicate pomegranate—almost as if it were a beverage composed of all sorts of aromatic spices, so that it tasted like spiced and mulled wine. My spirit called it not only new wine but also spiced wine. When I was given this wine to drink, it was like a purely distilled wine spirit whose yeast had been drawn off, its phlegma purely separated, and sublimated into such a tasty cordial that no tongue could describe it in words nor anyone say what it was except those who had tried and tasted it. It could refresh the life-spirit in an instant and make it vivacious. It flows forth from the heart through all the blood vessels, strengthening and refreshing, and draws the heart, the fount of all life, into the highest realm of joy. This delicious drink was so enlivening and pleasant for heart and soul (as wine tends to be when it is poured into the glass) that it could only be Wisdom's elixir of life. In that same moment I tested, felt and experienced that it had been extracted by chymical art, refined and sublimated to this excellence by her own hand. It not only cures and truly heals all sicknesses in the soul and spirit but also, as an incomparable cordial, gives powerful strength and new life to the heart, refreshes the spirit and draws the senses to a higher level of joy that, even with all [26] one's thoughts and fantasies, is unimaginable.

Here I experienced the earnest will to observe the difference between the oil and the wine of Wisdom. Her oil eases all aches, alleviates all pain, subdues all fear, and soothes all the fiery hunger and painful thirst of the spirit instantly. It refreshes the languid spirit as well as the wheels and energies of the soul and spirit. When they are lubricated and coated with it, they function more easily, quickly and gently. Sophia's wine, on the other hand, is a compounded or mixed tonic of life, a pure spirit and elixir, a quintessence. It refreshes the senses, invigorates and enlivens the heart, restores the spirit and brings it to the highest realms of joy. It revives moribund life, causes fear and sorrow to flee, and fills the spirit with unspeakable joy. It heals all sickness and banishes every tribulation and ailment for a time. It takes away all fatigue and frees us from weaknesses. A single drop accomplishes this work by strengthening the heart and refreshing the spirit. After I had drunk deeply of it, I said that it would be good always to dwell in the wine cellar of Wisdom. For the more I drank, the more joy I felt, and the more I approached a state of ecstasy, while the more I desired to drink of it, the more amazed I was at myself. For I could not drink too much of it nor become drunk; it did not make my heart nauseous and my spirit did not become bloated. There was clearly no danger, even if one drank deeply from the chalice of the spiced wine of Wisdom. There is nothing in this earthy Principle that can compare with this divine nectar and heavenly beverage. It is incomparably more glorious than one can describe with words or attain with the thoughts or imagination. The greatly exalted pleasure of this wine can only be recognized and experienced by those who drink of it. [27] Its most noble effects can only be described by those who have tasted it and by no one else. From my own experience I will say this: All the pleasures of this world, all wines, refreshments and compositions that have been created by the most experienced artists and imbibed by the emperors and kings of this world cannot restore the spirit in the way that a single small drop of this spiced wine can do. All the others are worth nothing compared to this wine. O gracious Wisdom! Grant my spirit always to drink from the chalice of this spiced wine. May I run my course to the end and not grow weak, fatigued or exhausted!

CHAPTER 6

June 28th

When I awoke, I experienced the oil-fire flame up and burn within my heart like a fiery oven and felt that the Day of Wisdom had come, on which all unpure earthiness was burned away and consumed from my old heavens. I felt the burning heat of the fire rise up to my head, where the old heavens had their seat, and which consisted of the circle of my intellect, will and senses, and which all together made up the old heavens within me. Hereupon Wisdom quoted and interpreted the words of *2 Peter* 3:12, saying that the day of God had now arrived, through which my old heavens had truly been set ablaze, their unpure earthiness dissolved, along with such elements as the earthy properties that had attached themselves to my intellect, will and senses. [28] These properties were now being smelted by the intense heat of the oil-fire and their dross, scum and filth consumed by the flames that burned so sharply within me.

This moved me to pray: "O do Thou purify me! O purify and refine my old heavens and separate out from them the old husks of earthy properties! O ride through the circle or perimeter of the heaven of my intellect, will and senses! O sweep my threshing floor thoroughly that it might be utterly purified by the devouring fire that I have felt burning therein! O by the fiery, differentiating flames that I have felt in my old heavens, eliminate from them all their unpureness, stains and contrariety which, against their pure nature, had inhabited them.

At this, Wisdom indicated and caused me to understand that the reason why she had not moved in my heavens and their energies was that they were unpure and tainted heavens. Now, however, she had come to those same heavens with the purifying and refining flames of her burning fire in order to purify them of all their stains and unpurenesses and to refine them. At this my spirit cried out even more fervently: "O make my old heavens clean and pure before your countenance! Destroy all the idols, the graven images and visions of pleasure, all of the antichrists and altars, and cast them away from the circle of my intellect! Burn down all the green orchards or the sacred pagan groves by this purification-fire! Cleanse my eyes, my ears, my taste and all my senses with this burning purification-fire, that all the vessels of my own house and heaven might be effectually cleaned and purified by your refining- and purification-fire! By this may they be prepared and made acceptable for your presence, O divine Wisdom! Let my sun, moon and stars be dissolved and melt away through the intense heat of your purification-fire, in order to make room for your New Heaven [29] to dwell therein! O establish your sun and moon, your stars and seven fiery lamps in their order! For this is the day of dissolution and purification which must take place before the great and marvelous day of your advent within us, with

CHAPTER 6

your New Heavens and your celestial constellations, in order to reign over my New Earth. This is the great and terrible day for which your servant has looked and desired, on which all idols, graven images and false gods, together with their names, shall be utterly tilled out by your destruction- and purification-fire. As the apostles and prophets of olden times predicted, they shall creep away into the clefts of the rocks and into the caves of the earth when you rise up to shake our Old Earth with terror and to stir our Old Heavens, together with all their hosts. For this purpose I shall endure these purification-flames until my heaven and earth are thoroughly purified; until they, like silver and gold, are purified of all their dross and unpurenesses, and are refined; until all things have been made new and all their earthy scum, filth and dross have been purely separated out by your fire and discharged by you, O divine Separator! Advance your work of purification by fire and continue it until all my heavens and their elements are purified from all properties that are contrary and abhorrent to their nature. Come then into me and dwell in my New Heavens, which have been formed and prepared as a dwelling for you yourself to abide in, together with your Principle. [30]

CHAPTER 7

June 29th

While my intellect impelled me to be careful and make good provision, Wisdom revealed to the inner eye of my intellect that she had come to make me a philosopher, according to her earlier prophecy. She had now appeared to reveal me to myself within myself. To be a philosopher was to know myself and my own nature. It was to know God and Wisdom within me. It was to recognize her Depth and the key which would open that Depth of hers which was moving in my depths.

She told me that I myself was my nature and my nature was I myself. The nature of my inward man was created from and consisted of not more than two things, namely of heaven and earth. The heaven within a man was his eternal spirit with his eternal energies, capacities and senses, which had their residence and seat in his head. The earth within a man, however, was his soul or heart with their associated affections and passions, or feelings of desire and wrath, which had their seat in his breast. Therefore, to know my inward man was to know my own heaven and earth. To know my own heaven, however, was to know my own eternal invisible spirit, together with my eternal intellect, will and senses within my head. And to know my own earth was to know my own invisible soul with its affections and passions, which have their seat in the breast. [31] To know God and Wisdom and to understand that both were present within me would be to know that God and divine Wisdom were working and moving in my heaven and earth, that is, in my spirit and its energies and capacities, and in my heart and soul with their affections and passions.

To know the great Depth of Wisdom would be to recognize the ground-less depth of her oil-fire, namely her fiery essence, which was mixed with oil into a nature and essence that penetrated and permeated my heaven and earth, that is, my spirit and soul.

To know the keys of Wisdom, which unlock her great fiery and viscous Depth and allow her to move in my heaven and earth, my spirit and soul or heart, is nothing other than to recognize the essential touches of her divine power that flowed directly from Wisdom herself into me. They touched my spirit and soul, entered them and penetrated them. This is Wisdom's act of unlocking.

These are the golden keys that are fashioned from no other metal than from bright, native gold. They are pure golden keys; that is, all of their contacts are touches of pure, refined divinity, even purest divinity itself. These secret keys are the keys that lock and unlock Wisdom's great Depth, as well as all the secrets and wonders that lie concealed in her fiery realm and ground. With these keys Wisdom locks and unlocks our heaven and earth, our spirits, with her energies or capacities, and our souls or hearts with their affections. These divine touches or energies

CHAPTER 7

from her oil-fire are the hidden, secret, magical keys that eternally hang by her side. It is with these that she desires to lock and unlock our spirits, souls and hearts. She entrusts no one else with this task, but desires [32] to accomplish it herself. Her hand of power knows well how to use these keys: when, where and with whom to apply them, according to time, place and person. She opens every lock with these keys and is able to insert them in any keyhole. All doors and gates fly wide open when they are used; all brass or iron bars are broken by them. Wisdom possesses the energies of these keys and they are in her power, not in the power of any creature, nor in our power, that is, not in the power of our eternal spirit nor that of our eternal intellect, will and senses; nor in the power of our grace-gifts of hope, faith and prayer; nor in the hunger of our own wills; nor in the avidity of our own struggles; nor in our own righteousness; nor for the sake of our own righteousness. Rather, these keys are efficacious and show forth their power only in our heaven and earth, that is, within the compass of our intellect and in the perimeter or forms of our souls, according to the pleasure of Wisdom's will and good pleasure. This is so in terms of time, place or location and with regard to the persons in and for whom they wish to work. They work at certain times and hours, not at the times convenient to men, nor when men or creatures desire, but when it pleases Wisdom to work with them. In using these keys, Wisdom is a free and voluntary agent. She does not work out of necessity, nor from coercion, but from her own free will and out of her innate goodness, and out of pity for and mercy upon eternal souls or spirits. Who is it who could oblige or force her? Who is above her? Who is stronger than she? Who was before her or higher than she? All spirits are subject to her. She is higher than all eternal spirits, whether of angels or of men. Therefore, it is alone on Wisdom's own account that she chooses to act and to work, to lock and to unlock, how and when it pleases her. She possesses a [33] wise and insightful spirit within her. She knows well when she should make use of those keys and when not; when she should work with them and when she should not. Thus all the children and apprentices of Wisdom come to know and recognize that all of the openings of Wisdom through these magical touches or keys not only happen in an instant but also when, where and in whom she will. Thus Wisdom's efficacious motions, her circulating or ascending and descending fire, her penetrating oil occur anytime, whenever she wishes or pleases. Day and night are one and the same to her; she works any place she likes—all places and locations where she can find and enjoy rest and quietude of spirit are equally welcome to her. The same is true for persons—they are equal in her eyes, whether rich or poor, honored or despised, learned or unlettered, male or female. With Wisdom our mother there is no difference between them, because all eternal spirits, in conjunction with eternal souls, are her children through birth and natural generation, and she is their mother. Thus, there is neither difference nor respect of persons as long as they have been marked with the divine signature, and their eternal spirits and souls are earnest and industrious seekers after Wisdom, and investigate her ways. Such persons possess will-spirits that hearken to Wisdom and

CHAPTER 7

desire to learn from her. They are obedient to her and subject themselves to her disciple and instruction, and steadfastly seek after her and long for her. It is to such as these that Wisdom chooses to appear, lets herself be discovered, and confides herself.

Thus did Wisdom reveal to me that she had descended with her viscous, fiery Depth and had entered into my heaven, into my spirit or intellect, will and senses, as well as into my earth, [34] that is, into my soul and heart with all their affections and passions. She came there to live and to move, to work and to penetrate, to circulate or ascend and descend with her viscous-fire, in order to purify and refine them, to dwell eternally within them, and with her fiery region and habitation to take up residence, to work within them and to permeate them for the sake of their purification.

CHAPTER 8

June 30th

My spirit was still impelled to contemplate myself inwardly, namely my inward, invisible and eternal man, who is hidden and concealed by my exterior man, and to meditate upon how that inner man was created from and consists of a heaven and earth, a spirit and soul. While I was occupying myself with these thoughts, Wisdom revealed to me my inward eternal man and showed me that it was actually a globe or sphere, a *microcosm* or a miniature world. Just as the outward, visible heaven and earth are actually two different essences *per se* yet constitute one single globe in their union, even so the spirit and the soul, although actually two different essences, in their union create only one eternal man and only one globe. Thus, the inward, eternal man is but an extract and an abbreviated idea of the *macrocosm* or large world. [35] Just as the outer world consists of heaven and earth, so the inward man is made up of heaven and earth, that is, of spirit and soul. The heaven of the inward man is his intellect, will and senses, which are, therefore, placed above his earth, that is, above his heart or soul and above their affections and passions. His earth is ordered and established below his heaven, and in their union they make up a globe within the inward, eternal, invisible man. His earth is not set above his heaven, nor is his heaven set below his earth. For the spirit of Wisdom is a wise and understanding spirit. It is a spirit of order, not of disorder. Therefore has She set the spirit, with its intellect, will and senses in the head, above the heart with its affections and passions. In this way the spirit should reign over the heart and rule it. In contrast, the soul, with its affections in the heart, has been place below the head, so that it might be obedient to the spirit in the head and be subservient to it. The soul should be under dominion, obedience and subservience to the spirit in the head in the same way that the outward earth stands in subservience to the upper heavenly bodies and is ruled and dominated by their influences. Thus the heaven of the eternal man is not placed in his earth nor his earth in his heaven, since this would cause disorder and confusion. Therefore, the rational capacities, will and senses of the eternal man are not planted in his heart, nor are his heart or soul and affections planted in his eternal spirit because confusion and disorder would arise.

In order that I come to know myself, Wisdom further presented to my intellect the following passage from Scripture: "And Mary said: My soul doth magnify the Lord, and my spirit hath rejoiced in God my Savior,"[11] for spirit and soul are considered to be two different essences. And in another place [36]: "I pray to God that your whole spirit and soul and body

---

[11] *Luke* 1:46

CHAPTER 8

be preserved . . . "[12] Paul further emphasizes these differences in another passage: "For the word of God is living, and powerful, and sharper than any two-edged sword, piercing even to the dividing asunder of soul and spirit . . . "[13] The reason Paul makes this differentiation is that spirit and soul are two separate essences.

1. In their essences. If you ask what the difference is, and what the eternal essence of the spirit of souls is, I will answer that the soul-spirit is an eternal essence that contains life, motility and sensitivity within it and consists of an eternal intellect, will and senses. Thus it is a seeing, hearing, smelling, tasting and touching spirit. The soul, however, is only an eternal essence, which indeed contains life, motility and sensitivity within it, but consists only of various affections and passions. Thus, there is a difference between them in terms of their eternal essentiality and autonomy.

2. Secondly, the two essential parts, spirit and soul, are differentiated essentially by locality, by their established places or seats. The eternal spirit, namely, with its energies, capacities and senses, has its seat and location in the head; the soul, on the other hand, with its eternal affections and inclinations, is established in the breast or heart, and we carry it in our bosom.

3. Thirdly, these two essential parts, spirit and soul, have been differentiated essentially as two particular and diverse essences by the purposes of

---

[12] *1 Thessalonians* 5:23
[13] *Hebrews* 4:12

their creation. The spirit was created by God to be the lord and ruler over the soul; the soul, however, was created to be ruled by the spirit, to submit to the spirit in subservience and obedience. Therefore, the spirit is placed over the soul in order of position. For this reason the energies or capacities of the reason and will and the life of the senses have been implanted in the spirit. To the soul are given only the affections [37] and passions, which are to be governed by the spirit alone.

4. Fourthly, these two essential parts, spirit and soul, are truly and essentially two diverse essences because the spirit must give an account to God for all the workings and movements of the soul, whether good or bad, orderly or disorderly, just or unjust, according to the will of God or against it, in accordance with nature or against the rule of nature, according to the letter of Scripture or against it. The spirit must take responsibility for whatever the soul does in the expression of its affections and passions in this outbirth, seeing that the spirit has been commanded by God to be the highest lord and ruler over the soul, with its affections and passions. The spirit has been endowed with power and authority to tame the soul, to subdue it and to exercise dominion over it. Thus, if the spirit allows the soul and its affections and passions to dominate it, if the spirit permits this and hands over its superior power to the soul and its affections and to the spirit of reason, so that they obtain power over the spirit and dominate it, that spirit will be called to account for its actions.

5. Fifthly, spirit and soul are two diverse essences in terms of their birth. The spirit is considered higher

CHAPTER 8

than the soul. The spirit is the immediate seed of God, the Spirit of Eternity. It is the Son of God, who from Him was immediately generated and begotten; who is essence of His essence, a Son of His essence and Being; who is none other than the eternal spirit of the soul. The essence or being of the soul, however, is considered lower and is of a lower grade of being than its spirit. For it does not come directly from the divine essence of God but is born immediately from the four eternal elements that have been breathed out and extracted from God's divine *Chaos*. The essence of the eternal soul takes its primordial cause [38] and origin from the mixture and coagulation of the four eternal elements in number, weight and mass, through the magical art of the spirit of the Eternal Wisdom of God. It arises as an essence born in equal temperature from the mixture of the four. The eternal essence of the soul is neither fire, nor air, nor water, nor earth, but rather a fifth essence generated from the four. It is identical to none of the four but is a quintessence that, by the creative *Fiat* of Wisdom, has been combined and composed as an element different from the four eternal elements. The spirit of virginal Wisdom is the mother of souls, just as the spirit of eternity is the father of the eternal spirit. The soul is a generated essence, generated from the mixture and coagulation or clotting of the four eternal elements. Wisdom is the soul's begetting mother, and it is born from her body. 2) The soul is an eternal generated essence because it is generated by Wisdom out of eternal material, namely from the material essence of the four eternal elements. 3) It is considered lower than its eternal spirit, or of a lower grade of being, because the eternal spirit was generated immediately from God's own divine essence. The eternal soul, however, has been generated immediately from eternal nature and is, therefore, a lower essence with regard to the essentiality of the spirit.

Since this is the case, we must not confuse the spirit and the soul nor mix them with each other nor consider them to be one and the same. They must remain without mixture or disorder in our cognition. For the spirit is not the soul, nor is the soul the same as the spirit, although both are eternal essences. To know that spirit and soul are diverse essences in their birth and origin is true philosophy, and to recognize this is to be a true philosopher.

Nevertheless, these two diverse essences [39] and eternal beings do not result in two different persons. Rather the two, in unity and harmony (whereby the spirit rules and the soul is ruled), constitute one single person, that is, one inward eternal, invisible man concealed beneath the outward visible man. If the spirit in the head is separated or divided from the soul in the breast or heart, it does not constitute a person or man. For then he is a mere abstract spirit and nothing more. In like manner, when the soul within the breast or heart is separated from its ruling spirit, its lord and king, it also does not constitute a person or man. When spirit and soul are united in an invisible, eternal body that is appropriate to them, they constitute an eternal person and an eternal man. In this fashion the three diverse parts, in the order and course of pure nature according to their initial establishment, constitute a single inward, eternal, invisible man, who is the subject of eternal beatitude.

CHAPTER 8

These two twins, the spirit and the soul, were indivisibly and inseparably united with each other by the magical art of Wisdom, in order to constitute a single eternal person and inward man, never to be divided or separated from each other. Henceforth, an eternal, abstract, naked spirit, when it has once been united with the soul by the art of Wisdom, cannot be without that same soul and cannot exist without its soul. Likewise, the soul cannot exist without its spirit. Rather, they exist in a precise unity in harmony with each other, and yet they are different. Further, spirit and soul cannot exist in unity with each other without a spiritual body. These three heavenly parts, spirit and soul in a spiritual, heavenly body, constitute an individual or undivided [40] person and an inward eternal man. Therefore these three, body, soul and spirit, exist and remain eternally in an indissoluble bond, one always subordinated to the other in obedience. They should never be separated or divided from each other. Rather, where one of them is, all three must be. They remain together as one person, whether they are in the Principle of darkness or in the Principle of light; whether in the *centrum* of God's anger or in the *centrum* of His love. Where one is, there all three are. For they are eternally together in the course of eternal nature by the decree of the divine Wisdom of God. Hence, the spirit cannot rejoice and the soul be in anguish at the same time, for the spirit and the soul are inseparable companions. If the soul is in a state of anguish, then the spirit is also in anguish. When the spirit is in a state of light and joy, then the soul is also in a state of light and joy within the spiritual body. Know, therefore, that from henceforth not only are the souls of the prophets, patriarchs, the apostles of Christ and the true saints of God in the kingdom of glory with Christ, but their spirits and bodies, along with their souls, are within them and with them. For where one is, all three are present. And of the same nature are those also who dwell in the anguish-ridden kingdom of the Dragon. Their spirits do not exist there without their souls. Neither do they exist there without their spiritual bodies, which have been formed and created from the nature of the dark body out of dark, angry wrath. Thus, where one of them is, so shall all three be indissolubly together for all eternity. [41]

CHAPTER 9

July 1st

The viscous, fiery wheels of Wisdom still impelled the eternal intellect of my eternal spirit to meditate ever more deeply upon the mystery of my self-knowledge. It was then revealed to me that the outward heaven of this visible creation was only a figure and fore-image of the eternal heaven of the inward man within me. Just as in the outward, visible heaven of this out-birth, there is a firmament and high up in that firmament a circle of light. That circle is formed by the sun, moon and stars, together with the constellations and the waters above the firmament. All of these have been arranged in their order to rule over the lower earth, to send down their influences upon and into the earth, and to make it fruitful or to remove infecundity from it. The intellect represents the upper firmament in the heaven of the eternal man, and it is in the firmament of his intellect that I, Wisdom, must place my circle of light. I must set my sun in my circle of light so that it can establish its eternal day, and so that the darkness of fallen night might be swallowed up by the clarity of my eternal day. I must establish my moon in the eternal man so that the motion of all his inward senses, that is,

SOPHIA

his countenance, hearing, taste and smell, as well as the entire sensitive life of his eternal senses might be ruled and directed by the splendor of my moon. I must set that moon in the [42] eternal firmament of man so that nothing else but the brilliance and reflection of my lights can rule over and give pleasure to the senses of his New Heaven. The stars and sidereal constellations of the New Heaven of the eternal man are the workings of his thoughts, and all the movements of his desires, and all the imaginings of his spirit, which are all good, pure and ordered. For these all have been awakened by the divine constellations that rule over them in his heavens. This must be so, because all of the workings of his intellect and will and all of the divine constellations in the heavens of his newly born intellect are under the dominion of his seven fixed planets, namely under the seven fiery lamps, their rulers. And the spirit of Wisdom is the bright Morning Star, the high ruler of all his divine constellations, which are placed principally and immediately under the rule of the Holy Trinity. The upper springs and clouds of man, which contain the water of life, those vessels of heaven from which the early and the late rains come forth, and from which the honeydew drops down, are set in the firmament and heaven of man himself. The hand of Wisdom's energy has set those stars all in their order for good intentions and purposes, namely to rule over the lower earth of man, his soul and heart. They are set there to send down their influences into the heart of man, to make it fruitful, and to banish from it all sterility and infecundity; to take away all hunger and thirst, to till out all nettles, thorns and thistles, and to prevent all weeds, so that they cannot grow in his closed or fenced-in garden and holy ground. In this way, grain, wine and oil can grow abundantly, increase and multiply in his heart, the eternal earth of man. This was presented to me as a work that still [43] had to be accomplished in my spirit and in my own heaven. It was presented not as a work that had already been done but as a work that was being carried out and would be effectually performed. It had not been performed but was shown to me as something still to do. This was done in order to inflame my heart to ponder its accomplishment.

CHAPTER 10

July 2nd

Because my spirit continued to importune and press me from within to achieve a greater level of self-knowledge, Wisdom revealed to me that the outward heavens were a figure and fore-image of the eternal heavens. Similarly, the outward earth of this visible world was a figure and image of the eternal earth within the inward man himself, namely of his eternal soul or heart and affections. She said that just as the earth is the ground upon which mankind walks, so the heart or soul of man is the earth or ground of the inward man, upon which his eternal spirit moves. And just as it is said of the spirit that it flies into its own heaven by the movement of its intellect, will and senses, even so it is said of the spirit that in the movements of the various passions of its heart it walks back and forth upon its own earth. Just as the outward earth has many pleasure gardens planted within it, even so out of the newly regained earth of the inward man, that is, out of his renewed heart and regenerated soul, rise the lost Garden of Eden and [44] the lost Paradise. The soul or heart is not Paradise itself. Rather it is Eden, the true Garden of Paradise, which emerges from man's own earth, which is his own heart. Just as other gardens blossom forth from the earth, Paradise springs forth from the soul and from all its affections in unity with divine love. Thus, the lost Paradise shall never be found outside of man, that is, outside of his own heart or earth. Rather, it must blossom and spring forth verdantly out of his own inward ground and earth, that is, out of his own heart.

On the other hand, the outward earth is the *matrix* or womb wherein the vegetable seed has been sown by the hand of the sower, and out of which grass, herbs, rooted vegetables, plants, trees and fruits blossom and grow forth, along with all sorts of fragrant flowers, things good to look at and delicious to eat. Various herbs, fruits, seeds and flowers grow forth for food, for medicine and for enjoyment, from this vegetable realm. It is the same with the eternal earth of man, that is, his soul or heart of the inwardly enclosed or verdantly surrounded ground and earth, wherein Wisdom sows her vegetable seeds. This is a type of seed that contains its life within itself, a living eternal seed. Therefore, flowers and lilies and rosebuds blossom forth from the heart or soul of man. These are his gifts of grace and his divine virtues. These are the herbs that grow from his own ground and earth. These are the herbs of gentleness, friendliness, mildness, benevolence and charm. These heavenly, paradisal herbs contain no tartness, bitterness, sourness or wrathful property or taste. His plants grow out of his own soul as out of his own earth, namely from the fruitful vine of the pomegranate tree, along with [45] all fragrant spice trees, such as the myrrh tree, the aloe-cassia and the

CHAPTER 10

cinnamon tree.

This is the vegetable realm of the eternal man. If his eternal spirit has been taught and instructed by Wisdom to be a noble, wise philosopher, and if he has become a subtle artist and a master of the arts through her art, then he can call himself a worthy natural scientist and a medical doctor to whom honor is due.

If his soul-spirit were an experienced botanist in these matters, or were the one who had planted science in the nature of his own herbs and plants, he could accomplish anything. If he were a true chymist who could separate the pure from the unpure, then from his own seeds, herbs, plants, trees and fruits, which grow forth from his own garden, ground and terrain, he could extract a powerful liquor. This liquor, the elixir of life, could become a juice from his own pomegranate tree, and a strengthening wine from the juice and grapes of his vine that grows in his own earth. With the power and virtue of this liquor, or the spirit of this wine, he could enliven, refresh and strengthen his spirit, and with that tincture bring the spirit to its highest state of joy. He could produce from the vegetable garden within him a precious oil, imbued with such healing power that it could heal all sicknesses and weaknesses, and free his eternal spirit from all complaints, troubles and sadness, as well as from all melancholy, pain and agony. This liquor can be made as precious as a divine medicine, can evince such a beautiful golden color, and can produce such a wonderful aroma and scent of incense, that it surpasses all the compounds and confections of the apothecary's art.

SOPHIA

These seeds, spices, herbs, plants and fruits grow as food and sustenance [46] from the earth of man. They can be employed as food, sustenance and medicine for the soul-spirit, as well as for pleasure, adornment and joy. The eternal man with his eternal spirit can not only find pleasure in his own garden but also discover his food and sustenance growing in his own earth. In that garden he can gather and drink the new spiced wine from his own vine that grows within him. It is the unknowingness of the eternal spirit of man that causes him to seek outwardly for his nutrition, medicine and pleasure, rather than within him. For the magical hand of Wisdom has planted all root vegetables, herbs, plants and fruits in him, and for this reason they grow freely and spontaneously, without toil and trouble. The eternal spirit does not need to plow or to sow. The products of the earth have been sown by the art of Wisdom and are irrigated by the upper springs with the water of life, which exudes from itself warm beams of fire that penetrate those fruits with its energy and tincture. Moreover, Wisdom has planted a central fire in her own earth so that the spirit of man has to do nothing else but know the gate and the path that leads to that earth and how to take and eat those products for his sustenance, and that he alone should know how to draw forth and extract their saps for medicinal purposes and to drink in abundance from their powerful juices. In this way he shall bring his spirit to a state of highest pleasure and joy, and also teach it how to bear these products as an adornment. Wisdom said that man's eternal spirit would be blessed and happy in its own vegetable realm and paradisal garden within it, and would not need to depart from its own earth. For its earth is a fruitful earth, a happy and beautiful land. There is a garden fountain in this land flowing with milk and honey. It is always spring and summer there. Grain, wine, oil, honey and milk [47] are ever present in abundance in man's renewed earth. When the earth of the eternal man is renewed again to its primal state, then the Paradise within it will burst forth verdantly. It is his abundantly fertilized land; it is his fertile field, ground and soil. All of his twigs, shoots, sprouts and blossoms burst forth from his own eternal heart and soul within him, when they have restored and renewed. O where has the soul-spirit been absent for so long that it does not even know its own hidden Paradise? It does not know that it is concealed within its own heart, which is its own ground or earth within it.

These visions of Wisdom that occurred within my eternal spirit took place solely to bring me to self-knowledge and to turn my eye inward, so that I might come to recognize myself and know and enjoy what lay within me. Wisdom told me that this was the basis of true philosophy and the sole path to becoming a philosopher. She also said that she had descended with her own fiery ground and had entered my eternal soul or inward earth, in order to renew them and to cause the eternal Paradise to blossom and become verdant again from my infertile wilderness, overgrown with useless thickets and weeds. Not that the work had been accomplished and perfected. Rather, Wisdom had come to perform this and was now in the midst of the work, seeing as she was capable of turning an arid and sterile desert

SOPHIA

into a fertile field. We must not tarry in these visions, however, for they have been given to the intellect, and stand before it, solely to awaken desire and to draw the will-spirit to seek after Wisdom, so that Wisdom might effectually and essentially accomplish that work. Many have deceived themselves by remaining trapped and caught by revelations and visions. They have contented themselves with the pleasant desire for Wisdom, before they have experienced it being [48] effectually accomplished and worked through within them.

CHAPTER 11

July 3rd

As part of my acquisition of self-knowledge, Wisdom then presented to my intellect the idea that the outward earth is where the realm of animals exists, where beasts and cattle dwell, and, together with the crawling worms and other living creatures, live, move and nourish themselves from its grass. This outward earth, according to her, is a figure and fore-image of the eternal earth of the inward man, in which his animal realm exists. Out of the eternal heart or soul of the eternal, invisible man, which is his earth, his living creatures, his cattle, his wild beasts, his living animals, and all living worms that creep in his earth, have their primordial origin and from it derive.

Do you ask what these crawling, teeming worms are? Know that these are each and every creeping earthy movement, each and every earthy inclination that stirs, and each and every lustful desire that rises up and creeps forth from the heart which is man's own earth, that either incline the soul away from heaven toward this earthy out-birth or raise it up away from all earthy creatures and toward heaven. What are then his living cattle, and his animals that live upon and in his own earth, and which were created for the use, comfort and office of the eternal spirit, such as the horse and the donkey, created for riding and for man's use and service, [49] according to his good pleasure and free will? These are the avid affections and passions of his own heart, his hopes, his desires, his love, his joy, together with the rest of his useful and serviceable passions. We also find his lions, bears, wolves, and rending beasts of prey, which prowl back and forth on his earth, roaring wrathfully. These are his fiery or angry passions, namely his wrath and ire, his wickedness and envy. These wrathful furies desire to kill and murder, and all of them are found living in his earth. All of these lively bestial, animalistic and brutal passions of his lower sensual and sensitive nature must be ruled, governed and guided by the eternal spirit of man's intellect, and not the eternal spirit dominated by them.

I truly saw that the animal realm of man had been born from his own earth and all his animal affections and passions had emerged from his own heart, which is his own earth. I beheld the wise provisions of Wisdom; for by Wisdom's order the inner beasts of man were not placed in his heavens, to dwell, move and seek their nourishment; nor were they in his intellect, will or senses. Their designated dwelling place is in the human heart, in the earth of man, to dwell and graze therein, in order to be tamed and ruled by the intellect and will of the eternal spirit of the inward man.

These visions or revelations were given to my intellect by Wisdom alone to guide me toward thorough self-understanding. She proclaimed to me

CHAPTER 11

and let me see clearly that she had come down to my earth to strengthen my eternal spirit and instruct it in how to house and tame my birds and beasts of prey, that they might no longer rule over and dominate my spirit. Thus my spirit should live no more from the flesh of [50] animals or the flesh of birds but solely from the roots, herbs and flowers that grew in its own farmland, fields or garden.

CHAPTER 12

July 4th

Then as guidance for my intellect toward self-knowledge I was told that the outward earth was a figure and fore-image, in whose mines, veins and intestines the mineral realm was hidden. Therein was contained the rich treasures of the earth, namely veins of gold and silver, seeds of gold and various precious gems, such as pearls, rubies, sapphires and diamonds of inestimable value, both for practical use and as jewelry and adornment. For these have all been created by God and laid in the deep center of the earth by Wisdom, so that they could be worn by the inhabitants of the earth for decoration, honor and adornment, and men thereby be made rich, noble and handsome. Likewise, these jewels are also valuable for their usefulness, application and service in medicine, for they are endowed with the highest power and efficacy against all toxic sicknesses, as well as the greatest ability to strengthen and refresh the heart and spirit of the outward man. God has devised it so that the highest and most refined healing power and virtue should be contained in mineral seeds and metals that far exceed the energies of the seeds of roots, herbs, plants and all heart-strengthening flowers and fruits.

This virtue is made serviceable to the extent that the reason-spirit, as a noble chymist, is able to draw out and eliminate the toxic qualities and properties from the [51] mineral earth. In the same way that jewels are drawn from the outward earth, spiritual energies may be drawn from the inward earth, that is, from the heart and soul, the eternal earth, of the inward eternal man. For the hand of Wisdom has sown her mineral seeds in that inward earth, namely the pure, immaculate gold-seed, so that man possesses a mineral realm and bears a rich treasure within his own earth. In this earth of his is present the material essentiality of the stone of Wisdom, the elixir and the transformative stone, which is called the stone of the wise or the philosophers' stone. O you devotees of Wisdom! This precious stone of divine Wisdom is such a pure treasure hidden in the field of man's own eternal earth within him, that is, in the inward eternal ground of his heart. This treasure is more precious than rubies; its acquisition is more desirable than gold; it is utterly incomparable. It brings riches and honor to the inward man; it confers abundance and beatitude; it liberates the inward man from all scarcity, hunger and thirst; it drives away all trouble, sorrow and sighing. Blessed and happy is the inward man who discovers these mineral gold-seeds within himself.

The reason why so few men have discovered this treasure is that they have not sought it, nor have they dug deeply enough into the depths of its earth, for it lies very deep. Herein my spirit perceived what sort of philosopher a man must be in order to accomplish this task. The eternal spirit of my inward man was

CHAPTER 12

the material of this stone, its pure mineral gold-seed. My eternal spirit was also the place and location of the treasure, namely because it could be found only in the depths of its own earth, seeing as the gold-seed had been sown therein. I also saw the philosopher's furnace, which was threefold. The first furnace dissolves the glue of mortality, since the outward man is [52] subject to disintegration by death, even before he has discovered and discerned the stone. The second furnace is the heart itself, in which this pure gold-seed lies mixed with much earthiness, filth and slag, things that must be separated out and discharged. After it has been purified, the seed is sealed with a hermetic seal and placed within a crystalline vial of pure glass. It must remain therein until it has been brought to the proper garnet red color that can tincture the spirit-man and transform him, so that he becomes pure, immaculate gold and thus perfectly perfected.

In addition, my spirit was also shown the true philosopher's fire as well as the central fire lying hidden within the gold-seed itself. My spirit was also instructed in the regulation of the fire, that it must neither be too hot nor too cold, that it must never go out, neither by day nor by night, and that it should always be kept at a gentle yet constant heat. Sometimes the fiery furnace must be heated with an intense fire and sometimes with a gentle flame. At times the seed itself might arise or be awakened to life, sublimate itself and transform itself from its own central fire, depending upon whether it had been properly regulated by the artist, the eternal spirit. This was the key to the work. After this I was shown the instigator and instructor of the work, without whose counsel, warnings, teaching and instructions it would be impossible to discern and complete. This instructor was none other than the spirit of Wisdom itself, which must be united with the eternal spirit of the eternal inward man. Otherwise, the stone could never be brought to perfection by the spirit of the eternal man. Finally, in the end, I was shown the way and manner in which it was created, as well as how to separate the pure from the unpure. The entire process was demonstrated to me, including the difficulties that could arise in the work of separation. I was shown, as well, how much constant, persistent effort was required before the work could be fully accomplished. At this my eternal [53] spirit fainted and no more energy remained within it. However, I received the consolation that half the battle was already won, once the will-spirit had decided to approach the work earnestly. Let no one deceive himself, however. The beginning of the work is strenuous and difficult, but toward the end it becomes easy and pleasant. In this way, my intellect was presented with the fact that the visible heaven and earth of this visible creation are merely figures and fore-images of the inward, invisible heaven and earth that belong to the inward, invisible, eternal man.

At this, it was revealed and presented to my eternal intellect who was the primary heart or king of this invisible globe or terrestrial ball, which consists of heaven and earth, that is, of an intellect, will and senses; for this is heaven. The heart or the soul, with its affections and passions, however, constitutes the created earth, whose ruler and lord can be none other

CHAPTER 12

than the eternal spirit. Its intellect, will and senses are its own created heaven, and the eternal spirit itself is the sole heart and overlord of its own intellect, will and senses, also heart and affections. It is in itself an eternal, invisible spirit. Therefore, its heaven and earth are also invisible, according to its own image and likeness. The inward eternal man is a magical spirit. Thus his world, his realm, his heaven and earth are all magical. I would say that his intellect, his will and senses are all magical. Therefore, the objects and products of his intellect, will and senses are all magical. Even his countenance, his flower, the sound of his voice, his nutrition, his eating and drinking, his perfumes and incense, his gardens, meadows, his strolls, his wine, elixir, nectar and ambrosia are all magical [54] as he himself is. His body, air, fire and earth are all magical, bright and clear. They are, like him, crystalline and transparent, so that he can pass through all gates and Principles without hindrance. Under the guidance of the holy Trinity, the spirit of the inward eternal man is God's heavenly *magus*,[14] His heavenly scout and messenger or interpreter. It is a ministering spirit and a pure flame of the fire that shines through. How crassly do those persons err and deceive themselves who make the object of their investigations the outward, coarse, visible, mortal human being or spirit, with his rational spirit, intellect, will and senses, which are occupied with visible things of this visible world and out-birth. Such men see only the pleasant pictures or images of this

---

[14] One who consorts with divine Wisdom and has illuminated spiritual senses and heart (J.G. Gichtel)

world, only hear the sweet harmonies and sounds of this world, and live solely from the flesh of animals, birds and fish. This outward, visible man has an outward, visible world that corresponds to him, over which he is lord alone. He is a mortal spirit and possesses, therefore, a transient, mortal kingdom. For this reason he is nourished with perishable food and, in his mortality, dies or passes away like the animals. There is, however, an inward, eternal, immortal man hidden within the outward, mortal man. For that which is mortal is a mere husk or shell that covers over the inward, immortal man. This is the man who is lord over his own heaven and earth, who rules over his own world or globe. He is a spirit who rules over his own intellect, will and senses, as well as over his own soul or heart and affections. This eternal spirit-man, after he is extracted and separated from the outward, mortal man, can no longer eat perishable foods. This is so not just when he is outside the body but also during the time that he is still in the body, for he eats no perishable food nor drinks any perishable beverage in eternity. This inward, eternal spirit-man is the sole ruler and lord over his own invisible heaven [55] and earth, just as the mortal man is lord over his own visible heaven and earth.

These representations took place and were shown to the spirit of my intellect solely with the intention of furthering my self-understanding, so that I might come to know how to examine myself, to recognize what was hidden within me and what might be found within me. They let me comprehend that Wisdom had come down and descended into my ground or earth. Wisdom had appeared in order to effect its

CHAPTER 12

spirit-tincture and to create its mineral stone in the realm of man, insofar as the spirit of the eternal soul was willing to earnestly request this of her. These representations, these prophecies, these visions and revelations occurred as an encouragement and inducement to persevere in earnest desire, and not to slacken in eager seeking and desire for Wisdom (as the greatest confessors of the faith since the days of the apostles have done in recent times) until we truly have come to possess and enjoy her.

CHAPTER 13

July 4th

While the thoughts of my intellect were still occupied with the eternal spirit of the inward, invisible man and his heaven and earth, Wisdom further revealed to me that in the way that this eternal spirit existed in its fallen and relapsed state or in its renewed state, its heaven and earth were in the same condition. To the extent that his eternal spirit [56] existed in its fallen and lapsed state, its heaven and earth would be in a fallen and relapsed state. To the extent that the eternal spirit itself had fallen, its heaven, that is, its intellect, will and senses, as well as its earth, namely its heart or soul and all its affections and passions, would exist in a fallen state. If man's eternal spirit exists in a renewed state, however, then his heaven, that is, his intellect, will and senses, as well as his earth, that is, his heart or soul and affections and passions, would also be renewed.

First of all, Wisdom encouraged my intellect to meditate upon the eternal spirit of the inward man with its heaven and earth in their fallen and relapsed state.

It is said of this spirit that it is tainted and unpure in its fallen and relapsed state. Thus it is said of its intellect, will and senses that they are also unpure and tainted. It is said that its earth is also unpure, tainted and corrupted, that is, that its heart or soul, its affections and passions, are as unpure and tainted as its heaven, its intellect, will and senses. This is the state of the inward eternal man with his heaven and earth in his condition of having fallen away from God and apostatized. He exists in an evil condition, in a tainted and unpure state, a state of absolute weakness and imperfection, in a state of affliction.

This eternal man in his fallen state is called the Old Man, the old Adamic man, or the First Adam within us, for the First Adam in his fallen condition is a figure and fore-image of this fallen man within us. This is our own fallen man, a fallen Adam, who is corrupt within, according to deceitful lusts.[15] [57] In this condition he becomes a spirit of disobedience and a son of disobedience.[16] Further, he is referred to as the man of sins because he is in a state of astrayness and selfness. He is also called the son of corruption because this state of astrayness within destroys him. He must be freed from this condition. Otherwise, he will corrupt and utterly destroy himself. In this state he is also called an Antichrist because, in this state, he stands in contrariety and opposition to God, the Holy Trinity, Wisdom and the Spirit of Jesus. Furthermore, in this condition he is called a mystery of unrighteousness because he lies hidden within all the deceptions of unrighteousness. In this state he is incapable of receiving the truth in love and is given

---

[15] *Ephesians* 4:22; *Colossians* 3:9
[16] *Ephesians* 2:2

CHAPTER 13

over to serious errors, so that he believes in delusions and lies and has pleasure in unrighteousness.[17] In this, his first natural birth, his mortal fleshly body is united with the outward spirit. Through his natural birth, even if he is the Son of God, he is nevertheless in himself the son of fallen Adam, a lost man, a corrupted and wretched human being. He is a natural man and cannot comprehend the things of God. He is an angel of darkness, an angel of the groundless abyss, an incarnate spirit of error who dwells in the body of the flesh. He is the servant of idols because he stands united with the Dragon and the Beast. He is a worshiper of false gods and of graven images. He is the servant of his own will because he bows down and prostrates himself before his own will and desires, like the heathen before Baal. He is an atheist who perhaps confesses God with his mouth but denies Him both with his deeds and his works. He is an adulterer whose spirit has turned away from the only true God and now commits adultery and harlotry with the nature of the Dragon and with the spirit of this world by loving himself and the lusts [58] and pleasures of this world more than he loves God. He is a liar, a miser, an unbeliever, just as the heathens and unbelievers of antiquity were. He is an angel who did not maintain his primal state. He is a disobedient, rebellious spirit who breaks and violates all of the commandments of God. He is a cynical Ishmael, an unholy Esau, an uncircumcised Philistine, a cloud without moisture, a tree without fruit, a wild sea wave, a comet or meteor. He is a dead spirit who is

---

[17] *2 Thessalonians* 2:11-12

dead in astrayness and transgressions, one who lives according to the way of Cain, a spirit who follows after the error of Balaam with avid desire and who walks according to the rebellion and dissension of Korah. He shall be kept in this condition of darkness, in bonds and chains, preserved for the judgment of the Great Day.

Numberless spirits in this state shall be excluded from the gates of the New Jerusalem, according to *Revelation* 22:15. Outside you will find dogs, magicians, whoremongers, murderers, idolaters and all liars. Why is this so? The reason and cause is that no unpure spirit can enter in.[18] Nothing shall enter there which might defile its ground or earth, for God will not work and cannot dwell within an unpure and tainted spirit. In this way, you may behold in what sort of unpure and tainted state, in what a miserable and wretched condition, the eternal spirit of the inward man dwells in its fallenness. Namely, that it comes from its father, the spirit of error; that it bows down before the Beast and worships it; that it bears the name and image of the Dragon and the Beast; that it makes itself into a god through its own selfness; that it prostrates itself before the lusts of its own will as before Baal-Peor; that its religion is hypocrisy before God and a mere external, assumed, slippery appearance of holiness, an appearance assumed to appease its guilty conscience. The spirit itself has chosen this appearance, and has formed and shaped it according to the letter of Scripture. [59]

My intellect was further confronted with the

---

[18] *Revelation* 21:27

CHAPTER 13

unpureness, corruption and pollution of the realm, the world, the *centrum* and Principles of the Old Man, areas that must, of necessity, resemble the Old Man himself. That realm, world, *centrum* and Principles, like their lord and king, must inevitably also be unpure and tainted in their fallen state, a fact to which Scripture gives clear witness. Such conditions, in this fallen state, are called the Old World, that is, the old, wicked world, which is full to overflowing with abominations and unpureness. Its kingdom is a realm of inherent darkness, a realm of thick, murky turgidity. The Old Man lives, eats, drinks and walks in darkness and is a child of darkness, and is held captive in chains and bonds by the power of this darkness for the judgment of the Great Day, that is, for the Day of Conviction. On that day the eternal spirit itself is consigned to a state of darkness and not to a state, realm and Principle of light. The eternal spirit is then brought over from the state of eternal darkness and affliction and translated into a kingdom of light.

Afterwards I was confronted with the unpureness, corruption and pollution of the heavens of the Old Man in his fallen state. For his heavens fell with him. It was impossible that the eternal spirit should fall away from God without its heavens also falling away and becoming unpure with it. This is because there is such an essential unity between the spirit itself and its heavens, which are an essential part within it. The inward heavens of man are inherently unpure in this fallen state. This is so in God's eyes as well as in his own. The early prophets spoke about these unpure and sinful heavens in the eternal man when

SOPHIA

they cried out: "Give ear, O ye heavens, and I will speak."[19] Give ear, ye heavens, for this did not occur in the outward, visible heavens outside of man. These fallen heavens are the dark heavens in the inward man, to which [60] we sometimes cry out when we mourn our abominations. Mourn ye heavens, covered and clothed in darkness! The eternal spirit shall be held in these, its own dark heavens, and in the fog of the darkness within itself until the day of its judgment comes. The eternal spirit may well say to itself inwardly: "O Lucifer! I was once a morning star, a son of the dawn. How am I now fallen from my primal radiant heavens! How have they now been transformed into darkness?"

In addition, it was revealed to my intellect that the hosts or generations or peoples of his inward heavens had also fallen into a state of evil and disorder along with him. His sun, moon and stars, which are the hosts and peoples of the fallen heavens within him, had fallen into a condition of unpureness, darkness, disorder and confusion along with him and in him. His sun had darkened, his moon had become obscure, and his stars had fallen into disorder and confusion with him. The entire course of his inward heavens had been reversed, all its order had fallen, with him, into disorder and into a confused state of evil and affliction. These are the old fallen heavens within the fallen man himself, which are being preserved unto the Day of Judgment for the fire. The allusive expressions and parabolic words of the ancients were thus powerfully revealed to my spirit by the fiery eye

[19] *Deuteronomy* 32:1

CHAPTER 13

of Wisdom. This is the fallen state of the eternal man along with his heavens.

The apostles in the New Testament report that the heavens within the fallen man are his intellect, will and senses, which have their seat in the head. His eternal intellect and his rational capacities are the heavens of the eternal man within him. Since he fell away from God, his own heavens within him fell away with him as well. Accordingly, let us consider what the apostles of Christ say concerning the eternal intellect in its fallen state. [61] Namely, it is an intellect that has been obscured, that walks in the darkness, not in the light. It is an intellect that is unstable or given over to a perverse understanding; it is an intellect that is without judgment or comprehension, an intellect that serves the law of sin. It is a carnal intellect with carnal attitudes which orientates its will, senses and intellect to the things of the flesh. It is a fleeting, inconstant intellect that walks in the way of vanity, an earthy intellect that loves earthy things. It is a proud intellect that is puffed up in arrogance, a corrupt and tainted intellect, an intellect that is hostile to God and to the good. It is a blinded intellect, an obscured, ignorant, perverse and corrupt intellect. You see herein that the inward heaven of man, namely his own eternal heaven within him is, in his fallen state, utterly evil, darkened and corrupt.

Another portion of the heavens of the inward man within him is his will. This will is in the same fallen state as man himself, as the apostles clearly demonstrate and instruct us in their doctrine and teaching. The will stands in contrariety to and enmity with the will of God. In this will that opposes God, man is an Antichrist and the will of an Antichrist. It is a disobedient and rebellious will opposing all the commandments and exhortations of God. This will-spirit is an idolatrous will because it is united to the nature of the Dragon and the nature of the Beast. It is an adulterous will because it commits spiritual adultery with the idols of silver and gold and of the flesh in this earthly out-birth. It is a stubborn will that raises up its own will in the place of God's will, thus making itself its own God and guide. Thus the will is a renegade will, a will established in evil and selfness and alienated in itself from the life that comes from God. [62]

The third portion of the heavens of the inward man within him is his senses. They are in the same fallen state as he, since they are essential parts of him. His senses are unpure, tainted and corrupted.

His eyes are evil, terrible eyes. They are vain eyes that find their pleasure in sin and vanity. They are dimmed eyes, blinded by darkness. Such eyes can see nothing other than what they see by the light of the sun, moon and stars, that is, the perceptible objects and forth-castings of this outward visible world and creation. In their fallen state, however, they cannot see the things and objects of the invisible world and creation with such eyes. It is said of them that they have eyes yet cannot see.[20] They have unfaithful eyes, eyes full of adultery,[21] lustful eyes that look for and lust after the desires of the flesh, prideful life, bestial life and earthly forth-castings. They look for and lust

[20] *Psalm* 115:5
[21] *2 Peter* 2:14

CHAPTER 13

after the idols and pleasant images of this present world.

His ears are uncircumcised ears in this fallen state, that is, unpure and tainted ears. His ears are deaf ears, that is, ears that have been closed and deafened. These are ears that cannot hear the voice and inspiration of divine Wisdom; such ears are stopped to all exhortations of Wisdom, especially to her friendly invitations. These are itchy ears that turn away from truth and listen to lies and fables. They give heed to the invocations of the Beast and the False Prophet and obey them. They obey the voices of men and creatures but not the voice of God. They are vain ears that find their pleasure in the sounds and music of this visible world and yet are deaf to the lovely harmonies of the invisible spheres.

His sense of smell in this fallen condition is unpure [63] and imperfect. They have noses and nostrils, yet they do not smell;[22] that is, in this fallen state they can smell neither the gentle, sweet and pleasant odors nor the powerful wafting of the garments of Wisdom; nor the strong aroma of her precious ointments; nor the incense of the myrrh, aloes and cassia of her pure body; nor the sweet aromatic vapors that ascend from the mounds of incense and from the beds of spikenard that rise up from the invisible creation within him. Such noses are capable of smelling only the unpure miasmas of the corrupted air in which they live. They can smell only the stinking manure vapors that rise up from this visible out-birth and the pleasant odors that have been artfully created from the spices of the

---

[22] *Psalm* 115:6

merchants of this world. The heavenly scents, divine and crystalline, that stream forth from the body of the Holy Trinity, which envelop the spirit with joy, yea that are absolute pure, immaculate Godhead itself, such noses can, in their fallen state, neither smell nor enjoy.

His sense of taste, his tongue, lips and mouth, are completely unpure and corrupt in their fallen condition. His taste is imperfect, he cannot taste what he eats. His palate cannot distinguish what he savors. He partakes only of the dust of mortality, the food of serpents; he consumes only the husks or residue, that is, the residue of this visible earth, the lusts and pleasures of this visible creation in union with his outward man. However, the sweet fruits that grow in his own Paradise he cannot assay; he can neither eat of the apples of love nor drink of his own spiced wine that should grow in his own garden. This is the case because he exists in a fallen state and therefore cannot eat of his heavenly and divine sustenance. Rather, his food is earthy, perishable and corruptible, just as it grows on this earthy, forbidden tree of mortality. [64]

In his fallen state his tongue cannot distinguish whether he is eating of life or of death, that is, whether he is eating of the living fruit which grows on the tree of life or from the forbidden fruit that grows on the tree of the knowledge of good and evil. With his tongue he eats from the arts and sciences that grow on the tree of death while he imagines that he is eating of the fruits of the tree of life. He convinces and deceives himself that his life depends upon the understanding of the history and knowledge of the mystery of Holy Scripture, instead of upon the essential possession of those things to which the knowledge of the history and the mystery beckon him.

His tongue is a terrible and evil tongue; for in his fallen state there is much unrighteousness within it. It is a viper's tongue whose words bite like a snake or like the sting of an adder. It is a deceptive tongue that flatters with the words of its lips. It is a backbiting tongue that calumniates with words that are the lashes of the tongue. It is a dumb tongue that cleaves to the roof of the mouth and is incapable of calling, crying, praying or speaking as the Spirit gives it utterance. It can only pray from artifice, intellectual knowledge and out of its own spirit. It is a dumb tongue that cannot speak of the hidden things of God, nor of His mysteries and wonders in the invisible world or creation, although it knows how to speak with artifice and knowledge of God's wonders in this world. It can talk about all the secrets contained in this out-birth yet is incapable of addressing a single mystery of God's invisible creation because such a tongue is dumb. A tongue that is dumb can neither pray to God nor extol God with songs of praise as it ought. It cannot sing or raise a song of praise to Him, even though it enjoys singing common songs and spiritual canticles artfully composed by spiritual men. [65] It is a senseless, impetuous, scolding, gossiping tongue that spews out argumentative and blasphemous words, as well as bad names, smut and filth. It is an undisciplined tongue. It is an untamed tongue, an uncontrollable tongue that cannot be tamed. It is a terrible and perverse tongue that speaks nothing but evil, sin and unrighteousness. It is a vain tongue that cannot keep from expressing vanities and vain words, and is incapable of speaking anything good. It is a vengeful tongue whose words are like swords; such a tongue is sharpened like the sharpest sword, in order to strike, to destroy and to murder. This is a malicious, envious, noxious and murderous tongue. It is a false and insincere tongue that speaks lies in the name of the Lord. It is a perverse tongue whose joy it is to speak of perverse matters. In the fallen state there is a variety of tongues, and yet all are still only one tongue, namely the Egyptian tongue. When the tongue is inflamed by the angry or wrathful Principle or from the earthy Principle, it is a world full of unrighteousness and evil. And so we may well say of the fallen tongue: "What shall we do with you or say about you? O evil and deceptive tongue!" And the words that come forth from an evil tongue in its fallen state—how can they be anything but evil words, idle words not seasoned with the salt of Wisdom, that they might become wise words? Instead they are vain, empty and foolish words that contribute nothing to the edification of the listener.

In their fallen state his lips are like unto his tongue. Therefore, the lips of the eternal man in his fallen state are terrible, unpure lips as are the fruits of his lips. His fallen lips are unpure lips, and under his lips unrighteousness and transgression are found. Who is the one who does not sin with his lips in his fallen state? Who may keep [66] his lips in check in this fallen state? His lips are flattering, insincere, hypocritical, sinful and deceptive lips before God. Such lips are destructive, thoughtless, perverse and sinful lips. His lips are quarrelsome lips, the cords wrapped around his own soul. They speak injury and vanity and are feigned, false lips. The fruit of fallen lips can be no better or different as long as the poison of asps is under them,[23] that is, as long as the speech of the lips is impelled by the wrathful anger-fire that is under them, and as long as unrighteousness is found under his lips.

His mouth must be sinful, unpure and tainted in this fallen condition, a mouth that is full of unrighteousness; an unbelieving, unfaithful mouth; a sinful and transgressing mouth that is full of curses and swearing; a flattering and vain mouth that speaks vanities; a perverse and hypocritical mouth, a mouth that is smoother than oil. In its fallen state the mouth is wicked, for it speaks from the jaws of the Dragon, and from the jaws of the Serpent, and from the jaws of the Beast and from the mouth of the False Prophet. Therefore, in its fallen state, the breath of this mouth must be an unpure breath, an evil, destructive, venomous and infectious breath. And what must the words be like which are the fruit that emerges from a mouth in its fallen state? What must be the fruits of a mouth in this fallen condition? They must necessarily be awful, unpure and tainted words, impregnated with an evil tincture that is destructive to others as well as to itself. They would have to be vain words, idle words, harsh, bitter, wrathful and angry words; earthy, carnal, bestial and infernal words, because they are spoken by the mouths of the Dragon, the Beast and the False Prophet within the one who [67] says them. They are foolish words lacking Wisdom because they are not spoken by Wisdom. They are

---

[23] *Romans* 3:13

flattering, dissembling words, deceptive and insincere words, envious and malicious words, transgressing and sinful words. There is a variety and multiplicity of words: dubious questions and aggressive words; invented, nuanced words; peevish words that are hard to bear and which cause chagrin and pain to the heart. All such words emerge from the spirit of the inward man in his fallen state.

In this way you may behold the sensory, sensitive life of the heavens that belong to the eternal man in his fallen state, and see that they are all in an evil and wretched condition. This is a fact that is amply attested to by passages in Holy Scripture. His eyes are so blinded that he cannot see the invisible world or creation within himself. His ears are so stopped that he cannot hear the voice of Wisdom within him. His tongue is so utterly unable to taste that he can neither savor nor enjoy the fruits of the tree of life within him. His sense of touch is so lost that he can feel and experience only anguish or perhaps the vain pleasures and joys of this outward world, this out-birth.

Thus his own senses become his jail and prison cell in this fallen state. The heavens within him are dark heavens, and his own eternal spirit becomes a prisoner in his own dungeon and jail house. In this fallen state the inward man is a dead man. In him the threats and warnings of God are realized when He says: "On the day that thou eatest thereof thou shalt surely die."[24] And therefore the eternal spirit-man is a dead man; that is, he is truly dead to the divine and heavenly

---

[24] *Genesis* 2:17

CHAPTER 13

life within him, the paradisal life, the life of Wisdom within himself, [68] for he does not perceive them. He hears nothing, tastes nothing, smells nothing and feels nothing of them within him, just like a dead man. He is, within himself, a blind, dumb, mute, insensitive, insensate spirit. He is hungry, thirsty, a naked spirit with no garment to cover his nudity. He wanders back and forth in this world and is hidden behind the mask of a carnal form. Like swinish men he lives from husks; like bestial men he grazes on grass, herbs and roots, and is utterly unknowing. For the true spirit of understanding has departed from him just as it departed from King Nebuchadnezzar. Nevertheless, he still considers himself rich, even in this dead, fallen state of his. He thinks himself to have been furnished abundantly with all good spiritual gifts, namely with understanding, prayer, hope, faith and good works, such that he lacks nothing. He has no idea that he is inwardly wretched, poor, blind, dumb, mute, naked and miserable. The ground and cause of this is that his sensitive life and the life of his senses live from the tree of death. He is still eating from this forbidden tree, and his intellect and will, his countenance, hearing, senses of smell, taste and touch are still occupied with this outward world outside himself. He nourishes himself from the fruits that grow on the twigs and branches of this tree, all of which fruits give him pleasure. He enjoys the vanities of this external Principle within himself. He is satisfied with presenting a good appearance and with walking in his own eternal Principle of eternal life within him. Therefore, he never seeks true eternal life or considers that he is in this fallen state.

SOPHIA

This is the first gate, through which I, Wisdom, am in the process of bringing and introducing your eternal spirit. This is the Gate of Conviction where I shall convince you of the unpureness of your old heavens, that is, how unpure, tainted, evil and sinful your intellect, will and [69] senses are, such that they must be dissolved and destroyed if they are to be renewed. Hereupon, as a preparation for the Gate of Conviction, Wisdom revealed and demonstrated to me what the old earth is in man in his fallen state. It is the heart or soul with all of its affections and passions, and an unpure, corrupted earth in its fallen state. The earth of the inward man in its fallen state is evil and unpure, just as unpure, tainted and corrupted as his heavens. This earth is called man's dry land or *terra firma*. This earth within man bears and brings forth nothing but weeds; nothing but thorns and thistles and bitter roots that serve no other purpose than to be fuel for the fire and to be burned. This earth is filled with evil beasts, powerful animals and birds of prey. No rain falls upon this earth and no sun illuminates it. The eternal spirit itself wanders aimlessly upon this fallen earth. The ancient giants and the abominable peoples are the inhabitants of this earth. This earth is a corrupted earth before the face of God and is filled with iniquities and sacrilege. It is inherently a meager, arid, unfruitful ground and soil, and there is no fatness within it. Nothing but wild beasts, lions, bears, tigers, wolves, dogs, and foxes live in and upon this earth. This is the restless, turbulent earth—there is neither rest nor repose within it but only agitation and bother. When the eternal man considers this earth, behold, there

CHAPTER 13

is nothing but disruption, disquiet and darkness within it. It bears and produces nothing but the grass, hay, stubble, weeds, husks and dust from which the inhabitants live. There is no other sustenance for an eternal spirit than all of these perishable things. This is the inward earth of man, which suffers, mourns and longs. This is the earth within man to which the prophets cried out that it [70] should hearken to the voice of Wisdom within it, should pay attention to it and obey it.[25] This is the evil earth which the Lord has abandoned; peace and joy have been removed from this earth. Grasshoppers, beetles, caterpillars and lizards dwell and nest here. This earth within man has become a desert and a wilderness where neither God nor Wisdom dwell. Therefore, it has become an overgrown wilderness. It has become an arid desert and a parched land wherein no springs of water may be found. It has become the dwelling of the Dragon and of the seven abominable nations, so that they might abide therein. It is the home of unbelievers, heathens and uncircumcised Philistines, and nothing is found there but wrathful, rending beasts. This is the cursed earth of man, the inward land of man, which, in its fallen state, lies under the curse, threats and judgment of God, as may be read in Holy Scripture. In this land the seed is sown in vain, for our enemies eat it up and devour it—those enemies, namely, whom you were to dominate and rule over. "I will make your heaven as iron, and your earth as bronze."[26] "And I will send the sword, the famine, and

---

[25] *Jeremiah* 22:29
[26] *Leviticus* 26:19

SOPHIA

the pestilence upon this land,"[27] and your land shall be made a desert and you shall die in the land of your enemies. This shall be on account of your astrayness and unrighteousness which have been committed upon this earth, because it is a wicked earth. This inward eternal earth of the inward eternal man is called Egypt. It is called Sodom and Babylon. It is also called Babel, a place and city of confusion. It is called the land toward midnight. In man it is like the outbirth of this world; it is Babel, Babylon, Egypt and the land of midnight. In this wicked, fallen earth God has no temple; its inward court and sanctuary have been trampled underfoot by the heathen, and the vessels of the House of God have been led away captive. The holy of holies has [71] been polluted, and in its place a false church has been erected, a synagogue of Satan, a false magisterium or teaching office, false worship, false prophets, a false Christ, false statutes, arbitrary offices, an outward, self-chosen and self-confirmed, slippery, deceptive appearance of blessedness that is without power, a self-appointed righteousness, a self-willed, self-chosen holiness that has been thought out and formed by rational invention according to the letter of Scripture. This is a religion constructed by man from man. This sort of Christianity does not consider, however, that God neither accepts nor takes any sort of pleasure in anything in man that His divine Wisdom itself has not cooked, prepared and set before Him. Further, this wicked earth, which the teachings of the prophets and the Old Testament depict through allusions and parables, is

---

[27] *Jeremiah* 24:10

CHAPTER 13

also described in the doctrines of the apostles and in the New Testament thus: it is nothing other than the heart, with its affections and passions, together with its sinfulness. This is the wicked earth of man and man's own unpure earth, which is filled with all sorts of unpure spirits and wicked desires.

Firstly, with regard to the unpureness of the heart in its fallen state, it is attested that all the movements and inclinations of the human heart, all of its thoughts and aspirations, are evil, that is, continually evil.[28] This is the state and condition of the eternal soul and heart in their fallen state. It is a hardened and stubborn heart like unto the heart of Pharaoh. We have been exhorted to seek God with our whole heart, with all our affections and energies. It is a stiff-necked, rebellious heart. It is an uncircumcised heart whose foreskin must be circumcised. It is a deceptive heart which cannot be trusted. It is a heart that has turned away from God and toward the creatures of this world. It is a double heart that [72] desires to possess the Kingdom of God and the Principle of this world as well. It is a heart that is unprepared to receive the seed of life within it. It is overgrown with fat and lard, and has been fattened with the delicacies of this world. It is a rebellious, idolatrous and adulterous heart, for idols and graven images have been set up within it. Christ said: "From the abundance of the heart"[29] (in its fallen state) come forth terrible thoughts, awful words, evil suspicions and evil movements and inclinations toward sin and earthy forth-castings.

---

[28] *Genesis* 6:5
[29] *Matthew* 12:34

From the heart go forth terrible thoughts, homicides, adulteries, harlotries, thefts, false witnesses, revilings, etc.[30] This old, wicked earth is nothing else but the heart of man with all its unrighteousness, that is, whoremongering, covetousness, malevolence, etc.[31] Behold the fruits that emerge from the fallen earth or heart of the inward eternal man. It is an unbelieving and disobedient heart that can do nothing else but walk in the way of unrighteousness and selfness. Satan has come into this heart to fulfill these things within it. It is all one and the same for heart and soul.

Further, as concerns the unpureness of the affections and passions of the heart or soul in its fallen state, we may say that these affections and passions are utterly tainted by unpure properties. They exist in complete confusion and disorder. They have turned away from God absolutely, and they whore after the spirit of this world and after the Principle and *centrum* of this visible out-birth. They run away from the realm of eternal blessedness. In this fallen condition they are referred to as disdainful, contemptuous, evil, sinful and unpure affections, inclinations and desires.[32] God has given them over to disdainful, unpure desires or caused them to fall into such affections because they have longed more for the creatures of this world than for God. These various affections or passions and inclinations of the heart or soul are called natural affections [73] because they were essentially implanted in the essence or substance of the soul

---

[30] *Romans* 1:29
[31] *Galatians* 5:19-21
[32] *Romans* 1:26

CHAPTER 13

and formed in the first birth and primordiality of the soul. They are like so many stirring movements, like feet within the soul which carry it from one object or forth-casting to another by its own natural desires and inclinations, which either attract it to or repel it from these objects. They are called evil affections or desires because they incline to things below, that is, to the earthy forth-castings of this world, and not to the things above, namely to eternal forth-castings. These natural affections and passions of the heart or the soul are called lusts and desires in Saint Paul's *Letter to the Galatians*.[33] Those who are in Christ have crucified their passions and affections, which are only the different desires and various inclinations of the heart or soul toward a forth-casting or object, natural desires and cravings that are awakened in attraction to or aversion from a thing. In this fallen state all of these primordial desirous movements or inclinations of the heart are only evil and thoroughly evil. Mortify, therefore, your members which are in and upon the earth.[34] This is the apostle's exhortation to kill or mortify these members. What sort of members? The affections or passions or cravings and desires of the earth. What kind of earth? Their inward fallen earth, which is the old earth within them. Saint Paul explains his own understanding and opinion and says that he knows that these members are nothing but the natural affections and passions of the heart and the natural cravings and desires of the soul that were born with them in their first

---

[33] *Galatians* 5:24
[34] *Colossians* 3:5

formation. With regard to their fallen state, however, the apostle calls them disordered affections and evil desires and longings. He does this because they are now so corrupted that they are beyond all order, rule and regulation and stand in complete disorder. They cannot be kept in check, nor can they be confined, [74] but have become inherently disordered desires and passions. They refuse to be reined in or be tamed by taking the bit between their teeth. Instead they carry their rider along at breakneck speed, whether he will or not, because they are too refractory and stubborn to allow themselves to be led. These passions of the soul are dumb animals and irrational lusting beasts, the untamed and unbridled young cows or calves who refuse to take on the discipline of the yoke of Christ and do not want to bear the cross of crucifixion and, in their fallen state, do not acknowledge the teachings of Christ. These are the living creatures, the cattle and beasts, the crawling worms which this fallen state brings forth, according to their species. These are the evil, dumb, bestial passions; these are the disdainful, contemptuous and unpure cravings of the soul with every sort of evil, creeping desire or movement of the soul. In and upon this fallen earth the roaring lion, the rending bear, the sly fox, the biting, bloodthirsty dog, and other such animals and beasts walk. They walk now in and upon the evil, disdainful earth of man. What are these evil, dumb beasts? They are nothing other than evil spirits that live upon this fallen earth in man and walk back and forth. Namely, the spirit of wrath, the spirit of anger; the spirit of evil and envy; the spirit of murder and the spirit of hatred; the spirit of strife and argument, disunity and war; the spirit

CHAPTER 13

of adultery, harlotry, lechery and lasciviousness; the spirit of drunkenness and gluttony; the spirit of gossip and slander; the spirit of lying, cursing and swearing; the spirit of arrogance, pride and self-exaltation; the spirit of covetousness and self-love; the spirit of idolatry and heresy; the spirit of turmoil and rebellion; the spirit of sorcery, and many others like them. What sort of an earth do you think these bestial animals live and move in and upon if not in and upon [75] the fallen earth of man, which is the old wicked earth within him? Where do you think they have their caves and dens if not in the various lusting affections of the fallen soul of man? Where are to be found the creeping, crawling serpents, namely the spirits of hypocrisy, slipperiness, falsehood and crafty dissimulation that slither and teem upon the earth if not within the inward fallen earth of the heart of man? Out of the fallen, lusting passions of man, as out of hidden caves, they creep forth to pursue and to deceive. These are the seven abominable nations or tribes of whom Moses speaks, namely the unbelievers and heathen who had to be driven from the land by Joshua, a fore-image of Christ. Although these same tribes or nations are long since dead, the evil spirits that inhabited them in their day are not dead but live still. From time to time they still live and dwell in and upon the fallen earth of man to the present day. They were merely figures and fore-images of these dumb beasts or of these bestial spirits and devilish spirits that dwell in the fallen earth of man and may be found within the fallen soul of man as so many inhabitants. They pass back and forth, to and fro, therein. They have freedom in their going out from and their coming into the affections and passions of man, which have fallen away from God and into his own desires and cravings.

In this fallen earth and in this desirous property of the heart or soul of man was planted the lost Garden of Eden, namely a garden of pleasure and joy. Now, however, let us see what sort of garden is revealed in the fallen heart of this inward eternal man in place of the former paradisal garden. If you earnestly examine it, you will find that there is nothing in the fallen heart of man except a garden full of weeds, only stinking flowers and tasteless, disgusting herbs, tart and bitter [76] plants; nothing but thistles and thorns, spiked and prickly roots, even the roots of bitterness. There is not a single plant of God's own planting to be found in this garden that has fallen away from Him. Nevertheless, the eternal spirit of the First-fallen Adam must live and nourish itself from these herbs, roots and plants, for he has nothing else from which to live. Now then, tell us, what sorts of herbs are found in the fallen earth of man, or in his heart and soul? Only evil, unpure, unhealthy and injurious herbs, for therein grow the herbs of anger, wrath, evil and hatred; the herb of evil suspicion, distrust and envy; the herb of arrogance, self-love and selfness; the herb of covetousness; the herb of impatience; the herb of anguish, sadness, sorrow and suffering; even the herb of lechery, lasciviousness and animalistic bestiality. These are the flowers, herbs and roots which blossom forth in the fallen heart of man, which is his inward fallen ground and earth. This is what his eternal spirit must eat and live from or die. Thus every fallen eternal spirit, which lives from nothing else but

CHAPTER 13

the abovementioned tart and bitter herbs, roots and plants, must become a wrathful, fiery, angry nature and a miserly, earthy spirit, a worldly-minded and repressive spirit. This must be the result because its nourishment and sustenance, namely the herbs and roots from which it lives and eats, transform that spirit into their own same property in the course of natural nature. In addition, there are other herbs, weeds and noxious vines which grow forth from Adam's fallen earth, that is, from his heart, which has fallen away from God. These are the herbs of self-righteousness, sanctimoniousness, self-chosen service to God; the herbs of a self-appointed, forced, outward appearance without inward essence or being. If someone eats of them, [77] they turn his inward eternal man into a slippery, flashy hypocrite who confesses only with his mouth. He is turned into a false Christian; a mere formalist; a facile, rote dissembler; one who prides himself on external knowledge and actions and whose faith is mere words; a Christian who knows only the history and the letter of Scripture; at best, a Christian who insists upon mystical knowledge; a member alone of the false church of Christ; and a slave who observes the times and attempts to please men. Such a man does everything out of the Principle of egotism and selfness which is within him. Everything he accomplishes he does in and through selfness for his own profit and purposely for his own particular advantage. How can it be otherwise? In his fallen, renegade state he lives and sustains himself from such husks, dregs and herbs as self-righteousness, self-sanctity, his own energies and capacities, his own duties and merits, his own statutes, and his self-willed or self-chosen worship of God. As the prophet Isaiah describes it: "To what purpose is the multitude of your sacrifices unto me? saith the Lord. I am tired of your burnt offerings. When ye come to appear before me, who hath required this at your hand, to tread my courts? Bring me no more vain oblations; incense is an abomination unto me; the new moons and sabbaths, the calling of assemblies, I cannot bear; it is iniquity. Your new moons and your appointed feasts my soul hateth; they are a trouble unto me; I am weary of bearing them. And when ye spread forth your hands, I will hide mine eyes from you; yes, when ye make many prayers, I will not hear. Your hands are full of blood. Wash yourselves, make yourselves clean, etc."[35] The ground and cause of the entire reproach in these words is: Your old hearts have not yet been washed; your fallen, evil earth has not yet been purified of its unpureness. The primary ground or cause why God rejects men who daily seek after Him, [78] who study to know His ways, who gladly desire to approach God in His institutions as a people that has already performed righteousness; and why all of their fasting, their mortifications, anguish and the humbling of their souls; their church meetings and associations, their church statutes and canons; their church prayers and praises had proved to be not acceptable and pleasing worship before Him has been described for our instruction by the prophet Zechariah: "When ye fasted and mourned for those seventy years, did ye at all fast unto me, even unto

---

[35] *Isaiah* 1:11-16

CHAPTER 13

me?"[36] Was my name and honor the end purpose of your fasting? And when you ate the bread and drank the wine (or performed the ceremonies and signs signified by those things), did you not do it for yourself, that is, from the Principle of selfness within you? And did you not have your own intentions and end purposes for your actions, which aimed at your own blessedness? In this way, the soul-spirit in its fallen state cannot go beyond its own Principle in its religious duties and in the observance of holy commandments; nor can it, through its own righteousness, perform any righteous work that would exceed its own energy and capacity and go beyond its own righteousness. For this reason, all of his good works shall be rejected if they are not performed out of a heavenly Principle of eternal life as their true source and origin; likewise, if they are not done in obedience to God's will and from God's will, Who Himself commanded these things of men. Otherwise the inward man becomes a mere outward, simulating believer and a Christian who confesses with his mouth alone. Such a man is neither hot nor cold but merely lukewarm. He is good for nothing else but to be spewed forth out of the heart of God; for in his own outwardly fashioned and presumed sanctity and power he thinks himself rich and blessed. Yet before God he is poor, naked, wretched and miserable. The reason for this is that [79] man lives and nourishes himself from the weeds and husks of divine service and duties and from the coarse outer rinds of these His institutions, and from the herbs of outward appearances as a form

---

[36] *Zechariah* 7:5

of self-sanctity and self-capacity. These herbs grow forth from his rebellious and fallen heart or earth and transform his nature into a mere form and appearance of blessedness that is totally without energy and power. He becomes a carnal, sensual Christian who confesses God, to be sure, but lacks the spirit of blessedness and true sanctity. Thus I truly saw that all of man, the whole man (and here I speak of the inward, eternal man), is in a rebellious, fallen state, for both his complete heavens and earth had fallen. This means that his heavens, his intellect, will and senses, seated within his head, had fallen. His earth, his heart, with its various affections and passions, whose seat has been placed within his breast, that is, the entire inward man, consisting of soul and spirit, was utterly fallen and corrupted with and in all its efficacious energies, capacities and properties. David understood and recognized well the fallen state within him when he prayed: "Create in me a clean heart, O God, and renew a right spirit within me."[37] He understood his heart and spirit to be his earth and heavens. In his spirit he includes his intellect, will and senses. In his heart, however, he comprehends his affections, desires and longings.

These presentations or persuasions took place solely to lead me toward self-knowledge. It was not enough that I recognize within myself that I consisted of heaven and earth, of spirit and soul. It was necessary that I understand that my entire man was fallen, and that my heavens and earth, my spirit and soul, were in a fallen [80] state. I had to comprehend

---

[37] *Psalm* 51:10

CHAPTER 13

gradually what this fallen state was, and that it was a tainted and unpure state, and thus a wretched, miserable, utterly corrupted, lost and pitiful state before God; for it was a wicked state, alienated from life and from the presence of God. It lacked free participation in God and intimate, familiar fellowship with Him. Therefore I was commanded to search in Holy Scripture and to look into that mirror and see what it had to say about this fallen state. I was told that Scripture's words were utterly true and certain, no matter what worldly Christians and the church of Babel within Christianity might say against them. That which I have here written to them is clearly founded upon the true sense and convictions of the prophets of the Old Testament and the apostles of the New Testament.

CHAPTER 14

July 5th

After this presentation and persuasion it was demonstrated to my spirit that the holy of holies has been erected in the heavens of my intellect, in order that the Holy Trinity with its saints and angels, and with Jesus in the radiance of his love, should dwell therein. Mount Zion and the New Jerusalem should be opened within the circle of the intellect or dwell therein and inhabit it as the temple and tabernacle of God. In this fallen state, however, the holy of holies is polluted and tainted with false gods. The Antichrist and the Dragon, the Beast and the False Prophet, and the Whore of Babylon reigned as gods in the temple [81] of the intellect, and all of the golden vessels, that is, the sensory energies and capacities, were polluted and desecrated. The Dragon, the Beast and the False Prophet were worshiped in the holy of holies. It was also shown to me that in the earth of my spirit and soul the holy place was erected, wherein the true worshipers of God worshiped Him in spirit and in truth, and sacrificed all their meat offerings, drink offerings, burnt offerings and freewill offerings to Him. They were to be offered to God as acceptable and holy offerings when they were consumed by the fire. Now, however, in this state of apostasy, the holy place was defiled, the altar trampled underfoot, and the inner sanctuary desecrated by the heathen and by unbelievers, that is, by wicked spirits and evil peoples who worship false gods and have established their idols within it. In this fallen state, the holy place and the temple of the human heart have become a false church, a defiled temple, a desolate sanctuary, a synagogue or school of Satan; and the holy city has been trampled underfoot by the heathen. The outer court, however, which is outside, has been given to the heathen. This outer court is the outward man.[38] Wisdom showed me, however, that she had come to re-establish the tabernacle, the booth of David and the inner sanctuary in the heart of man, so that she might bring down God's heart into the human heart; and so that the human heart might again become a holy place; and that the holy of holies might be built up again in the intellect and heavens of man; and that she might bring down God's intellect into the human intellect and God's spirit into the spirit of man.

These prophecies or presentations were simply exhortations and encouragements to beseech Wisdom that she might effectually perform this. I continued begging her, and allowed myself neither rest nor repose, [82] until she had achieved and accomplished this. This is not a matter of visions, prophecies, predictions or promises, however, but of essential possession alone. There is no fixity or ongoing constancy or satisfaction in the desiring of it. This only comes with the achievement of the

---

[38] *Revelation* 11:1-2

CHAPTER 14

work and the possession of the essence. This was all revealed to me only for my self-understanding.

CHAPTER 15

July 6th

My intellect was shown and my spirit reminded that I should search in Holy Scripture and ponder what it said concerning the inward eternal man, his heavens and earth, and his spirit and heart or soul in his renewed and re-established state. Thereupon, I investigated Scripture and discovered that if the spirit were renewed, then its heavens and earth would be renewed also. If his heavens and earth were brought to a renewed state, then his intellect, will and senses would be renewed along with them, and afterward also his earth, that is, his heart and soul, together with all his affections and passions, or desires and longings.

First of all, I had to contemplate the eternal spirit itself in its renewed state. Accordingly, it is said of the spirit itself in its renewed and proper state that it is a pure spirit, a new creature, a new man, the Second Adam, a life-giving spirit created in righteousness and true holiness, after the mirror-image of Him who created it. [83] It is the spiritual man who weighs and judges all things but who himself is judged by no one. He is the son of God through his second birth. He is the angel of light in whom the spirit of God resides, for God is his Father. The spirits of Abraham, Isaac and Jacob, Joseph, Moses, Joshua, Caleb and Enoch have been made alive in his spirit. The spirits of Elijah and Elisha rest within and upon him. He is a spirit in whom there is neither astrayness nor deception. A good spirit, a faithful spirit. A broken and contrite spirit. An excellent spirit. The spirit of the holy gods is within him and in him is the spirit of the saints of God. He is driven by the spirit and walks in the spirit. The spirit of life is in him and the spirit of truth is with him. All of these particular marks are predicated of and testified by the inward man in truth in his renewed state.

Secondly, when the inward eternal man is renewed, his own heavens are renewed with him. He is a New Creation in himself and has created, through Wisdom, a New Heaven within himself, a new world, a new kingdom and Principle within himself. The prophets of old evoked the New Heavens within man, heavens that should rejoice and break forth in singing.[39] God's will dwells within this New Heavens and fills it with His radiance. The bright lights of this New Heavens within man are not the sun, moon and stars. Rather, the light of the glory of the Lamb and the Morning Star are their lights.[40] It is a heavenly, divine kingdom within man. The renewed spirit has a claim to this Kingdom of Heaven, and there is great reward for him in this heaven. God the Father is in this heaven. There are few who enter of themselves therein, for very few are so perfectly renewed and regenerated

---

[39] *Isaiah* 49:13
[40] *Revelation* 21:23; *Revelation* 22:5

CHAPTER 15

as to be able to claim possession of it and enter in. The will of the Father shall be done in this heaven. [84] There are treasures laid up in this heaven for the newborn saints who are born into it. In this heaven we may sit down and sup with Abraham, Isaac and Jacob, with the patriarchs and prophets, and with Jesus and his apostles. There are also mysteries that belong to this restored kingdom within us. Here there are keys that belong to this Kingdom of Heaven, to lock and unlock, to bind and to loose. O how blessed are they who find and possess them! These are the joyous heavens that are commanded to rejoice and be glad. "Therefore rejoice ye heavens, and ye that dwell in them."[41]

The renewed heavens of man within him consist of the renewal of his eternal intellect, will and senses, which have their seat in his head.

Accordingly, let us first consider the eternal, renewed intellect of the eternal man and what its nature is in its renewed state. It is a good, true, pure, illuminated and transformed intellect. It is an intellect that longs for God, an intellect with God, an intellect surrendered and yielded to God's intellect. It is a heavenly intellect which does not contemplate the things of the flesh but rather the things of the spirit. It knows the intentions and will of God. It possesses the intellect and mind of Christ and of Wisdom. It is a fervent intellect and a willing intellect. It is a renewed and regenerated intellect. It is a constant, unchanging intellect with regard to goodness and eternal life. It does not meditate upon earthly things but upon

---

[41] *Revelation* 12:12

heavenly things. It does not strive for the things of the flesh. It does not walk in the vanity of its own intellect and reason. It is in truth a healthy intellect, free from all schism and heresy. The commandments of God are written upon this intellect. Those who have been renewed in their intellects preserve and hold them pure and untainted from the world and its devices. [85] Their intellects shall not become weary or faint. Their intellects are sober, moderate and humble in all things. Their intellects are vigilant and faithful intellects, free from all doubt. They are peaceful and joyful intellects, filled with peace and joy in their faith. They are steadfast intellects and, at all times, wise and understanding intellects, for they possess the intellect and mind of Wisdom.[42] Such a renewed intellect is an understanding intellect. The spirit of Wisdom and of understanding is in their intellect. The spirit of understanding is in the intellect. His intellect is possessed of a good understanding. Truly, it is possessed of a sharp understanding. His intellect has an understanding of visions, revelations, dreams, of divine mysteries, and of parables and obscure words. He, the inwardly renewed man, serves God, prays to God, praises and glorifies Him with songs in his spirit and understanding. This is the intellect of a renewed and regenerated spirit which has been re-established in its original condition. The heavens of such an intellect have likewise been renewed with it. His eternal intellect is filled with divine light, and there is no darkness within it. He walks with God in the light, like unto God, Who is light and free from all

---

[42] *Revelation* 17:9

CHAPTER 15

darkness.

The renewed will of the inward eternal man, when it is restored, is described thus in Holy Scripture: It is a pure, holy and untainted will. It is no unpure or tainted will. It touches nothing that is unpure. It is a will that is separate and apart from the unpure tree and from the forbidden tree and its fruits. It does not partake of unpure animals and does not pollute itself. Nothing unpure ever enters its gates. It is a mighty will that possesses power over unclean spirits within itself. The unclean spirit has departed from it. It commands the unclean spirits to depart from it and from others. The renewed [86] will comes into contact with no unclean thing. No tainted and unpure will can enter the holy of holies. It is a clean, pure will that has been cleansed of all its unpureness by the blood of the Lamb. It is no idolatrous or adulterous will. It is a virgin will. A virgin will must receive Christ and be the true mother of Jesus. It is an oppressed, tempted and tested virgin. It is a true virgin and thus the daughter of Zion. The virgin will loves Wisdom. The renewed will is, within itself, a free, voluntary will. It rejoices and finds its pleasure in doing God's will. It does God's will in its own earth, just as this occurs and is done in its own heavens. It is a will that is surrendered and yielded to the will of his Father. It strives to do not its own will but God's will. It is a will that is born not of the will of the flesh, nor of the will of man, but out of and from the will of God.[43] He does not seek to do his own will but the will of his Father, and the will of Wisdom, his mother. It is an eager

---

[43] *John* 1:13

SOPHIA

will, always prepared to desire good and not evil, and not to crave from the forbidden tree. Such a man has power over his own will. It is a will that is perfect in the will of God. Through our willingness to do the will of God, and by the mystery of His will, which is the power of will within us, we are sanctified. This is the unification of wills that enables God's will to be the human will and the human will to be God's will in all things. It is a free and voluntary will, a will that has been made willing. The obedience of the spirit resides in this willingness of the will. It is willing to participate, to be in fellowship and to live honorably. The renewed will is the throne of God and of Christ. Nothing reigns therein but God and Wisdom. The Dragon, the Beast and the False Prophet have been expelled from that throne. No self-will and no selfness rule within such a will. [87]

The renewed senses or sensual energies and capacities are the third part of the heavens of the inward man. With him and beside him, his senses have been made pure, clear, bright, transfigured and shining senses. Through the purification of his senses he comes to the point where he can experience and feel the divine mind, a divine feeling, and an understanding in divine power. Thus his senses are heavenly and spiritual, and know how to distinguish things. They can differentiate between good and evil, between heavenly and earthly matters. They are heavenly senses that do not busy themselves with earthy, bestial and devilish matters, but rather with things which are divine, heavenly and supersensual.

CHAPTER 15

His eyes

His renewed eyes are eyes that see, illuminated eyes which can perceive the invisible worlds and creations of God. They can see invisible spirits and deal with them. Such eyes can see the invisible God; otherwise they could have no free access to or free fellowship with Him. They possess, from the spirit of faith, the eyes and the vision of faith. They do not see by way of reason, for reason represents a mirror that is all too dark to see into. Everything which they see they see through the clear mirror of faith, wherein invisible things are made visible, absent things are made present, and faraway things are brought near. In this mirror things that are in the future and yet to be performed are made present and already accomplished. It is a mirror in which impossible things are made possible. This is the seeing eye and the countenance of faith. Such eyes do not see by way of outward sensory abilities but through the mirror of faith. They have opened eyes, eyes that see according to divine impartations, divine visions and revelations, and according to heavenly discoveries. These eyes are capable of perceiving hidden secrets [88] and mysteries. They are blessed eyes which have found favor and grace before God and before His Wisdom. The vision of their eyes is a blessed vision; they are blessed eyes. Their eyes behold the blessedness of Mount Zion. They see God's invisible wonders with their invisible eyes in the eternal world of Mount Zion within them. They have neither thorns nor prickles in their eyes. They do not have eyes that fail or deceive them. They are not darkened eyes but bright, shining eyes. Their eyes are fearless, alert eyes, eyes that wait upon God and His revelations. Their eyes do not slumber. They are dove's eyes, chaste, loyal and constant. Their eyes behold Mount Zion and the New Jerusalem in their splendor, and their king in his beauty. They take pleasure in the desires and longings of their eyes. Their eyes are burning lamps, clear and brightly shining eyes. For they see their own blessing and blessedness in the blessing of Mount Zion within them. They have anointed eyes in order to see the anointing itself.

His ears

The renewed ears of the inward man, or the ears that have been re-established in their original state, are ears that hear. They hear with their ears. They can hear invisible spirits and speak with blessed spirits. From the spirit of faith they have received the ears of faith, and can, therefore, hear the voice of God and the Word speaking inwardly within them. They have ears that are open to hear the invisible voice of God, His speaking Word, His sweet tuneful tone and His charming, harmonious music and melody. They hear His predictions and prophecies concerning the things that are to come, as well as His promises and warnings. [89] They have circumcised ears, ears that are open to all of God's exhortations and invitations. They are unstopped ears, ears that are inclined toward the laws, words, chastisements, invocations, warnings and discipline of Wisdom. They are ears which are closed to the spirit of this world, the Dragon, the crafty serpent and the False Prophet, as

CHAPTER 15

well as to their invocations, their temptations, their enchantments, and their lies and deceptions.

His sense of smell

The renewed nostrils, or instrumental olfactory capacities and energies of the inward man, have a strong ability to smell delicate and pure aromas. They smell the delicately aromatic odors and incense of the eternal Godhead. They smell the charming odor of the garment of God. They smell the sweet-smelling scents of God's anointing. They trace the scent of Lebanon; the odors of the vine and the pomegranate tree; the scent of myrrh, aloes and cassia. They smell the aromas of the spice beds and the spice mountains. They scent the garments of Wisdom and her sweet-smelling body, as well as Mount Zion and the body of the Holy Trinity. They smell only pure air and pure exhalations. They take in the pure influences of the eternal world through their purified nostrils.

His sense of taste

The inward man's renewed sense of taste is a very rich and joyous taste. He savors what he eats and drinks. He tastes the hidden manna and eats of the apples of love. He tastes the oil, honey and butter which he eats and savors the bread of life. He assays the fruits of his own energies or virtues and gifts of grace that are within him and tastes that they are utterly sweet and delicate. He tastes that the fruits of Paradise are exceedingly lovely and delicious. He experiences that the water of life and the spiced wine which [90] he drinks strengthen his heart and fill him with joy. He tastes that the heavenly gift and the kind word of God and the energies of the future world that he samples are delightful and sweet. Now he eats only of the tree of life and its fruits and from the tree of love and its fruits. He does not desire to eat from the tree of death. He desires neither to touch, savor nor sample of the evil, forbidden tree and the fruits that grow upon it. Now he eats only of the fruits of immortality and no longer from the fruits of mortality; he eats no longer a perishable fruit but an imperishable fruit coming forth from the Godhead.

His tongue

In the inward man's renewed state the tongue is a holy, good and pure tongue, free from all unrighteousness. It is not a lashing tongue. It is no adder's tongue. It is a tongue that speaks no deception. It is neither a flattering tongue nor an injurious tongue. For there is no evil under his tongue. It is not a proud, boastful tongue, and it produces nothing arrogant or haughty, nor does it magnify itself. It is not a slanderous, gossiping tongue. It is a kind tongue, a healing tongue. It preserves itself from evil so that it does not sin with its tongue. It is not a mute tongue but rather a speaking tongue. It speaks of Wisdom and Wisdom's paths. It is neither a lying tongue nor a false one. It is a righteous tongue that speaks what is righteous and upright. It is a wise tongue that is able to speak of the secret things and the hidden mysteries of Wisdom. It is a subdued and bridled tongue. Although it is a small member, when it is inflamed by the fire of divine love it is prepared to speak of the wonders of God and to proclaim his praise with thanksgiving, like the pen of a ready scribe. It is a new tongue. It is a divided, fiery tongue.

His lips

In man's renewed state his lips are [91] like his tongue. Therefore, his lips and the fruit of his lips must necessarily be pure, good, holy and righteous. They are bridled lips; they have a bit between them. They are alert lips; they watch and have a great care for what goes into and out of them. The do not sin with their lips and therefore they are not sinful lips. They are not lying lips which speak deception. They extol and praise God with joyful lips. They guard the gate of their lips. They have the lips of wise men. The speech of their lips is turned to instruction. Their lips are sweet lips that drip honey. They honor God with their lips. They are righteous lips that speak truth and righteousness.

His mouth

In the inward man's renewed state the mouth must be a pure, unspotted holy mouth. It speaks through God and through Wisdom, and through the spirit of Christ, not from itself and from man's reason. Men can speak from mouth to mouth with God and God with them. The law of God is in their mouth. God has placed His words in their mouth. Love-fire-flames go forth from their mouth to consume those who oppose them. Their mouth is a righteous mouth that speaks justice and truth but nothing of error. They extol and praise God with their mouth. A two-edged sword goes forth from their mouth. The fruits of their mouth are more precious than rubies. The kisses of their mouth are sweeter than honey. They preserve the gate of their mouth from evil. They sound the Lord's trumpet with their mouth. Their mouth speaks from the abundance of their heart. There is no falsehood found in their mouth. They speak not from the mouth of the Dragon, the Beast or the False Prophet, but from the mouth of Wisdom.

The breath of his mouth

The breath of the mouth of the renewed man is a pure breath of air. [92] It is an inflaming, enkindling breath, a tincturing breath, that is, a penetrating and sharp breath that can go through every gate. It can invade and penetrate the innermost places of the heart and its inner energies, although the doors are locked. It is a mighty breath because it takes its primordial cause from the fiery Principle of the gentle love-fire that has been kindled within its heart.

His words

The words of the mouth of a renewed man must be pure words, for pure words are the fruits of a pure mouth. Their words are the words of the saint. Their words are righteous words and thus expressly energetic words. Their words are few in order that they do not sin with their words. Their words are wise words and their speech is in parables, so that they have need of an interpreter. Their words are charming and gentle words. The words of the pure are delicate and sweet words, as delicate and sweet as honey. The

CHAPTER 15

words of the wise are sage and judicious words and words of understanding. They speak no hasty words. Their words are healthy and healing words.

Thus you may behold the sensual, sensitive life or the life of the senses in its renewed state and see what sort of life it is. It is a pure, blessed and happy state. They behold Paradise blossoming again and restored in the spirit of their intellects. They behold the invisible creation of Mount Zion and of the New Jerusalem within themselves. Their ears hear the voice of God, Christ and Wisdom, and the lovely harmonies and sounds of the heavenly spheres. They sing songs of triumph which none other than they may truly sing. They eat and live from the tree of life alone and feast upon the joy of its fruits. Their own senses are their own redemption and freedom. Their heavens [93] are full of light; in them there is no darkness. Such a man is a spirit resurrected from death and the grave, who lives again essentially in the life of God and in his own paradisal life. He sees, recognizes and experiences himself to be a true living spirit, clothed in his new, spiritual body. He is rich and lacks nothing. He enjoys the various paths in the Principle of eternal life within him. He is greatly satisfied by this, is at complete peace and desires nothing further. For Mount Zion itself has come down to become this sensual, sensitive life within him, a life that flows forth from the obedience of faith and that can be enjoyed by no one but man.

Know now and be persuaded of what a heavenly, blessed state the state of the renewal of your heavens within you must be. I have come down and have entered into your old heavens in order to transform them into New Heavens. I have done this so that you might possess and experience this divine and heavenly life in the movement and working of your senses in their renewal and re-establishment.

CHAPTER 16

July 6th

I was further commanded to observe what Holy Scripture said concerning the earth of the inward man and what sort of earth this renewed earth might be. I found therein that it was his New Earth, his created earth, created by Wisdom, a plant created and formed by God Himself. It is God's New Creation [94] in man. It is a fruitful earth which bears herbs, vegetables, plants, flowers, grain, wine, oil and honey for those who inhabit it. It is a land where milk and honey flow. It is the true spiritual land of Canaan, of which the former outward Canaan was but a figure and fore-image. This is the earth that is filled with all sorts of delicacies and tidbits for the taste and with all kinds of charming and pleasing wonders upon which the eternal senses may feast. This is the pure, unspotted earth which is free from all sin, selfness and evil. This New Earth is full of God's wonders and of His eternal goodness. This earth shall stand eternally and shall never be destroyed. Within this whole earth there is only one pure language; it has but one name and only one nature. It is no Babel, no divided tongue or speech. There is no Egyptian tongue within it, but everything it contains is pure harmony and unity.

SOPHIA

This is the blessing with which Isaac blessed his son Jacob: "Therefore God give thee of the dew of heaven, and the fatness of the New Earth, and plenty of grain and wine."[44] This earth, this New Earth, is the Lord's. Only the Lord and His saints inhabit this earth. No one but He rules in and upon this earth—neither the Dragon, nor the Beast, nor the False Prophet. It is the Lord's earth, a *via excellentiae et praeeminentiae, via juris et proprietatis*,[45] or is the greatest and highest way and a way of law and property. It is a blessed earth because it is an obedient earth. God has promised to bless it. Therefore, it is the Promised Land and the land of blessing. This land receives rain in due season, it brings forth its growth, the trees in the fields produce their fruits, and one grape harvest leads straight to the next. There is abundance of bread, and man dwells securely in this land, free from all evil and injury. There is peace in this land. Man lies down and rises up again and needs fear no one. [95] There are no evil beasts, no beasts of prey, and no rending animals in this land. The sword does not pass through this land. It is a fruitful land that multiplies. Upon this earth man will see his redeemer at the last day, with Job.[46] Only God and His saints live upon this earth. The earth is the Lord's and it is full of His goodness; all the inhabitants in and upon this earth fear the Lord, serve Him and call upon Him. This entire earth is filled with rejoicing and gladness. The Lord is the lord of this whole earth. He formed

---

[44] *Genesis* 27:28
[45] A way of excellence and transcendence, a way of law and propriety.
[46] *Job* 19:25

CHAPTER 16

this New Earth by His creative word. None but the righteous, the upright and the humble shall inherit this earth. This earth is full of the knowledge of the Lord. God fulfills this New Heaven and New Earth in man. God is the laud and praise of this entire New Earth, and is the joy of the whole earth. The Lord shall never forsake this earth. It bears no suffering but is always joyful. This earth is illuminated by the splendor of God. There are no grasshoppers or scorpions, no lions, wolves or serpents upon this earth.

Out of this New Earth blossoms forth the Lost Paradise, the faded Garden of Eden, and the Tree of Life with its twelve-fold fruits, and the Tree of Love with its fruits. Upon this New Earth no desert or overgrown wilderness shall be found, because it is like a garden of God. The seeds of life, the elixir of life, the highest tincture, all grow here. Here, too, grows the fruitful vine that produces highly pleasing spiced wine which rejoices the spirit. Here man drinks the pure blood of the grape, the libation of the New Testament. Here the spice tree grows, from which is derived the holy, fragrant oil, the precious anointing oil that makes the countenance shine with brilliance. Out of this New Earth grows forth the mineral gold-seed, which bears its life within it, and which can awaken itself to life and glorify [96] itself, until it forms itself into a wise, red stone. This stone is known as the transforming stone of the philosophers, the stone that can transform man from a beastly form into an angelic one, and can restore all things to the state in which they first and originally existed. The head of the serpent is crushed by the seed of this virgin stone, according to the first promise of God, given to the first fallen Adamic man.

In this New Earth and Heavens God established His lost tabernacle, His temple, and his holy place, and His inward court and sanctuary, and Mount Zion and the New Jerusalem and His triumphal Church. It is here that God will walk with His saints, and His saints will walk with God. God and man shall enjoy inward, intimate fellowship with one another, and His laud and praise shall ever be proclaimed.

The New Earth, this holy place, has been placed in the heart of man. Therefore, when that earth is once again restored and renewed in the renewed state of man, then the heart of man is a pure and holy heart. The heart of man has become the heart of God, and the heart of God lives within the heart of man. Then there is a unity of hearts and Paradise inhabits the heart of man. Then there is an abundance of grain, wine, oil, milk and honey, which all multiply in the heart of man. Then there is only spring and summer in man's heart. Then the grapevine, the lily, the rose bush and pomegranate tree all begin to bud. The myrrh tree, the aloe, cassia and cinnamon trees all burst forth. Then the spices spread their fragrance in the heart of man. Man then eats nothing but the apples of love and the fruits of the vine. Then he drinks only the blood of the grape and the powerful juice or sap of the Tree of Life. In this way, the heart of man is eternally glorious and inexpressibly filled with peace [97] and joy. To graze upon the hills of the earth is the inheritance of Jacob. Now there is no lack of energy or any fatigue in this heart, for it is a circumcised heart. This heart seeks to love and fear

CHAPTER 16

God with all its faculties and energies. It is an upright heart, a heart that has been tested and proven. It is a flaming heart that burns with love for God. It is a heart that has been purified by faith. The law of the Lord is written upon their hearts. Love, life, nature and the name of God have been poured into their hearts. These are the marks of a wise, willing, merciful and courageous heart. There is an altar within their hearts. Their hearts are in accord with God's own heart and are perfect hearts. The new wine of the kingdom has transported them into an ecstasy of joy and carried them up beyond themselves. They are hearts that have been strengthened and confirmed in the love of God; they are truly sealed hearts. Things both old and new come forth from the good treasures of this heart. The pure in heart see God. It is a simple heart and not a double heart. They do the will of God with all their hearts. The covering has been removed from their hearts.

This New Earth and the holy place have been established in the renewed soul of man. In the renewed state of man the eternal soul of man is a pure and holy soul. Everything that has been said concerning the heart applies to the soul as well. Equally, everything that can be applied to the soul may also be applied to the heart. Let us see, however, what Scripture has to say regarding the renewed soul that has been restored to its primal, original state. It is, so Scripture says, a living soul that has the seed of eternal life within it. It is a pure soul, free from astrayness. It is a sinless soul, purified of all taint of sin, without spot or infirmity. It is a redeemed and [98] ransomed soul, a saved and blessed soul. It is a converted soul, a justified and sanctified soul. It is a renewed soul, an assured soul, a soul that has been healed and released again. It is a soul that rejoices greatly. It is a conquering and triumphing soul, a blessed and blissful soul. It is a contented soul. It is a paradisal soul; that is, Paradise blossoms forth and becomes verdant within it. It is a chastened soul that has been raised in the chastisement and discipline of Wisdom. It is a preserved soul. It is a righteous soul—otherwise it could not be a soul which had been justified. It is a pure and holy soul without infirmity—otherwise it could not be a healed soul. It is a fattened soul and there is no leanness within it. It is a soul which has been placed at rest. It is a soul that has been freed from all bonds and imprisonment. It is a loving soul. It is a purified soul. If it is a purified soul, then it is also a satisfied soul. The Lord leads this soul at all times and satisfies it in the arid places and blesses its limbs with fatness. It is like a watered garden and like the springs of water which never cease flowing, or dry out, or lack water. This soul has its pleasure in the Lord and soars above the heights of the earth and grazes in the inheritance of Jacob, its father. This soul is a watered garden that knows no more sorrow. Its suffering and tribulation have been turned into rejoicing, and it has become joyful after its sorrow. It has been fed with fatness and is satisfied by the bounty of the Lord. It sings upon the heights of Zion; it runs to the goodness of the Lord, for it possesses wheat, wine and oil in abundance. It is the redeemed of Jacob and has been freed from the

CHAPTER 16

hand of one who is stronger than it.[47]

As regards the various affections and passions of the heart or soul, when the soul is a renewed soul, then the affections and passions are renewed with it. [99] For the latter are not renewed without the former, and the former is not renewed without the latter. The natures of these eternal affections and passions are also renewed in this renewed state, such that they become holy affections and pure passions. They are as useful and serviceable to the soul as legs are to the body, for they are the feet of the soul, so to speak. They are the cart upon which the soul rides. In their renewed state they are all heavenly affections and passions. They ponder the things which are above, which are eternal and are free from earthy matters. They are no longer disdainful, contemptuous, earthy, sensual or lustful and bestial affections. They are no longer bestial or devilish passions, but pure, heavenly, supersensual and virginal affections. All the lusts, desires and inclinations of the renewed soul become pure, holy, and virginal desires, longings and inclinations. They are orientated to the high state of Mount Zion and the New Jerusalem. All desires and longings of the soul must rise up to Mount Zion and continue toward the Lord their God. Now, in their renewed state, these affections become well-ordered affections; they remain within their limits and confines and exist in their proper order. They are no longer evil desires but good and pure desires, which all incline toward their true forth-castings and all yearn and long for God. They are no longer bestial,

---

[47] *Jeremiah* 31:11-14

animalistic passions and are no longer compared with unruly calves, with rending wild beasts, or with lions and wolves. Instead, they are compared to horses and donkeys, that is, to horses which the affections might ride and to the donkeys which might carry their burdens. Beasts of prey, such as lions, bears and foxes, the evil spirits which inhabited the lusts of the passions, have been expelled, and they have become pure, virginal affections. They now live and move, dwell and work as pure spirits within the passions. The seven abominable peoples [100] have been driven out of these affections and no longer dwell within them. Each and every creeping thing or lively impulse within the soul or heart is now, in this renewed state, a good, pure, virginal impulse. Now we have said enough concerning the purity of the affections and passions of the soul or heart.

This is the New Earth. The lost Garden of Eden and the Paradise are to be planted in this new earth and property of the human heart or soul with its essential desires and longings. Yet therein shall be no weeds, no thistles or thorns, no infertile deserts; no hunger, thirst or scarcity; no impotence of soul or spirit; neither infirmities of the soul nor spiritual weaknesses and incapacities; neither anguish, nor sorrow, nor sighing. If only such seeds as contain eternal life within them grow in the enclosed earth and ground of the heart or soul of man, then this is truly a good and glorious Paradise. It is such a Paradise when the herbs of grace alone, herbs that have life within them, namely herbs of gentleness, humility, innocence, harmlessness, uprightness, piety, purity, mutual love, brotherly love and other similar godly virtues and heavenly plants and sprouts of grace, grow forth from the heart of man. Likewise, when nothing else but trees of righteousness, the tree of life, and the tree of love with its twelve-fold fruits grow therein. They shall all grow forth from the midst of the paradisal earth in the human heart, when nothing but the plants of peace, of joy, patience, faith and confident trust, like lilies and rosebuds, are found in the heart of man. Then shall the grapevine bloom in the human heart, so that he might drink of the new wine and might quench his thirst with the pure blood of the grape. Then the olive tree will give its precious oil in abundance. [101] Then the spice trees will spread their delicate, delightful fragrances, so that the heart might be purified, sanctified, dedicated entirely to God and offered up. His wine, grain and oil shall satisfy him with their abundance. Then the heart of man shall enjoy the blessings of his New Heavens. All of the prophets prophesied concerning the expectation of the renewal of the New Heavens and Earth of man. As we read in Isaiah: "The wilderness of the human heart and the solitary places of the heart shall be glad; the desert of the heart of man shall rejoice, and blossom like a rose. The heart and the spirit shall blossom abundantly, and rejoice even with joy and singing . . . For in the wilderness of the human heart waters, the waters of life, shall break out, and streams in the desert and in the dryness of the heart of man. And the parched, scorched ground and earth of the human heart shall become a pool, and the thirsty land springs of water . . . Their hearts shall be filled with joy and gladness, and sorrow and sighing shall flee away."[48] When will this happen? When the heart has been restored to its proper condition and has been transformed into a New Earth. On that day truth and might shall spring forth and blossom in the heart of man, and the external appearance of Christianity shall vanish away. The heart rejoices and, in its renewed state, partakes of the essence and the autonomy of pure Godhead itself. The heart and spirit nourish themselves no longer from husks, appearances, words, images, signs and ceremonies. Rather, they partake of the pure elixir of pure energy and of pure Godhead. On that day, no self-righteousness, no self-proclaimed sanctity, no own-power, no self-earned works or merits, no self-established institutions, no self-defined worship of God, no self-willed gatherings, will be any more seen in the heart of man. In its renewed state, the inner court and the sanctuary stand open in the heart of man, [102] along with the holy altar, in order that the meat offering, the drink offering and the entire burnt offering might be offered by fire. And the holy of holies shall be opened within the spirit of the soul, so that God might dwell therein. Then shall the New Heavens and the New Earth be made new in man. And after the holy place and the holy of holies have been opened in man's New Heavens and New Earth, man will then possess and partake of the hill of Mount Zion; and the state of the New Jerusalem shall be effectually occupied and taken into possession by man within man. Then all prophecies will be fulfilled,

---

[48] *Isaiah* 35:1-2, 6-7, 10

CHAPTER 16

all promises redeemed or confirmed, and effectually enjoyed: the seed of the virginal Wisdom of God has truly crushed the head of the serpent, for its attack has been interrupted and thwarted. God and man have again become one heart and one spirit. God has His pleasure in man and man has his pleasure in God. God walks with man and treats him as would a father, and man walks with God as would a son. The entirety of Holy Scripture, from *Genesis* to the *Revelation* of Saint John, is effectually and essentially fulfilled in man. For the New Heavens and the New Earth are formed within man, that is, within his spirit and soul, and the first heavens and first earth are passed away. The holy city, New Jerusalem, has come down from heaven. And the tabernacle or booth of the holy place and the holy of holies are both revealed in the heart or soul, and in the spirit of man. God dwells in man and man dwells in God. God shall be filled and satisfied in man, and man shall be filled and satisfied by God. Holy Scripture proclaims nothing greater than the state of the absolute perfection of man, both within himself and in God, through this exalted, mutual, essential unification of man with God as his Father and of God with man as His son. Therefore, [103] the revelation of all the prophets and apostles finds fulfillment in this complete re-creation of New Heavens and a New Earth within man and in the perfection of man in becoming a renewed creature.

This revelation was imparted to me for my self-understanding, whereby I was told that it was necessary that I come to know myself, that I come to understand myself within myself, to know what I myself was, and how I was created from and consisted in the heavens and earth that are within me. I was told that I was a globe or microcosm, and that there was a spherical small world within me which consisted of heaven and earth. There was revealed to me the direction toward which this heaven and earth were drawn and toward which they pointed: namely the heavens were related to my spirit, in union with my intellect, will and senses, which were located in my head. The earth was related to my heart or soul, in union with its affections and passions. Not only that, but I also had to know and understand what my heavens and earth were, both in their state fallen away from God and in their renewed state in union with God. It was not the case that this revelation alone sufficed to understand all of these things, or that the presentation which had been made to my intellect represented the essential possession of the thing itself. No, this was not a place of rest for the spirit or for the soul, that they should content themselves with visions, contemplation, revelations and proclamations concerning self-understanding. Many had done this, had not aimed far enough, and had fallen short of the goal. Instead, these revelations were given to the purpose that man should entreat, move forward, struggle and battle, in order to effectually take possession of it and enjoy it. The purpose of self-understanding itself and the goal of prophecy was that this state of renewal should be enjoyed by those who seek after it earnestly and yearn for it. [104]

CHAPTER 17

July 7th

The First Gate

All of my previous representations, said Wisdom to me, have taken place in order to make you into a divine or Christian philosopher, with knowledge of yourself and of your own creation within you, consisting of a heaven and earth. This was done that you might understand what their nature is, both in their fallen state and also in their renewed state. Now I am come to bring you in through all of my gates which lead into the holy city, New Jerusalem. My first gate is the Gate of Conviction. I have entered within you to convince your spirit that your heavens and earth are still in a fallen condition, that is, in a state of astrayness and selfness. They are still tainted and unpure, and therefore in a miserable and pitiful state. Upon this conviction my spirit was so dismayed that I almost fainted. At the same time, however, I gave this answer to Wisdom, my visitor: "How was I to think that my heavens and earth were still in such a fallen state?" Wisdom answered that either they were fallen or they were all in a re-established and renewed state. Now, if they were all in a renewed state, then

CHAPTER 17

her work was already accomplished and perfected before it had even begun. For this reason it was absolutely necessary that this Gate of Conviction be thrown open, so that [105] I might recognize where I stood, and that I was still in a fallen state, because my heavens and earth were still in a fallen condition and had not yet been renewed, but still were awaiting renewal.

She told me that this was not a work which had already been completed or accomplished, but had still to be done. I had yet to earnestly and diligently seek and strive before such a work could be done by and through her. Secondly, such a conviction was necessary, in order that I come to recognize, love, honor and be amazed by divine energy, when I considered and meditated upon the things from which I had been saved and freed by it. I ought to ponder upon how I had been renewed and where I had been brought by that energy, namely out of a state of astrayness and selfness and affliction—out of a state where I had been alienated from most intimate fellowship with God. On the other hand, I should also think upon where I should be brought, namely to a renewed state, to a state of absolute perfection, to the state of highest purity and beatitude in the fullest enjoyment of God upon Mount Zion. "You must come to understand the way and fashion in which your eternal man has been thus renewed," she continued, "and the means by which this happened, as well as the most noble instrument which accomplished this. All of these things must necessarily be preceded by this conviction, so that you might surely understand that the work has not yet been accomplished but is yet to be done." For if the work had already been done, instead of still to be done, then this conviction would be both unnecessary and false.

Because Wisdom had stopped my mouth in such a manner, I replied and said: "What have I been doing during this whole time and for the entire last twenty years? I have acted according to the persuasion of the Father and in the conviction of sin, and of my sinful [106] state of affliction, according to the Father's works of the Law. I have lived a life of repentance, remorse and suffering, and contrition of heart. I have humbled myself greatly because of my sins and affliction, yet I, along with my heavens and earth, am still in a fallen state? If my heavens and earth have not been renewed, then what have I accomplished in the office and work of the Son? Regarding the many divine actions, teachings and instructions, and faith in the works and office of the Son (in trust, namely, that I had been renewed and was in a state of renewal), what have I done, if I have truly not yet been renewed?"

Wisdom's answer to my questions was this: "The work of the Father and the Son are only works of preparation for this, my Gate of Conviction. Secondly, you ask me what you have done. I answer that you have been effectually in the process of renewal and you still are. I know very well that you have been effectually in the process of renewal in the work or dispensation and office of both the Father and the Son. Nevertheless, you have not been effectually and fully renewed or reconstituted in either of them. Therefore, I have come to persuade you and to demonstrate the difference between renewal *per se* and the renewal of the self, so

CHAPTER 17

that you might understand it. Your own conscience will tell you that your heavens and earth are not yet effectually in a state of absolute perfection and have not yet been renewed to a state of glorification. In the works of the Father they were effectually revitalized and prepared for restoration to their first, primal condition. In the office of the Son they were further and more intensively prepared for renewal, and further strengthened through faith which is grounded in Jesus and rests in Him. And yet renewal is fully perfected through neither of them. I am now [107] come to bring them, effectually and essentially, from their fallen state, and to establish them in a different state, namely in a state of perfect renewal."

Upon this my spirit again replied: "I acknowledge that before the work of the Father and the Son my heavens and earth were old heavens and earth, in a fallen state of astrayness and affliction. However, after the work of the Father and of the Son was realized upon and within me, I considered them to be newly created heavens and earth, redeemed heavens and earth, justified heavens and earth, sanctified heavens and earth, and therefore renewed heavens and earth."

Thereupon she answered: It is absolutely certain that your heavens and earth were effectually redeemed by the Father's divine teachings and instructions. They were justified, they were sanctified, they were perfected and effectually revitalized. And in the Son's office within you they were further, more intensively and in a greater measure and degree, redeemed, justified, perfected and revitalized. However, neither the Father's nor the Son's work has fully, completely and perfectly redeemed, justified, sanctified, or returned and restored from their fallen state, your heavens and earth. And the ground and cause is this: both the foregoing work of the Father and of the Son have left your heavens and earth in a commingled condition, in a mixed state. In this state they are in part good, in part evil; partly in a state of sin and partly in a state of grace. They have, therefore, neither been fully redeemed and freed from all astrayness and selfness, nor perfectly renewed and established in a state of goodness, where they might be free from all immixture with astrayness and selfness. Thus, in the office of the Father and the Son, your heavens and earth were partly old [108] and partly new. It is my office, however, to completely and perfectly renew them, so that they might become utterly new and that the old might pass away.

You must further know that astrayness and selfness still remained within your heavens and earth during the office of the Father and the Son, and insofar as astrayness and selfness remained within them, they were still old. Insofar as astrayness and selfness were tilled out of them, they have been made new. Astrayness and selfness shall never be completely rooted out from man's heavens and earth during the days of the Father and the Son. Rather they still remain (in accordance with the figure and fore-image of the abominable nations) in the heavens and earth of man during the office of the Father and the Son. For the Canaanites and the wicked peoples were left in the land of Canaan as thistles in the eyes and thorns in the sides of the Israelites, and as a test and a trial for them. They were not utterly driven out and expelled

CHAPTER 17

until the days of Solomon, who was a figure and fore-image of the Lord Jesus in the spirit. This conviction is right and truthful altogether, and you are still in a state of astrayness and affliction during the work of both the Father and then Son, until the office of the third day begins, which is the dispensation, office and work of the Holy Spirit. That office shall utterly expel astrayness, selfness and all of the wicked nations from your heavens and earth. Then your heavens and earth shall be completely freed from all astrayness, evil, selfness and affliction, and shall be renewed. Thirdly, your heavens and earth are both in a state of constant struggle and warfare during the work of the Father and the Son because the seed of evil or malevolence struggles with the seed of good; the seed of sin and the seed of grace war against each other; the seed of life and the seed of death are ever in a state of rivalry. The reason for the everlasting warfare between these [109] nations, these mutually hostile seeds, takes its primal cause from the reasons given above, namely from the immixture of astrayness and selfness in and with your heavens and earth. During the office of the Father and the Son this warfare is never ended. It goes on constantly. They wrestle and struggle with each other to see which of them shall gain victory, conquest and domination over the other. At times the evil seed conquers the good seed, at times the good seed is victorious; at times the light gains the upper hand over the darkness, and at times the darkness is triumphant. As the antitype indicates, the war between the two seeds shall have no end, neither during the office of the Father nor during the illuminations of the Son, until Solomon's kingdom

SOPHIA

is established, that is, until Jesus begins to reign in the spirit. You are, and shall remain, in a fallen state until the victory is won, and until full dominion has been obtained over astrayness and selfness, and over all darkness, evil and affliction. Although there is an effectual struggle and concern for renewal in your heavens and earth, yet the work has not yet been essentially performed and accomplished. Rather, it is in the process of being done, and who knows which of the seeds will obtain the upper hand and bear away the victory? Therefore, compare all of these things, one with another, within you, and do not refuse to undergo this necessary conviction within.

After my mouth had been thoroughly stopped and I had nothing more to say, there arose within me a desire to know what would have happened to my soul if I had died in this fallen state, this state of struggle and warfare, this state which was mixed and not yet fully purified. In what sort of place would I have ended? In heaven or in hell? This question was floating in my spirit when the spirit of Wisdom replied that I would not have [110] ended in hell, because the work or the office of the Father had saved me from the kingdom of the Dragon and from eternal anguish. I had been redeemed and freed from entering hell by the work of the Son, by the sowing of the Son's grain of wheat and precious mustard seed, which are the eternal, immortal and imperishable seeds of the Godhead, and which ever struggle and battle against the evil seed of the Dragon.

Thereupon I asked further, whether I would have been able to go directly from the body to heaven, that is, to the exalted state of glorification, to Jesus the

CHAPTER 17

mediator of the covenant, and to the holy prophets and apostles? I received the reply that I would not have been able to go there, for I still had many gates to pass through. Wisdom had come down to invite me to follow her, because she wished to lead me through them. Until this happened I would be completely unsuited to such a degree of splendor. If I had died in such a state, I would have died in my minority during the office of the Father and the Son, like the children of Israel who died in the desert before they could enter the land of Canaan. I would thus have died in a state of grace, but in a mixed state, not yet fully purified, and in a state of struggle and warfare. I would not yet have come to the state of the complete conquerors, the state of the martyrs and confessors. Now Wisdom had come to call me to those same princes upon their thrones, if I were willing to follow her. She had to lead me, because no one can come to that place or ascend until all astrayness and selfness have been tilled out root and branch and utterly destroyed, and all seven abominable nations have been overcome and slain.

This instruction awakened another question within me, namely where I would have gone if I had died in this fallen state, since there is no intermediate place, no purgatory. If I could not have entered either heaven or hell, where would I have gone? To this question Wisdom replied: [111] "You would have gone to heaven, to the heavenly, eternal world, which is the Father's house and habitation. Although there is no purgatory or intermediate place between the worlds of darkness and light, yet there are many dwelling places in the light-world prepared for those who die still caught in the disordered affections and passions

SOPHIA

of their souls and intellects, during the work, office and dispensations of both the Father and the Son: habitations for those who die before the work of their conversion, regeneration, redemption, justification, sanctification and renewal have been fully perfected. Thus you also would have entered into the particular habitation which the Father has prepared for you. For you must know that in the heavenly world of light there are many dwelling places. The number of such habitations in the Father's house is incomprehensible, given the immeasurability of the eternal world. How else could one star be differentiated from the others in splendor and glory and exceed them? The ground and cause is this: there are degrees of grace and degrees of splendor and glory. Therefore, the degrees of the habitations in the Father's house are like to the degrees of grace and glory. Secondly, there are also degrees of saints and Christians. There are children and babies who die during the Father's dispensation or office and during the days of the Father. There are also habitations prepared for them. There are also strong men who die during the dispensation or office of the Son and during His days. Comfortable dwellings have also been prepared for them. And then there are the elders and the fathers who progressed so far that they achieved a holy, divine understanding. For these the state of Mount Zion and the state of the New Jerusalem in splendor have been prepared. Just as the tree falls,[49] so it shall be taken up into the habitation which has been prepared by the Father for it in the light-filled, heavenly world. I would not like to

---

[49] *Ecclesiastes* 11:3

see you deceive yourself and [112] think that everyone who dies enters in immediately to the highest thrones in the holy of holies, for that is a dream, considering that no unpure spirit which has died in a mixed condition of good and evil can enter therein before it is utterly purified of sin, the war is completely ended, and the victory has been fully won. I also do not want you to impulsively judge eternal souls according to their election or reprobation, for that is a wicked doctrine. Therefore, neither judge nor condemn, for God's paths go forth in the whirlwind and His mercy is upon all His works. When children in Christ die, they enter into the dwellings and habitations of children. Strong men in Christ enter into the dwellings of strong grown men when they die. And the complete conquerors and victorious heroes, whose struggles and warfare are fully accomplished, enter into the dwellings and habitations of the fathers and elders when they die. The weak, who die in the fear of the Lord in the Father's days, enter into those dwellings prepared for the weak. The strong in the faith of the Gospel who, during the days of the Son, died in hard battle against the world, the flesh and the devil, enter into the dwellings prepared for courageous heroes who have died in battle and warfare. You, too, would have died in this state. Now, however, I have come to lead you up to the hill of Mount Zion and the New Jerusalem. Therefore, judge and condemn neither your brother, nor the children in Christ during the days of the father, nor the strong men during the days of the Son, who abide in faith and the obedience of the Gospel. Rather, strive much more after the high goals of your calling, so that you might attain it.

CHAPTER 18

July 8th

The Second Gate

[113] After I had passed through Wisdom's Gate of Conviction, I had become convinced that my heavens and earth were still in a fallen state and had to be renewed through her office, that astrayness and selfness still cleaved to them, and that they were tainted and defiled, despite the fact that the days of the Father and the Son had worked upon and in them. Nonetheless, I took heart anew because I heard that Wisdom had now come to lead me through another gate, which was called the Gate of Renewal. Through it my old, fallen heavens and earth would be made New Heavens and a New Earth, and my spirit would become a new creature, a renewed creature re-established in its first, original state.

In this work of renewal Wisdom revealed and presented to me what was to be made new within me, namely that my old heavens and earth would be made new. These were the materials of my renewal. She said that she had not come to create and shape entirely new heavens and earth, but rather to transform the old heavens and earth within me into

CHAPTER 18

New Heavens and a New Earth. They were to remain the same heavens and earth, but the old properties alone were to be destroyed and new properties were to emerge and be brought forth from the same place. The eternal autonomies and essences of heaven and [114] earth should remain eternal in themselves. The eternal spirit with its eternal energies or capacities and senses, as well as the soul with its inclinations, affections, desires and longings, should remain eternal.

She also presented and demonstrated to my intellect that destruction or dissolution must precede renewal. The old heavens and earth could not be made new before they were destroyed and dissolved. The old heavens and earth were not the old autonomies and essences in and of themselves, but only the old qualities. The old evil active properties had to be destroyed. Only then would the new active properties appear and reveal themselves. She underlined the necessity of this destruction and dissolution, and the fact that this must precede the re-creation and renewal of my heavens and earth, by reference to various scriptural passages, such as: "For the first heaven and the first earth were passed away,"[50] that is, the old heaven and the old earth in their fallen state must depart and make place for the new. Again: "The old heavens must dissolve and pass away before the new heavens and earth can be revealed."[51] And again: "The old heavens and earth must be moved and shaken before the New Heavens and Earth can

---

[50] *Revelation* 21:1
[51] *2 Peter* 3:10

be made fast and unshakable."[52] Again, Wisdom commanded me to observe the manner of their destruction, for they had to be destroyed. But how? And by what means? Must they be dissolved and destroyed by water? No, but by fire! "The old heavens and earth which are now kept in store, reserved unto fire against the Day of Judgment . . . The old heavens shall pass away with a great noise and the elements shall melt with a fervent heat,"[53] and the wicked earth shall be consumed with all its works. This dissolution and destruction cannot [115] occur without fire: "The old heavens, being on fire, shall be dissolved and the elements shall melt with fervent heat. Nevertheless we look for New Heavens and a New Earth,"[54] through the dissolution of the old. The fire is thus the instrument of their destruction and the means of their dissolution and passing away. By what sort of fire? It does not occur by means of the elemental fire of this out-birth. It does not take place through the infernal fire of the Dragon. For the Dragon would not want to ruin or purposely till out these heavens and earth in man, in which evil dwells and which are not the Dragon's own. Thirdly, these heavens and earth are not to be destroyed by God's wrath and anger-fire, lest their eternal essences and autonomies be dissolved and ruined, for these latter must not be destroyed and annihilated. Only the evil and wicked qualities that cleave inwardly to their eternal autonomies and essences should be destroyed

---

[52] *Hebrews* 12:26-27
[53] *2 Peter* 3:7, 10
[54] *2 Peter* 3:12

CHAPTER 18

and consumed by fire. Fourthly, they shall not be destroyed by the fire of Mount Zion in the severity and sharpness of God's judgment or of the divine justice of punishment. For that fire is sent by God's grace and mercy, in order to lead them to a more blessed state. Fifthly, the fire of this destruction comes from the fire of Mount Zion! It comes from the fire of the love of God. This fire destroys and consumes only weeds, husks, chaff, thistles, thorns and the tares of evil, that is, all astrayness, selfness, evil, and each and every evil quality and active property. All life must give up the spirit and be consumed in the flames of this fire—all life that had not been planted by God in the spirit; all life that is alienated from heavenly life; the earthy life, the bestial life, the irrational animal life, the sensual life, the rational life, the busily active life of selfness. All of these must now [116] be destroyed and consumed by the fire of Mount Zion.

Sixthly, this love-fire was described to me thus: 1) It is a consuming, devouring fire and thus an intense, powerful fire. It has been endowed with energy and power, in order to carry out the destruction for which it is sent. 2) It is a merciless, pitiless and terrible fire, whose eye spares nothing that is contrary to and opposed to its own nature. Astrayness and selfness, evil and earthiness must now become the tinder and nourishment of its flames. This would not have happened during the days of the Father and the Son because at that time astrayness and selfness were still too strong to be fully driven out. Now, however, on this day of their burning, they shall be consumed root and branch. No right eye, no Agag, will be spared, but everything which this fire cannot abide must

SOPHIA

be burned and reduced to dust and ashes. 3) This consuming fire is, nevertheless, in its own nature a mild and gentle fire, a pleasing and joyfully burning fire which may be compared to a refiner's fire. Such a fire is intended solely to refine and purify and to separate the scum or dross and tin from the silver and gold, and is not the sort of wrathful fire that would consume and destroy even the good. Thus, even this devouring fire is one that is not too hot, so that it might not destroy the essences and autonomies themselves of the old heavens and earth. At the same time, a refiner's fire cannot be so weak that it is incapable of burning away the scum or dross from the gold and silver and purifying them. It cannot be so weak that it could fail to separate astrayness and selfness, evil and unpureness from the heavens and earth. In Scripture this consuming flame [117] is compared to a refiner's fire.[55] That fire would refine and purify only the gold and silver, while smelting away their dross. The purified gold would remain. Earthiness, drossy qualities, and all slimy essences and filth of the old heavens and earth, namely astrayness, evil, selfness, self-righteousness, self-proclaimed sanctity and the self-assumed appearance of religion would all be refined, separated out and destroyed. The essences and autonomies themselves, however, would eternally remain. Recalling Scripture, I asked myself: "But who may abide the fiery day of His coming? And who shall stand when this fiery, consuming day appeareth?"[56] And I received the answer that

---

[55] *Malachi* 3:2-3
[56] *Malachi* 3:2

CHAPTER 18

the heavens and earth would suffer yet abide upon that consuming, fiery day, because that fire would be for them a refining and purifying fire. The chaff or dross of the heavens and earth, their astrayness, evil, selfness and the earthiness of mortality, however, cannot stand upon that fiery, consuming day, for then they shall be destroyed and consumed, and they shall not stand. The fire must not be too hot, for the heavens and earth of man could not bear it. Nor should it be so gentle as to be incapable of destroying and consuming astrayness and selfness.

Thirdly, [sic] she said, consider well what it is that is destroyed and also the universal quality of what the fire destroys. It does not destroy the eternal essences and autonomies, that is, the eternal spirit with its eternal sensual and rational capacities, nor the soul with its eternal, essential affections and passions. It is not that sort of intense fire. At the same time, it destroys and consumes all the old, evil qualities, all the self-actualizing properties that inwardly and intimately cleave to those essences and autonomies. This fire separates the precious from the vile, the good from the bad. Astrayness and evil [118] are consumed and destroyed by it. She remarked that I should mark well the universality of the destruction and consumption, the fact that these qualities and properties are rooted out thoroughly, root and branch. The roots of astrayness and evil are pulled out, root, twig and branch. On that day neither original sin nor sin actually committed shall be spared. During the previous work of preparation of the Father and the Son such things were spared, but on this consuming and flaming fiery day all astrayness, all selfness and selfness, all seven wicked, abominable nations, and everything which commits evil in the heavens and earth of man, must be ignited, devoured and burned like straw and stubble.[57] Saint Peter supports this: "The heavens and earth shall melt away by reason of the great heat . . . The earth with all its works shall pass away."[58] It shall be a complete purification of the entire heavens and earth that are within man. It is no half-purification, no partial or fragmentary destruction, but a thorough and perfect work of purification and refinement. It thoroughly refines and perfectly purifies man's heavens and earth, that is, the eternal spirit of man with its intellect, will and senses, and also his soul with its affections and passions.

Fourthly, [sic] she also encouraged me to consider who the destroyer was, who the refiner, who the purifier? Who was it who brought down this fiery smelting oven and established this hot, burning, devouring, fiery furnace and smelting oven in the midst of my earth and heavens? Who was it who commanded and maintained this fire? Who imposed law and measure upon it, and established goals and limitations? Who decided how wide those limits were to be and that they were not to be exceeded? Who brought it about that the oven should not burn hotter or more gently, faster or slower than was pleasing to Wisdom. Actually, that one could not be God the Father, for His day and office [119] was done and past. It also could not be God the Son, for His day

---

[57] *Malachi* 4:1
[58] *2 Peter* 3:7, 10-12

CHAPTER 18

was also past and accomplished. For He had sown the seed of the Godhead in the flesh. In His day it had striven and struggled in His heavens and earth, and it was now also accomplished and past. That divine seed had served its time and had not been able to free itself of all things—it had been too much weakened by the flesh, and the Dragon and the Beast were still too strong. This destroyer could not be the appearance of Jesus in the flesh, for that first appearance had occurred in weakness. His day: She told me that His first appearance in the flesh in weakness had already occurred, but was also in the past. I asked: "Is this destroyer, the one who refines by fire, Jesus in the spirit?" "No," she said, "for this refining and purifying fire only paves the way for Jesus' birth in the spirit and the day of the Holy Spirit or the Day of Pentecost." Accordingly, I was informed and given to understand that it was John the Baptist who performed the office of a forerunner, to prepare the way for the birth of Jesus in the spirit, just as John had performed the office of a forerunner in the spirit and zeal of Elijah before Jesus' advent in the flesh. This was a fiery office that prepared the way for the birth of Jesus in the spirit, and it was accomplished and carried out by the hand of an invisible spirit. That spirit did not consider it robbery that Jesus should be equal in divinity with the Holy Trinity.[59]

Fifthly, [sic] it was presented to my intellect and revealed whose fiery, burning, consuming day this was: namely that it was not said of the Father's days of conviction, with their anguished terror, fear and

---

[59] *Philippians* 2:6

dismay of conscience on account of sin, nor of His anger-fire in the soul. For these had already appeared in the soul and departed. This fiery day could also not be ascribed to the Son's work or office, through which He purified the soul from astrayness and selfness, [120] for the days of the Son in the soul have also passed and are gone. None of these previous days was able to redeem and fully free the soul from all astrayness and selfness. Therefore, they await the second advent of Christ in the spirit, and Pentecost and the Holy Spirit, and the final baptism by fire, in order to perfect the work in full purification and accomplish the transformation of all things. This is absolutely true and certain. Yet this is not the fiery day of the smelting and refining fire, which is the last, great, terrible day, the advent of the holy, and the birth of Jesus himself in the spirit. This day of refinement and purification is only a provisional day, an office of preparation for the last great day, namely for the day of Jesus in the spirit and the day of the Holy Spirit, on which it will appear as on the Day of Pentecost. Therefore, it is not the completion of all things but is a fiery day occurring after the days of the Father and the Son and before the day of the Holy Spirit. And so, this day is none other than the Day of Wisdom, on which she rises up and sits down and prepares her children for the state of Mount Zion, for the New Jerusalem and for their glorification. Although the day of the Father took place during the beginning of regeneration, and the day of the Son continued and further promoted the work of regeneration, now the day of the Wisdom of God is rising in the splendor of Mount Zion, in order to lead her children to the heights

CHAPTER 18

of Mount Zion and to prepare them for glorification in the New Jerusalem. For Wisdom knows well that, without her fiery, purifying and refining flames, such glory can neither be achieved nor enjoyed.

On this account Wisdom now said to me: "I have come down with my fiery, fervently burning refiner's oven and have entered your [121] closed heavens and earth to destroy and till out all astrayness, all evil and all selfness, and to bring to an end all self-righteousness and all self-defined worship of God and holiness. I shall reveal myself to you in your own heavens and earth, and you shall come to know me and feel me in my fiery Depth, in my fiery region, and experience my refiner's fire within you. This is my first garment, in which I shall appear to you, until your heavens and earth are thoroughly purifed from all astrayness and selfness, and refined from the ground up."

At this my spirit was startled, hesitated and answered: "I would have thought that this work of refinement within me had already been completed, that I had already undergone and moved beyond this process, and not that I still had to undergo and accomplish it." To this Wisdom replied: "This work could not take place during the work and dispensation or office of the Father, nor during that of the Son, because astrayness and selfness were still intermingled with the effectual seed of life during both of those dispensations. If this work had already been performed and dealt with, it would no longer need to be accomplished, for it could not be done in the absence of Wisdom. Yet I have never entered into you to perform this work until now. Therefore, do not

SOPHIA

deceive yourself. This purification and refinement of your New Heavens and New Earth has never yet happened and is still to be performed."

I replied to her: "You entered into my heavens and earth with your purifying flames, so many years ago, namely in this or that year, and in this or that place. For I felt them then just as I do now, because I recognize from the taste that they are the same as those in which I lay bound for so many hours and days." Wisdom answered in the following manner: "It is true that I prophesied to you on that same day, and revealed and demonstrated through appearances, visions and predictions [122] that this thorough and general destruction of astrayness and selfness would have to proceed and take place within before the great Day of Pentecost could ensue within you. At that time I immediately sent forth my love-fire-flames to court you and to win your favor and to draw you up to the heights of Mount Zion. You effectually experienced and enjoyed my purifying fire-flames. You did not remain within them, however, but departed on the same day from them and turned your spirit and the desires of your heart toward the forbidden tree and ate from the fruits of death. With many others, you ran after the spirit of this world and the evil spirit, and abandoned me and the tree of life and of love in my essence and being. Therefore, I left you and drew back into my Principle. Thus, until this hour, you, along with the others who have also been backsliders, have lived in the prophecy, that is, in the light and vision of that which you ought to be, and in longing for it. But you have not enjoyed the possession of the essence itself.

CHAPTER 18

Many others have been deceived in the same way. Now, however, I have come to begin the work of your inner purification and renewal, and to accomplish this effectually from the ground up in your old heavens and earth. To this end, I require nothing further of you than a willing and inclined will, a passive and ineffectual will, so that you might, with a willing intellect, permit me to accomplish and work this within you. I will fundamentally work and perform this in and for you. Do not think or imagine that this work, this dissolution of your old heavens and earth, is impossible. I know well that the False Prophet, which is reason within you, would like to convince you that this is so. Yet know that I am a subtle, penetrating energy and for me it is possible to work and accomplish all things. Do not let your heart be downcast, but be of good courage [123] for I am come to perform this. I desire to do this and am able to do so. I can do this easily, yet with joy and gladness. It shall be my entertainment to destroy the evil seed of the Dragon and the Beast within you, if you will but abide with me and persist with your will-spirit in my circle-fire. You shall stand with me and behold how I make all things new within you, New Heavens and a New Earth. For I tell you, it is not in the power or energy of an angel to accomplish such things. No one is commissioned to do this work but I, I who am the virginal Wisdom of my Father, the Father who creates nothing without me. I, too, can do nothing without the Father, Son and the Holy Spirit. Those men who confuse me, Wisdom, with the Father, and with the Son, or with the Holy Spirit, are foolish philosophers, for I am a spirit and energy that is differentiated from the Holy Trinity, but am yet one with the Holy Trinity. What I do, the Father, Son and Holy Spirit also do. I perform nothing from myself, but the Holy Trinity works in me. In this fiery day of mine, however, and in this my day of purification and refinement, the Holy Trinity accords me precedence for the sake of differentiation, so that Wisdom might be recognized, honored, admired and praised by her children." At this my spirit rejoiced inwardly and surrendered my soul and spirit willingly, in order that my old heavens and earth might be thoroughly and fundamentally purified in and through the intense, fiery refiner's oven of Wisdom. I felt this oven and its fervent heat effectually in my soul.

CHAPTER 19

July 9th

The Third Gate

[124] On this day Wisdom visited me again and said: "I have brought you to the Gate of Renewal, and you are going through the effectual dissolution of your old world, your old creation, your first heavens and earth. That which is earthy in that earth shall pass away and be devoured by my consuming fire, as I have shown you. Now I shall instruct you further, in order to turn you into a philosopher wise in the understanding of your own self-dissolution and in the utter annihilation of your old, evil selfness. I have come to teach you to understand the explanations of the old, secret symbols and fore-images, and to understand the sayings and obscure riddles of the wise. You should also receive knowledge of the prophecies and predictions of the prophets and of their allusive words and expressions, wherein they prophesied concerning my fiery day and this, my fiery office. On that day, the old world and the old creation shall be utterly destroyed; the old heavens and earth shall pass away, be subverted and burned with fire. Reason has not understood this day of dissolution

SOPHIA

and melting but has, rather, conceived of it as a terrible day for this visible creation and out-birth, as if the attention of the prophets' words and prophecies were trained solely or primarily upon the devastation of the nations, the desolation of kingdoms, and [125] the subversion of external realms and rulerships. Although there might be some truth to this in the literal sense of prophecy, I have come to you to instruct you in the truth of the hidden mystery which is concealed beneath the allusive words and expressions. These prophecies were actually all directed toward my fiery office, toward my fiery day, when the old heavens and earth in man shall be burned out, and shall be universally and entirely dissolved and destroyed on their last Day of Judgment.

Although the old heavens and earth, together with the evil, wicked, dark and earthy spirits, were judged during the day of the Father, those days passed away and the spirits were not completely driven out. Although they were also judged during the day of the Son, still they remained alive within man. Now, however, on my Day of Judgment, they shall no longer inhabit the heavens and earth of man, but must and shall all be destroyed, dissolved and melted by my devouring and eternally enduring love-fire. Man's old heavens and earth, together with all evil, wicked spirits, dark powers and earthy spirits, must perish in my fiery flames and be utterly tilled out on my final Day of Judgment. I have now come to your old heavens and earth, not to demonstrate their downfall merely through a vision or a revelation, nor by way of a prediction, as I did previously. Rather, I have entered essentially into your old creation in order

CHAPTER 19

to effectually destroy it by my fiery refiner's oven, which I have placed within the midst of your heart. That oven's intense heat shall ignite with fire your old heavens and earth together with their elements, consume them down to the ground and turn them into dust and ashes. This is my first garment, in which I shall reveal and make myself known to you. It shall be my fiery region, and you shall see me in my [126] fire oven alone. You shall feel that I am a spirit of burning,[60] for I shall burn out everything old by my fiery flames and make everything new. Although I am a spirit of burning for dissolving the old heavens and earth within you, yet such work should be attributed to each person of the Holy Trinity, as it is effectually ascribed in Holy Scripture, now to the Father, now to the Son, and at times to the Holy Spirit. For I, a spirit of burning, am pure Godhead and one with the Holy Trinity. Although they work nothing without me, I also can accomplish nothing without them. This work of destructive melting or dissolution of the old heavens and earth in man through the will and good pleasure of the Holy Trinity, as well as the glory or fame and excellence of the work of destruction, are attributed to my spirit of burning and to my fiery day and office in the heavens and earth of man.

This honor was granted to me by the Holy Trinity in the first promise, mentioned in *Genesis*: "And the seed of woman shall bruise the serpent's head."[61] I am this virginal woman, the virginal young woman. It is my eternal, fiery, virginal seed of love that effectually

---

[60] *Isaiah* 4:4
[61] *Genesis* 3:15

SOPHIA

destroys the great betrayal, the dangerous attack of hell, the serpent and the Dragon, by the tilling out of their old work of astrayness and evil, in order that this seed might create and introduce a New Heavens and New Earth. All previous women, all the famous women who are mentioned in Holy Scripture have been merely figures and fore-images of my spirit, namely Sarah, Rebecca, Deborah, Jael and the Virgin Mary; all of them merely figures and fore-images of me, as I have been known to my children at all times by the name of virginal Wisdom. [127] The ancient prophets prophesied concerning my fiery day using this name: "This is the word that the Lord hath spoken concerning him: The virgin, the daughter of Zion, hath despised thee and laughed thee to scorn; the daughter of Jerusalem hath shaken her head at thee."[62] This can be no one other than the virgin of Wisdom. And at *Jeremiah* 31:4: "Again I shall build thee and thou shalt be built, O virgin of Israel; thou shalt again be adorned with thy timbrels, and shalt go forth in the dances [128] of those who make merry."[63]

---

[62] *2 Kings* 19:21; *Isaiah* 37:22

[63] A timbrel is a type of drum. In other passages of Scripture it connotes an instrument that is used to express great joy after victories in war and during the high holy days, as a way of praising God (*Genesis* 31:27; *Isaiah* 5:12; *Exodus* 15:20, etc.). It also carries a deep mystical sense, pointing toward the sweet harmonies in our spiritual forms and energies. See *Jeremiah* 31:4 above. And also *Isaiah* 24:8: "The mirth of timbrels ceaseth, the noise of those who rejoice endeth, the joy of the harp ceaseth." The joy of this musical instrument has ceased because the prophet is describing great misery and tribulation. It is curious that the text of Scripture, in this and many other passages, uses the word "Topeth," which the

CHAPTER 19

This virgin of Israel, this virgin of Zion can only be God's eternal virgin of Wisdom. And again: "Then shall the virgin rejoice in the dance."[64] The virgin is, in outstanding fashion, a figure of the virginal Wisdom which shall rejoice greatly in the renewal and making new of all things. In the book of *Psalms* divine Wisdom is compared to the queen in gold of Ophir and to the eternal betrothed and bride.[65] The later verses of this psalm mention young women who are her companions, but she is their princess who rules over them all.[66] Everything which Scripture says concerning the Day of Zion and the dawn and

---

best scholars take to mean the fire of burning hell, because they are all unacquainted with the fiery Day of Wisdom. The ancient Hebrews expressed this in the book of *Job*: "I have been condemned to the fires of hell before my time, a thing which happens to other men after their death." The words of *Isaiah* 30:33 are particularly worth considering, according to their secret sense: "For Topeth is ordained of old; yea, for the king it is prepared; he hath made it deep and large. The pile (According to *James* 3:6 this is the spiritual wheel of birth) of it is fire and much wood; the breath of the Lord, like a stream of brimstone, doth kindle it." The translator wished to insert this information in order to address Christian teachers and to exhort them to act like the "muzzled oxen" of *1 Corinthians* 9:9, who tread and thresh the grain of Holy Scripture purely and carefully, and who demonstrate the deep grounds of scripture to their worthy hearers. Such teachers should be careful not to reject and condemn that which they do not immediately understand. With the term "oxen" Saint Paul alludes to the Hebrew word "Eleph," which connotes an ox, as well as a teacher, leader or guide.

[64] *Jeremiah* 31:13
[65] *Psalm* 45:9
[66] *Psalm* 45:13-14

brightness of that day, and of its splendor, is to be seen as referring to the Day of Wisdom. The Day of Mount Zion is the Day of Wisdom and the Day of Wisdom is the Day of Mount Zion. On her fiery day Wisdom shall effectually take up the hammer and nail in her hand, drive the nail through Sisera's head and nail him to the earth.[67] Among the spirits of this earth, Sisera was a mighty general over the Canaanites, who were handworkers and traders. Although this work was performed by the power of the Holy Trinity, yet the glory and fame of it was attributed to virginal Wisdom.

Here you will reply that in the New Testament this work of destruction is attributed to the name and spirit of Jesus. The answer to this is that those who distinguish my spirit from the spirit of Jesus are ignorant, for these are but one spirit. If my spirit performs a work, the spirit of Jesus does it as well. For the sake of differentiation in the work of regeneration, however, this work is attributed to my spirit. Because I am one with the Holy Trinity, you may attribute it to the Father, the Son or to the Holy Spirit, [129] whichever you wish. My fiery, burning office and destruction is only a office of preparation for the advent of Jesus in the spirit, just as were the office of Elijah or of John the Baptist before the advent of Jesus in the flesh. I only create New Heavens and a New Earth for the advent of Jesus in the spirit, in order that he might bring down Mount Zion and with it the Holy Spirit. Do you think that Jesus is going to bring down Mount Zion into the tainted, unpure

---

[67] *Judges* 4:21

CHAPTER 19

heavens and earth of man? Never! For my office points to Mount Zion and to Jesus in the spirit, and seeks to guide and lead you to Jesus in the spirit, which is a higher office. My fiery burning does not lead away from Jesus but toward the birth of Jesus in glory.

In passing, you must consider this admonition, that a Last Judgment shall come upon the children of Mount Zion and destroy their old creation, and shall expel from them everything evil, in order that a New Creation might be introduced, namely Mount Zion and the splendor of the New Jerusalem. This judgment does not, however, cancel or annul the great last Day of Judgment, which shall be universal and shall come upon the good and the evil, the righteous and the unrighteous alike. This prior judgment involves only the children of Mount Zion, the children of Wisdom.

The passages of Holy Scripture which I have collected concerning the final destruction of the old and first creation, namely of the world of astrayness and selfness, and about which the prophets prophesied, are the following: The entire second chapter of *Isaiah* depicts the destruction of the old heavens and earth in man, "for out of Zion shall go forth the law, and the word of the Lord from Jerusalem."[68] The law out of Zion and the word from Jerusalem are the fiery law and the spirit of burning which go forth from my mouth. Then shall my fiery law "judge among the nations, and shall rebuke many [130] peoples."[69] The wars of the nations, which arise out of the mingling of light with darkness, of flesh with spirit, shall come

---

[68] *Isaiah* 2:3
[69] *Isaiah* 2:4

SOPHIA

to an end. The state of war shall cease, for my office shall scatter the wicked nations, shall refine and purify the heart and spirit, and they shall walk in the light of the Lord.[70] Then shall the soothsayers and the Philistines, the aliens and foreigners,[71] be consumed by my melting fire, and shall be burned out of the heavens and earth of man, that is, out of his spirit and heart. Men's land, that is, their hearts, are filled with gold and silver and have no end of their earthly treasures[72] in the desire of their intellects and will for this outward Principle. Their hearts are full of idols, and they worship the works of their hands,[73] which are their own imaginings and desires. I tell you that their hearts, which are full of spiritual idolatry and adultery, shall all be consumed by fire. Then, in my destructive office by fire, the fear of the Lord and the glory of His majesty[74] shall begin to rise in their heavens and earth, that is, in their spirits and hearts. Then the lofty, proud looks of the human spirit shall be humbled, and the haughtiness of men shall be bowed down, and the Lord alone shall be exalted on that day,[75] that is, on the Day of Wisdom, in the fiery office of Wisdom. In my dissolving and destroying fire-flames, which are the day of my fiery office, the day of the Lord Sabaoth, of the Lord of Hosts, the day of the Father, shall be lifted up. For my fire shall be upon every proud and lofty spirit that has exalted

---

[70] *Isaiah 2:5*
[71] *Isaiah 2:6*
[72] *Isaiah 2:7*
[73] *Isaiah 2:8*
[74] *Isaiah 2:10*
[75] *Isaiah 2:11*

itself, and upon the cedars of Lebanon, and upon all the oaks of Bashan, and upon all the high mountains, and upon every high tower, and upon every fortified wall.[76] These all stand for the lofty [131] thoughts of the human spirit with regard to its historical and its mystical knowledge during the dispensation and office of both the Father and the Son. The spirits of men were subject to these dispensations in earlier times, but now my day of devouring fire has broken forth and risen up in their spirits. All the ships of Tarshish or of the high seas, all of their thoughts, imaginings and desires which, like fast ships, are driven forward by the strong winds, shall perish. All of the delightfully formed pictures that have been set up in their senses and all the charming forth-castings of their lusting senses shall be thrown down and destroyed.[77] The entirety of sensual life in man's spirit shall perish in these flames on my day of destruction. The loftiness of man shall be bowed down, and the haughtiness of men shall be made low,[78] and the Lord, the Father of spirits, the only true God, shall alone be exalted in man on that day, the day of my office. The goal of this is the destruction of the old heavens, that is, the spirit, intellect, will and senses of man. Now follows the dissolution or destruction of the old earth: "And the idols He shall utterly abolish."[79] All idols shall be thoroughly destroyed and rooted out. From where? From the land or the earth, that is, from the heart or soul of man, and from their affections

---

[76] *Isaiah* 2:12-15
[77] *Isaiah* 2:16
[78] *Isaiah* 2:17
[79] *Isaiah* 2:18

and passions. Their entire form and essence shall be dissolved down to the ground—all of them and not just some. There shall be a final and total destruction of all of them. Men shall freely cast from them the golden and silver idols upon which they had set their hearts and affections and which they had worshiped, when my day and my fiery, consuming office enters into and bursts forth in their old earth, shaking terribly whatever has been planted in their hearts and affections or desires. "Then they shall cease from man, whose breath is in his nostrils, for wherein is he to be accounted of?"[80] The evangelical prophet Isaiah prophesied concerning my fiery-burning day. [132] Now, however, I myself, with my fire-oven, have entered your land and earth, that is, your heart and affections, and come into your heavens, that is, into the spirit of your intellect and senses, in order to effect and accomplish this destruction in your inward man.

Throughout chapter 24 of the book of *Isaiah*, the abovementioned prophet prophesied concerning my day of dissolution and destruction of the old heavens and earth of man through fire within him, whereby the prophet begins with the destruction and melting of the earth and continues from earth to the heavens. "Behold the Lord maketh the earth empty."[81] What sort of earth? The old earth, the evil, wicked earth within man. He empties it out and turns it into a wilderness; He turns it upside down; that is, He alters its form and inverts its covering and scatters

---

[80] *Isaiah* 2:22
[81] *Isaiah* 24:1 (see also *Genesis* 1:2)

CHAPTER 19

its inhabitants, that is, all seven wicked trading and handworking nations, all evil, wicked and unpure spirits which lived in the lusts and affections of the soul or the heart, and which traded, bought and sold in this outward, visible world. "And it shall be, as with the people, so with the priest, the prophet, the prince; as with the lord, so with the servant; as with the mistress, so with her maid; as with the buyer, so with the seller."[82] All of them ought to and must perish; they all stand in Babel, in confusion and bewilderment. "The land or the earth shall be utterly emptied, and utterly spoiled,"[83] that is, not one single satanic or infernal spirit shall remain in the heart and the affections of the human heart. My day shall bring utter destruction and tilling out. "Now the wicked earth shall mourn, the old earth shall languish and fade away,"[84] that is, not one single evil spirit, [133] not one earthy spirit, shall inhabit the earth or dwell in the heart; there is not one of them that shall not perish and be destroyed by fire. It is appropriate, and righteousness itself commands that the wicked earth should be destroyed down to its foundations. The wicked earth and heart have been defiled by the inhabitants thereof; the evil spirits in the intellect of man and heart have transgressed the laws of Moses, and the laws and commandments of Christ. They have broken the everlasting covenant which God made with them.[85] Therefore the curse has devoured the land, and therefore the evil earth has been desolated.

[82] *Isaiah* 24:2
[83] *Isaiah* 24:3
[84] *Isaiah* 24:4
[85] *Isaiah* 24:5-6

Therefore the wicked inhabitants of the earth, the earthy spirits, shall be burned. "When it shall be thus in the midst of the land, among the people, there shall be as the shaking of an olive tree, and as the gleaning of grapes, when the vintage is done."[86] Who is among the small number of olives or grapes that still remain? Only the eternal spirit with its intellect, will and senses, as well as the heart with its affections. For all astrayness and selfness, and all of the evil spirits which dwell in the terrible, evil essence of astrayness and selfness, must and shall be destroyed in the fire. Then the spirit and the heart shall praise and glorify the Lord our God in the fire.[87] "The earth is utterly broken down, the earth is thoroughly dissolved; the earth is moved exceedingly. The earth shall reel to and fro like a drunkard."[88] Who is able to melt and dissolve this old earth? Only the Day of Wisdom and her all-powerful office can accomplish this by fire. Her fire melts the earth and dissolves it, devastates it so that it falls and does not rise up again.[89] That same fiery day shall dissolve and destroy not only the wicked earth but also the heavens, the hosts of heaven and the kings of the earth. The spirit of man with his desire, [134] intellect, will and senses shall be punished, as shall be the kings of the wicked earth, who are all the rulers of evil and wickedness, of thrones, powers and principalities, and who belong to the Dragon and the Beast. "They shall be gathered together, as prisoners are gathered in the

---

[86] *Isaiah* 24:13
[87] *Isaiah* 24:15
[88] *Isaiah* 24:19-20
[89] Ibid

CHAPTER 19

pit,"⁹⁰ and they shall be burned with fire. Then shall the moon—that is, the earthy life of the senses, which is the sensual-sensory life—become red with shame, namely when no one believes further in any of the idols of the earthy Principle and finds no pleasure in them any longer. The sun shall be ashamed; that is, the earthy life of reason shall no longer rule.⁹¹ What life shall rule then? Answer: The life of faith from the spirit of faith. The Lord of Hosts, the Eternal Father, shall rule and reign in the spirit of faith upon Mount Zion and in Jerusalem; that is, my day is a day of preparation; it is a preparatory office in and through the destruction by fire of the old heavens and earth in man. It prepares the way for the Kingdom and for the reign of God on Mount Zion; it is an introduction to the beginning of the reign of God and to the sending down of Mount Zion and Jerusalem in the place of the old heavens and earth. The destruction of the old creates space for the advent of the new. Then the Lord shall reign gloriously in the presence of the elders. These elders are the patriarchs and prophets from the days and office of the Father. The Lord of Hosts, the Eternal Father, shall reign gloriously, that is, in the splendor of His majesty. After all of the wicked powers and energies that inhabit the heavens and earth of man are cast out, and the only God reigns alone in the heavens and earth of man with none beside Him, then it shall inevitably be a glorious kingdom and government.

The prophet Isaiah also prophesied concerning my

---

⁹⁰ *Isaiah* 24:22
⁹¹ *Isaiah* 24:23

SOPHIA

day in the book of *Isaiah*, chapter 13, from verse 6 to 16. In addition, the prophets Jeremiah and Ezekiel spoke of my day and of my office in the destruction of all things, [135] as did Joel[92] and Zephaniah: "I will utterly consume all things from off the land or the earth, saith the Lord."[93] It is a terrible thing for reason to hear that all things are to be consumed and rooted out of the land. It is not the land or earth itself that is to be destroyed but the form of the land, that is, all the things that are in and upon the land. It shall have to be a complete and utter devouring and destruction, for the final Day of Judgment of the Father and of the Son have already taken place and are past. "I will consume man and beast."[94] By "man" the prophet means the sensual and rational human being, and by "beast" the animalistic, the bestial and brutal human being, the earthy man, the man of flesh and blood. This man must be destroyed and tilled out. I will till out the beasts that belong to this bestial man. These are all of man's bestial, animal affections and passions; for the disorder of both the angry and the lustful affections, together with all their evil desires, longings and cravings, may be compared to such beasts as lions, bears, wolves, foxes and other such predatory, rending animals. These must all be utterly consumed by the fire. "I will consume the fowl of the heavens, and the fish of the sea, and the stumbling blocks with the wicked."[95] The fowl are all the soaring thoughts, desires and imaginations of

[92] *Joel* 2:10-11, 31-32; *Joel* 3:1-2, 9-17
[93] *Zephaniah* 1:2
[94] *Zephaniah* 1:3
[95] Ibid

CHAPTER 19

man's intellect, will and senses. These are the fowl of his heaven. The fish of the sea are the running to and fro of his earthy thoughts. The stumbling blocks are all the idols of his spirit and heart with the wicked, that is, with all the earthy spirits and dark powers that inhabit his heart, affections and passions. I will till man out of the land. The land shall remain, but man shall be tilled out, so that he shall be no longer dwell and be active therein, says the Lord. [136] The Father has promised it and has prophesied it by His prophets during the day of the Father. Thus, it must be fulfilled. I shall root out man. To be sure, the Father prophesied this as something occurring in the future. I, Wisdom, am now come to fulfill this prophecy and to till man out of the land. What sort of man? All of man—the entire man. All of man, that is, everything which pertains to man, everything which goes forth from man, and everything which man has accepted from the spirit of this world and in which he has clothed himself. All of man, that is, every sort of life, shall be tilled out of man. His sensual-sensory life, his bestial life, his rational life—all shall be tilled out. Man's contemplative, meditative life arising out of the life of selfness; his self-seeking life; his idolatrous and adulterous life, which has fallen away from God and turned, instead, to the spirit of this world, with which he commits adultery; his self-righteous life; his outwardly adopted life of service to God, shaped precisely according to the literal commandments: each and every life that takes its cause and primal origin from man's own will and energies shall be destroyed and consumed by fire. "I will cut off the remnant of Ba'al from this place, and the name of the Chemarim[96] with the priests,"[97] that is, with all idolatry and worship of false gods, and with all self-conceived forms of beatitude in God and Christianity that are established by priests, servants and pastors. Their names, their self-willed offices and ordinances, established and instituted by and through men—these must all be tilled out by fire. They are merely a service of Babel, a disordered, confused service which must now be rendered powerless and then destroyed by my powerful, discerning office. On this, my Day, I have come in the zeal and power of Elijah against all [137] the priests of Ba'al, by whatever names they call themselves, in the several nations, tongues or kingdoms. "And those who worship the host of heaven upon the housetops"[98] are the same as all of the spirits which are heathen and unbelieving, which bow down and worship before the spirit of this world. These are the spirits which, upon the tops of their houses, open themselves to the influences of the stars with their spirits, intellects, will and senses, and submit themselves to those stars. All such spirits must be cut off by my flaming, fiery sword and be tilled out. All that which is man's and comes from man shall be offered up by me, virginal Wisdom, on my fiery day, as my sacrificial offering to the Lord. "And it shall come to pass in the day of the Lord's sacrifice, that I will punish the princes and the king's children, and all such as are clothed with foreign apparel."[99] Who are these princes? It is the eternal spirit itself,

---

[96] Pagan sorcerers who burned with zeal like an oven
[97] *Zephaniah* 1:4
[98] *Zephaniah* 1:5
[99] *Zephaniah* 1:8

CHAPTER 19

for it is the King of Kings. And who are these royal children? They are nothing other than the energies and capacities of the king, namely the eternal intellect and will, with all the eternal senses. All who are clothed with foreign apparel are clothed in a foreign nature which is contrary to and opposed to the divine nature. From now on, the spirit and the soul must be clothed with nothing else but the virginal nature of Wisdom, with the clear Godhead of Wisdom, seeing that none of the foreign garments can persevere and stand in the liquefying, destructive fire. We may be certain that all ecclesiastical fraternities, all church congregations and all ecclesiastical constitutions are to be considered as nothing but unpure garments, without the purity of the just nature of Wisdom. "All the merchants are cut down like grass, and all they who bear silver are tilled out."[100] All the spirits busily trading in the intellect and all who deal in silver or carry on trade in the outer Principle must be [138] destroyed and rooted out. All those that are settled on their lees and say in their hearts:[101] "We can do a great deal of good with this. We can become one in spirit with the world. It is neither evil nor unjust, nor is it a sin that we provide ourselves and our wives and children with decent things. We must not and cannot always be praying, seeking and waiting." Such tempters and temptations shall be tilled out. The great day is near for those who have endured and survived the day of the Father and of the Son, and who are children of the knowledge of the mystery—that day is very near

---

[100] *Zephaniah* 1:11
[101] *Zephaniah* 1:12

to them. The mighty man shall weep bitterly, as will the man who is rich in spiritual treasures, in gifts and graces, and in knowledge of history. The man who is mighty in reason, learnedness, and other natural gifts and qualities, and who is mighty in observance of his obligations and duties in his office to God—the man who is mighty in the mystery, in visions, in revelations and prophecies—that man will bitterly and wretchedly lament when he sees everything burning before his eyes. The mighty man who has been a teacher, a guide and leader for others; who has been a great and active man and who has acquired a mighty reputation and made many proselytes; or who has brought to faith those who were alienated from the knowledge of Christ—I declare that this man will bitterly and wretchedly lament when he sees all his earnestly practiced godly works burst into flames and consumed. "That day shall be a day of anger and wrath, a day of trouble and distress,"[102] when they see such a sudden work and when they see the land suddenly robbed and desolated of all the spirits, life and energy which had inhabited it.

The prophet Haggai prophesied concerning my day of destruction: "Speak to Zerubbabel, governor of Judah, saying, I will shake the heavens and the earth. And I will overthrow [139] the throne of kingdoms, and I will destroy the strength of the kingdoms of the nations; and I will overthrow the chariots, and those who ride in them; and the horses and their riders shall come down, every one by the sword of his brother."[103]

---

[102] *Zephaniah* 1:15
[103] *Haggai* 2:21-22

CHAPTER 19

What else are these heavens and earth than the old sinful heavens and earth within man? And what is this overthrow of the kingdoms of the nations other than the tilling out of the heathen spirits which inhabit the spirit of man? What are the chariots in which they ride other than the intellect and the will? And what else are these horses than our senses? Yet the horse and its rider must both come down. And who is Zerubbabel, God's servant, whom God will make as a signet ring?[104] He is none other than the eternal spirit of man. This is God's servant, who shall be sealed and preserved and delivered from all of his enemies. The ground and cause of this is that God has chosen him. The spirit of man has been chosen and elected by God for beatitude.

Malachi, the final prophet, also prophesies concerning my day and office: "Behold! I will send my messenger, and he shall prepare the way before me, and the Lord shall suddenly come."[105] The truth of history and of the literal meaning is this: This messenger was John the Baptist, who had to prepare the way for Christ's advent in the flesh as His first advent in weakness.

The truth of the mystery, however, is this: I, Virgin Wisdom, in my fiery office, am this messenger and forerunner. The office of Elijah and the office of John the Baptist were both merely figures and fore-images of my preparatory office. Just as John prepared the way for Christ's first advent in the flesh, my office creates and prepares the way for Christ's

---

[104] *Haggai* 2:23
[105] *Malachi* 3:1

Second Coming, the advent in the spirit. "Then the messenger of the covenant, [140] whom ye delight in and serve, shall suddenly come to His temple,"[106] after the temple has been prepared by me. "And I will come near to you to judgment."[107] This is the last Day of Judgment, on which I shall be, in the soul and spirit, a swift witness against all spiritual sorcerers who have been enchanted by the wine of this outward Principle and against all spiritual adulterers who have committed spiritual harlotry in their intellects, wills, senses and affections or desires and cravings with the created beings of this world. For, behold, the day is coming, it is truly coming, and my burning day shall come quickly. On that day I shall establish and open my fire- and refiner's oven, and it shall ignite and burn the heavens and earth of man; the proud and all that do wickedly shall be burned like stubble and shall be consumed. Root and branch, astrayness and selfness, the essence of sin and the wicked roots of evil from which the tares grow forth—they shall all be destroyed and tilled out. "Behold, I shall send you the prophet Elijah."[108] I, Wisdom, am the true Elijah. He was my figure and fore-image. My fiery, destructive office succeeds the office of the Father and the office of Jesus in the flesh as an intermediate office in preparation for the advent of the great and terrible Day of the Lord.[109] This great, manifest and glorious Day of the Lord is the Second Coming of Christ in the spirit, in the power of the Holy Spirit. My fiery, burning

---

[106] Ibid
[107] *Malachi* 3:5
[108] *Malachi* 4:5
[109] Ibid

CHAPTER 19

day is not the same as that day. My day precedes the Day of the Lord, and that day follows my day. My day is an office of testing or examination, on which all astrayness, evil and selfness shall be destroyed and tilled out of man. It prepares and makes straight the way for the Second Coming of Christ in the spirit.

These are the allusive words, phrases and sayings of the prophets, which the man of reason cannot comprehend. Rather, he [141] deflects them from himself and interprets them as referring to the kingdoms and nations of this world, and to outward wars, devastations and tribulations. Accordingly, I have told you that you need to become a son of Wisdom, and that you must be able to understand these allusive phrases and obscure enigmas. You must comprehend where, to what purpose and to whom their prophecies point, namely to the destruction and tilling out of the world of astrayness and selfness in man.

CHAPTER 20

July 10th

Wisdom said: "Now I must reveal to you and demonstrate how the teaching of Christ and the apostles agree with the ancient prophets who came before them, and how the teaching of the New Testament agrees and coincides with that of the Old Testament. Additionally, I will instruct you in how both testaments prophesied concerning my future day and office occurring by fire, and in how the apostles understood the obscure sayings and parables of the prophets who had come before them.

First of all, I will present the teaching of Jesus on this particular point. The disciples came to Jesus with two questions. The first was: What shall be the sign of your coming,[110] namely of your Second Coming in the spirit and in the power and glory of the Father? Jesus answers thus: "And then shall appear the sign of the Son of Man in heaven; and then shall all the tribes of the earth mourn, and they shall see the Son of Man coming in the clouds [142] of heaven with power and great glory. And He shall send His angels with a great sound of a trumpet, and they shall gather together His

[110] *Matthew 24:3-4*

elect from the four winds, from one end of heaven to the other."[111] The second question was: "What shall be the sign of the end of the world?"[112] What sort of world? He is speaking not just of this outward, visible world but also of the old world within man, the old world of astrayness, unrighteousness and selfness in man. He speaks of the time when this world will come to an end, or be dissolved, or be destroyed in man. Jesus answers: "Immediately after the tribulation of those days the sun shall be darkened, and the moon shall not give its light, and the stars shall fall from heaven, and the powers of the heavens shall be shaken."[113] We should not take this to be the visible heavens alone, but also the old heavens in man's intellect and the powers of the wicked heavens in man. These also shall be shaken, according to this prophecy.

The ground and occasion of this question arose from Christ's teaching, wherein he said to his disciples: Do you see this edifice, this temple? This stone building, this temple of Solomon, is a figure of all visible stone churches or temple worship in the outward man and in the Principle of this world. I tell you: "There shall not be left here one stone upon another that shall not be thrown down."[114] In other words, all outward stone temples and churches, all external worship in splendid ceremonies and majesty, such as outward baptism, preaching, chanting of psalms, bread, wine and church congregations, shall be torn down on my day of destruction, together with all fleshly statutes

---

[111] *Matthew* 24:30-31
[112] *Matthew* 24:4
[113] *Matthew* 24:29
[114] *Matthew* 24:2

and institutions. Babel, Babylon and Egypt cannot be destroyed without also overturning their external worship, which is established in the outward man [143] and in the stone temples of the world. Their outer court, which is the worldly Principle wherein their stone temple is established and which is a figure of the outward body and the outward man who prays in such temples, must be destroyed, together with their temple- and church statutes. Their inner court or holy place, which is the service of their heart, wherewith they think to worship God, must be destroyed. Their holy of holies, which is the service of their intellect and will, must also be destroyed. It was impossible to destroy the temple without destroying along with it the holy place and the holy of holies in their figures of the service of the heart and intellect, which have been established in Babel in, by and through the outward man. The ground and cause of the overthrow and casting down of all Babel-service and its stone buildings, as well as its outward institutions and its service of the intellect and heart is this: The abomination of desolation in the holy of holies has been set up in these outward worshipers. I, Wisdom, tell you that this is a prophetic prediction which shall be fulfilled. This outward service shall cease, for God desires to be worshiped in spirit and in truth in the inward man. According to this revelation, the type of gathering of the Quakers must also be destroyed on my day, for this is, in truth, merely an outward church. For my office makes preparation for Mount Zion, and for the church or congregation of the firstborn, and for the universal gathering of holy spirits, so that they might be established in the New

CHAPTER 20

Heavens and New Earth within man by the work of my hands. Therefore, everything which has been erected by and through man should and must be broken down and destroyed on my day of destruction. If another church should rise up, upon the foundation of the Quakers, and erect an outward form of blessedness in the Principle of this world, to which the outer man must be conformed and by which he must be guided, [144] I shall, nevertheless, destroy it. For if abomination and desolation dwell within it, how can it be a work of my hands? How can they say that I have built it if it has been built by man and erected by the creature? My office shatters and destroys all outward worship of God which is performed in the outward man and in stone churches, together with all their evangelical statutes and institutions, which have been established in this evil world. It is pure service of Babel which shall not stand on the day of my office. My office must destroy and utterly raze Egypt, Babel and Babylon, together with all service of the heart and intellect, for the abomination of desolation dwells in the midst of them. My office makes preparation for a different temple, for other priests and for a different liturgy and worship which shall be pleasing to God.

Saint Paul prophesied concerning my day and my office of testing, where everything is tried and proven. He writes: "Every man's work shall be made manifest; for the day shall declare it."[115] What day? The Day of Wisdom shall make all manifest through fire, and this fire shall test and prove. In the *Letter to the Hebrews* we read: "But ye are come to Mount

---

[115] *1 Corinthians* 3:13

SOPHIA

Zion, and unto the city of the living God,"[116] and to the church or the congregation of the firstborn. This is the church which must be established upon earth. This is the church for which my day and my office are preparing the way. On my day I shall tear down every so-called church of Christ devised by man. I shall overturn them and destroy them down to the foundations, in order to bring the Church of Mount Zion and its worship of God down into this world. Paul understood the implications of my day and what the effect and the energy of my office would be when he wrote: "Yet once more [145] I shake not the earth only"[117] but also the heavens—not only the wicked earth in man's heart or spiritual nature but also the old heavens in man's spirit and intellect, with their temples, with their false worship of God, and with their commingled forms and institutions. This movement or shaking is the effect of my office.

Consider also the witness of Saint Peter: "But the heavens and earth are now kept in store, reserved unto fire against the Day of Judgment."[118] Which heavens and earth? They are the old, wicked heavens and earth within man himself, the old world and old creation within him. These are reserved unto fire. For what sort of fire? For the fiery office of Wisdom, which shall be like a fire on the Day of Judgment. What kind of Day of Judgment shall that be? My fiery day, because on that day I shall judge the old heavens and earth. I shall convince and convict them. Then I

---

[116] *Hebrews* 12:22
[117] *Hebrews* 12:26
[118] *2 Peter* 3:7

CHAPTER 20

shall condemn them to dissolution and liquefaction in my everlasting fire, so that they shall be destroyed and smelted around. Their complete and universal destruction is expressed and described in the following words: "[On that day] the heavens shall pass away with a great noise, and the elements shall melt with a fervent heat; the earth also, and the works that are in it shall be burned up."[119] Not just this heaven, with its elements and its hosts, that is, the sun, moon and stars, and the firmament in which they stand, but also their wicked earth and all its works—not just their commerce and handicraft works but also their works of service to God, their obligations and institutions in service to God, their offices of religion and their churches, in which they hold their worship services, as well as their ecclesiastical statutes—all of these must be burned. Behold, all of these things in the heavens and earth of man must be dissolved and melted. When? Where and how? When? On the Day of Wisdom. [146] Where? —In the spirit and soul of man. And how, or by what means? —By fire, by my heavenly fire.[120] Look for this fiery dissolution of all things, as Peter looked for it within himself. Thus, every wise and perceptive Christian must look for the same within himself and await it.[121] Peter refers to it here as the Day of God, and it would seem that he understands this to be the day and office of the Father. That day may be called thus because I, Wisdom, am pure Godhead in my essence and one with the Holy

---

[119] *2 Peter* 3:10
[120] *2 Peter* 3:12
[121] Ibid

SOPHIA

Trinity. What I perform, the Holy Trinity in me performs. Thus you may ascribe it to each person of the Holy Trinity, namely to the Father, the Son or to the Holy Spirit. Now, however, the time has come that I can say and declare expressly, with clear differentiation and absolute explicitness, that this is my day. The Father and the Son have previously had their days upon the stage of this world, and their days are passed and gone. Now my day has come, however. It shall be revealed in man before the eyes of the world. My day consists of a day of destruction and of the abolition of everything which came before me and of the establishment of a new world and new creation within man. For the sake of differentiation, therefore, this day is called the virginal day or the Day of Wisdom.

This day of movement or of shaking, this day of overthrow, which is the day of virginal Wisdom, has been previously announced in the *Revelation* of Saint John: "And I beheld, when he had opened the sixth seal and, lo, there was a great earthquake."[122] Where else should this earthquake take place than in the wicked earth within man himself? What sort of shaking and quaking occurred in the heavens of man? Answer: His sun, namely the light and life of reason within man, became black, and the moon became like blood. The life of the senses in the earthy Principle [147] became as offensive to him as blood.[123] "And the stars of heaven fell unto the earth,"[124] that is,

---

[122] *Revelation* 6:12
[123] Ibid
[124] *Revelation* 6:13

CHAPTER 20

the thoughts and imaginations of his heavens ceased their movements, and the firmament of these heavens in man ran together and contracted, as things which are caught in the fire are wont to do. This is nothing other than a new prophecy and a repetition and renewal of all the things which all the prophets had previously said. "And I saw another angel fly in the midst of heaven, or in mid-heaven."[125] This angel is Wisdom in the exercise of her office. She is described as flying because she is a quick, penetrating power and energy in the midst of the heavens or in mid-heaven, that is, in man's New Heavens within his intellect. This angel possessed the Eternal Gospel, in order to proclaim it to those who inhabited these New Heavens. The proclamation of the Eternal Gospel is the aspect of renewal or the perfection of her office, the making new of all things in man's heavens and earth, that is, in his new intellect and senses, and in his renewed soul or heart and their affections and passions. It is a preparatory office, a office of renewal. It is the erection of the inner court or the holy place in the heart of man and of the holy of holies within his intellect. It is a office which prepares the spirit of man for the birth of Jesus in the spirit and for the day of the Holy Spirit. It prepares man's spirit for the descent of Mount Zion and the New Jerusalem, that they might dwell within his intellect and heart, and in his affections and passions. This is the subject and ground of the Eternal Gospel, namely the revelation and creation of man's New Heavens and Earth, which nothing but that Gospel's revelatory and creative

---

[125] *Revelation 14:6*

energy in man may bring about or create. It is a office that brings man's spirit to the point where it fears the only true God, [148] gives Him honor, glory and praise, and serves and worships Him, the One who has created the New Heavens and New Earth in his intellect and heart, in the holy place and in the holy of holies. This is the immediate evangelical office that precedes the advent of Jesus in the spirit, the coming of the Holy Spirit, and the state of Mount Zion and the New Jerusalem in splendor. It is a office that restores and renews all of those things which the First Adam allowed to decay and which the new Second Adam shall renew when He comes again. This restoration and renewal of all things within the spirit and intellect of man shall precede the glorious state of Mount Zion and the New Jerusalem.

We read in *Revelation*: "And I saw a new heaven and a new earth."[126] It is the evangelical office of Wisdom to restore the New Heavens and New Earth in man. Before this could take place, however, the first heaven and earth had to flee, be dissolved and smelted around. Their dissolution had to prepare the way for the restoration of the New Heavens and New Earth in the intellect and heart of man. The New Heavens and New Earth in man open the path for the descent of the holy city, New Jerusalem, so that it might dwell in the New Creation within man. For this reason, the office of Wisdom by fire, both in its property of dissolution or destruction by fire and in its property of renewal by fire, is different from the office of Jesus in the spirit, as well as from the descent

---

[126] *Revelation* 21:1

CHAPTER 20

of the Holy Spirit and from the state of Mount Zion in splendor. The former precedes the latter and the latter succeed the former.

Now I shall show you the *hieroglyphica* or secret symbols and fore-images of the ancients, which were and still are figures and fore-images of the downfall and destruction of the old world, the old creation, the old heavens and earth within man.

The first figure was the flood and drowning [149] of the old world by water. The second figure was Egypt and Pharaoh with his army. The third was Joshua in the conquest and occupation of the land of Canaan, the expulsion of the wicked nations, the burning of their cities, and the destruction of their idols. The destruction of Babylon and the downfall and destruction of Sodom and Gomorrah were all figures of my office of destruction. Moreover, all of the prophecies of the prophets concerning the destructions caused by the Egyptians, Babylonians and Assyrians are merely figures for the destruction of the wicked world within man, the world that must be rooted out of him.

Wisdom also showed to me the *hieroglyphica* or secret symbols and fore-images in the *Revelation* of Saint John. Egypt must be destroyed, and Sodom and Babylon must be burned by fire. They point to nothing else but the evil nature within man, which must be destroyed and tilled out of his intellect and heart. "And their dead bodies shall lie in the street of the great city, which spiritually is called Sodom and Egypt."[127] What sort of Sodom and Egypt? These are

---

[127] *Revelation* 11:8

SOPHIA

the Sodom and Egypt which dwell in man's intellect and heart, and which must (mystically understood) be destroyed. For the divine life and nature of the Godhead was crucified in them.

"Babylon is fallen, that great, that mighty city is fallen!"[128] In prophecy this effectually and truly took place. This Babylon can be none other than the Babylon in the heavens and earth of man. "Thrust in thy sickle and reap; for the time is come for thee; for the harvest of the earth is ripe."[129] What sort of harvest of the earth is it that is ripe? The harvest of the wicked earth in the heart of man. This harvest, this sickle and this reaping are simply my office of destruction by fire. At *Revelation* 17:16 we read of the condemnation and destruction of the Great Whore. This Great Whore is the corrupted, lascivious, salacious and whorish intellect in its evil [150] nature and essence. This intellect has turned away from God and has turned to the creatures of this earthy Principle, committing fornication with them. Their destruction and uprooting is simply my fiery office, which brings ruin and downfall upon them. My fire devours their flesh, which means that all their earthy desires are destroyed, consumed and devastated, and that they are despoiled of all their sensual desires, which are then burned by fire. *Revelation* speaks again of Babylon in chapter 18. The angel mentioned here is Wisdom. She is no created angel but a pure angelic energy. "Babylon the great is fallen, it is fallen."[130]

---

[128] *Revelation* 14:8
[129] *Revelation* 14:16
[130] *Revelation* 18:2

CHAPTER 20

What Babylon is this? It is the secret Babylon in the nature of man, in man's heavens and earth. It is the wicked Babylon in which wicked nature, the spirit of error, satanic spirits and evil spirits fly to and fro in their wicked movements in the intellect and will of man. Unpure animals and beasts do the same in man's heart and affections. Their effectual fall occurs when I, Wisdom, enter into them to destroy them and till them out, and to impose my fiery Day of Judgment upon them. We are called to come forth out of the wicked nature that is within us, which dwells within our intellects and hearts and within our affections and passions. The fiery call of Wisdom invites us to come out from among them by the actions of our will-spirits, or to pray with heartfelt desire that they might be utterly destroyed, smelted around and tilled out. This earthy nature in our intellects and senses and in our affections and passions or inclinations toward the Principle of this world, and toward the images and creaturely essences within it, is the inward secret Babylon and the Babylon in the nature of man. This Babylon must be thoroughly destroyed by fire, for the Godhead is mighty and strongly active in [151] Wisdom's fire, in order to burn it utterly. "And the kings of the earth, who have committed fornication and lived luxuriously with her, shall bewail her."[131] Who are the kings of the earth mentioned here? They are the royal energies and capacities of the spirit which lament her and bewail the destruction of earthy nature as they see the smoke of her burning. Who are the merchants of the earth who weep and mourn for

---

[131] *Revelation* 18:9

earthy nature and for its essence, because they can no longer do business and sell their wares?[132] They are the volatile senses of the intellect, which can no longer ogle or run after gold and silver, or creatures, or the riches and honors of this earth. They are the merchants, namely the senses, which had been enriched by these things. "For in one hour so great riches are come to nothing."[133] All of their wealth has been destroyed, for the interventions of Wisdom are quick and very energetic. In the heavens and earth of man there is great rejoicing over the downfall of this wicked, earthy nature. After this has been effectually accomplished, the spirit, the intellect, will and senses, the heart and affections are elated, although they do mourn because the work is still in progress. After the work is completed, they, along with the prophets and apostles, shall praise Wisdom for its accomplishment. Then the spirit, together with the senses and affections, shall see that God has avenged them upon Babylon,[134] for earthy nature has brought nothing but sorrow, trouble and tribulation to the inward man. It has severed man from God and God from man. Now, however, they shall be effectually avenged upon it. After the great city of Babylon within man, this wicked, earthy Babylonian nature in the heavens and earth of man, has been pulled down, it shall never rise again to inhabit man's heavens and earth. "And the voice of the harpers, and minstrels, and flute players, and trumpeters,"[135] and

[132] *Revelation* 18:11
[133] *Revelation* 18:17
[134] *Revelation* 18:20
[135] *Revelation* 18:22

the dance shall never again be heard in the senses or the affections. No business or commerce shall be conducted in earthy nature, and no word of marriage [152] shall ever be heard therein.[136] "And in her was found the blood of prophets, and of saints, and of all that were slain upon the earth."[137] In this evil, earthy, devilish nature and in human selfness, the divine life or the life that comes from God had been killed. The blood of the prophets, that is, the life and blood of their prophecies, had been killed in its nature. The heavenly life of all the saints who had died during the office of the Father and the Son was found in its nature, and it was the ground and cause of all this. Now, however, vengeance has descended upon it, now it has been desolated by the fiery office of Wisdom. At *Revelation* 19:1 God is praised for having judged this wicked, earthy nature which had poured out and corrupted man's heavens and earth, that is, his spirit or intellect and his soul or heart, and also the blood of the seed of life, which had been sown during the office of the Father and of the Son. For this reason it must now suffer justly during the office of Wisdom and because it had slain the Lamb and poured out its blood. "For the Lord God omnipotent reigneth."[138] He has occupied the kingdom and reigns therein. This means that God the Lord, God the Father, and the entire Holy Trinity in their almighty power, have begun to reign in this work of destruction of the earthy spirit and nature that inhabit the intellect and

---

[136] *Revelation* 18:23
[137] *Revelation* 18:24
[138] *Revelation* 19:6

heart of man. He is the beginning and opens the way to His almighty kingdom, and to the wedding feast of the Lamb, and to the birth of Jesus in the spirit, and to the day of the Holy Spirit, and to the descent of Mount Zion and the New Jerusalem. Then God shall reign in the Godhead-power of His omnipotence.

What is this visible world, this out-birth, this visible creation? It is the Babylon outside of us; it is the evil and unpure essence, the accursed essence. It is the forbidden tree of [153] evil, which we must no longer touch. It is the abomination, the curse, the accursed thing. It is the golden staff or the golden tongue. The Babylonian garment. It is the witch of Endor, the painted Jezebel. This world, as the forbidden tree, the tree of temptation, remains and is not destroyed by the fire of Wisdom within us. Rather, it is earthy, evil nature which shall be destroyed and tilled out.

Now I shall show you the devastation of Babel and the destruction of Jerusalem, together with its holy place and holy of holies. These symbolize the fact that all false worship, all false forms of adoration, all false churches and temples, which have been erected in the evil nature of man and in his earthy nature, in his holy place and holy of holies, together with their sanctuaries and mixed worship of God, must be destroyed. They shall truly and effectually be destroyed on my day. For my day shall bring down and introduce the Eternal Gospel, toward which the office of the patriarchs and prophets pointed during the days of the Father, and to which the office of Christ and His apostles referred. The advent and revelation of the Eternal Gospel must cast down and destroy all Jerusalem temples, all Babylonian worship, all mixed

CHAPTER 20

worship, all idolatrous worship and all the temples of the idols in the intellect and heart of man. All human inventions and institutions must cease when the church of the Eternal Gospel has been established in the holy of holies.

Here one might object and ask the question: Why did the prophets of ancient days prophesy the destruction and smelting around of the heavens and earth within man in such obscure sayings and metaphorical or allusive speech and expressions? Why has this been represented by such dark, mysterious symbols as the destruction of kingdoms, nations and cities, with their inhabitants? Why did they employ a metaphor such as the destruction of the temple of Solomon, with its holy place and holy of holies, to refer to [154] the decay of all outward temples, temple worship and temple statutes? Why did the prophets not use clear, explicit words, so that every common eye could see, and every spirit might perceive and understand? Answer: We wish to leave this question for the moment and answer it at a later time.

CHAPTER 21

July 11th

The Fourth Gate

When my divine visitor, Wisdom, returned to me, she showed me that she had brought my inward man through the gate of the dissolution and smelting around of the old heavens and earth within me and, thus, through the first part of her fiery office, which consisted of the destructions of the old heavens and earth. The heavens and earth *per se* remain, for they are intrinsically eternal essences and autonomies which are not subject to destruction or annihilation. Thus, nothing perishes except the old world of astrayness and selfness, together with the cities and all the inhabitants of those cities, and all their old, active properties and forms. These are the materials capable of being destroyed and consumed. Wisdom added that these were the tinder and fodder of her eternal blaze in the eternal nature of man, which consists of heaven and earth, that is, of spirit and soul or heart. Wisdom said further: "Now I shall also bring you [155] through my delightful, charming Gate of Renewal, which is the gate of restoration to the first or primal state. This is the second part of my fiery day or office, the part that consists in the creation of New Heavens and a New Earth, that is, in the making new of all things in those same heavens and earth. They do remain the same heavens and earth in and of themselves. The old heavens and earth *per se* are neither consumed nor destroyed by my fiery blaze. Instead, it is only the malign active qualities and properties of the evils of astrayness and selfness, everything that works evil, and each and every evil spirit, which shall perish. Thus, the same heavens and earth within man shall be renewed and brought back to their first purity. They shall be endowed anew with divine and heavenly qualities or properties, and with divine energies and heavenly graces. This is the creation of New Heavens and a New Earth in the nature of man: the making new of the eternal spirit, together with its eternal intellect, will and senses, in addition to the making new of his heart or soul, with their affections and passions. In the creation of New Heavens and a New Earth in the nature of man, consider the following aspects:

First of all, what name should be given to it? At times it is called a New Creation in man, despite the fact that it is still the same heavens and earth, in terms of their eternal autonomies. Yet all things are created anew within its New Heavens and New Earth. Within it there are new cities, new strong castles and fortresses, new inhabitants, new qualities, new active properties, new energies and graces, both within its New Heavens and its New Earth. All of these have been created in a magical fashion by my creative energy and by the *Fiat* of omnipotence. I must employ the word "magical" [156] because there is no other way of expressing it. The term is understood only by the children of Wisdom, however, who recognize and understand that Wisdom is active solely in a magical fashion in the heavens and earth of man. I mean thereby, however, that all things in those heavens and earth shall be made new truly, effectually, essentially and autonomously, and not merely in the imagination. On the contrary, everything will be accomplished and effected by my creative power, or in a magical fashion. Do not be disturbed by this expression. Do not judge too quickly, according to ignorant reason. Rather, wait until Wisdom comes to make new your own heavens and earth within you. Then you will recognize from experience and understand how divine Wisdom works all things in our heavens and earth by her divine magic. This is why what is established in the old heavens and earth of man is called a New Creation.

Secondly, it is called a restoration to the original state or a restorative work, because it truly and effectually restores the heavens and earth within man to the first state of creation, to the state of the First Adamic man. That same man was created to be a sanctified man in the mirror-image of God, free from all original and personal sin, from all evil seeds within, and thus free from all evil inclinations. He was placed in Paradise and was meant to live in Paradise, where all things grew spontaneously: all the things which he required for his nourishment, for his food and drink, and for his use and service. All this was to be enjoyed without the slightest labor, toil or trouble to his spirit or to his body. Yet now we know neither what the first state of the First Adamic man was, nor where

CHAPTER 21

this Paradise was located, nor where it is today. Nor do we know the nature of the first and original state of Adam, the first man, the state of purity, innocence and uprightness, [157] free from all immixture with astrayness and selfness. This could not be understood during the office of either the Father or the Son. For those who lived during those two offices lived and died in a mixed state. Although a seed of grace was sown in the hearts of some of the saints, yet a seed of evil and astrayness was mixed in with it, so that life and death struggled with each other within them, light and darkness were mixed, and the saints died in this condition. Their intellects were so blinded that they decisively concluded that it was impossible to be free of sinful life and to be redeemed from astrayness and selfness. Thus they died in their minority and immaturity.[139] Now, however, on my day my fiery office has come to restore all things in man's heavens and earth (which the first Adam had lost) and to renew the lost mirror-image of God, together with the lost Paradise. It shall re-establish man's heavens and earth, which presently lie under the curse because of man, and cause blessing to come upon them. It shall make verdant again the lost Paradise in man's heavens and earth; the faded, withered, vanished Garden of Eden in human nature shall again become like a garden of God. In his New Heavens and New Earth man shall again enjoy everything that the First Adam lost. On the day of my fiery office, all of these things shall be effectually restored, enjoyed and possessed again through essential experience.

---

[139] *Galatians* 4:1

Thirdly, my work of restoring all things to their former state and making them new is compared to the re-establishment of a building or to the erection of a temple, a church or a house. Man's [158] New Heavens and New Earth, when they are returned to their original, first-possessed purity, must become God's true church upon earth, the house and temple in which He chooses to dwell. It is my work to build this glorious edifice and grand structure in the New Heavens and Earth of man. My hands must lay the ground and foundations for this building. I must establish the true church of Christ upon this earth; I must reconstruct the lost booth of David; I must rebuild the holy place in the heart or soul of man and the holy of holies in his intellect and spirit. I must repair the breaches and close up the gaps. It is my work to raise up again this new and one true Christian church within man. No one else can do this, not even the angels in heaven. The greatly praised Holy Trinity has chosen and commanded me to rebuild the lost and devastated temple of Solomon in the New Heavens and New Earth of man, and to restore it to its original condition. It is my arm that must overthrow and destroy Babel, that is, all of the confused, self-established churches of human beings. It is also my arm that must rebuild the true temple of Solomon, which is a figure of the true church and temple of Christ in man's nature. What has Babel done within Christianity, therefore, that it desired to erect Christ's true church upon earth? This is something which is not within its power to do, for from the time that Jesus was killed upon the cross, the apostles died, and apostasy set in, there has never

CHAPTER 21

been a true, Christian, visible, gathered church upon the earth. It was impossible that there could be such a church. There could be no true, Christian, visible state or church of the Gospel; instead, there could only be churches of the Antichrist. There could be neither true servants in the church nor true services, neither true worship nor true worshipers, until I, Wisdom, descended with my fiery [159] office to make all things new and to establish a new, visible, true state of the church upon earth—until I restored the true church with my laws and statutes. This church shall be called the house of Wisdom, on account of those who worship within it. There shall be true worship, true priests, a true altar and a proper fire, so that all might be inflamed. Now then, if this is my work of restoration, and if it is incumbent upon me alone to rebuild the true church of Christ with all its decrees, then what has Babel achieved in Christianity, other than to erect churches of the Antichrist and outward pseudo-forms of blessedness? All of these shall now be burned with fire on my day, which is near. How have they set fire to Babel with their confused opinions and heated, fervent disputations with and against each other? Each one has raised his sword against his neighbor and persecuted him with bitter reproaches and accusations. They have driven each other out of the congregation and banished them. Each has accused the other of being false, and one church has cursed and damned the other. Why? For the sake of idle words and opinions. Each argues for his own established form or image and for his church. Each party has battled for and believed that their form was the true church of Christ upon earth, the one true church, to which belonged the promises of eternal life. Each party has cried out and proclaimed: "We are Christ's true church upon earth! All of the others are false churches of Antichrist! We possess the true keys to exclude or to let enter. We possess the true gate and entryway through which you must enter in. We possess true evangelical worship and evangelical priests. In fact, they are all churches of Antichrist and liars. Because of these things particularly, they shall be exposed as deceivers on my day of destruction [160] upon Babel. This shall occur on the day when I restore all things, when I come to rebuild the true church of Christ, which shall rise up again as a newly created church from the dust, ruin and ashes of the outward pseudo-churches. Then the church of the Quakers will be found to be a church of Antichrist, a humanly established church. Its form, and the door by which they let people into their church, shall be destroyed. They shall be found to be liars, since they claimed that they were the true church of Christ, possessed the sole path to blessedness, that their teaching was the right remedy and their form was the true gate to Christ's true church. I tell you and testify that they are just as much a church of Antichrist as are the other churches, which they despise. They shall be proven liars in their teachings, because they claim that they are free from astrayness and selfness. Yet they are not. They claim that they are perfect, but they are still imperfect. They testify that they have arrived at Mount Zion and the New Jerusalem before Mount Zion and the New Jerusalem have descended into them. That they testify to and claim such things as truth before I, Wisdom, have made them into new

CHAPTER 21

creatures is precisely what will brand them as liars on my approaching Day of Judgment upon them. Think about my names and titles: creation; restoration to the original state; renewal; rebuilding of the destroyed temple of Jerusalem in the New Heavens and New Earth of man; the figure and counterpart of the true church of Christ in the renewed nature of man.

Second consideration: Consider further the locality or the place of these New Heavens and Earth, and where they are to be made new. You do not have to gape at the outward, visible world as if its time had already arrived and it were about to be renewed or made new. No, these New Heavens and Earth [161] reside within the nature of the eternal man. The New Heavens which are to be made new shall be renewed in the eternal spirit and in its intellect, will and senses. These are the New Heavens of man which I shall make anew. His New Earth is his renewed heart or soul as well as his affections and passions. These New Heavens and Earth, which shall be made new, are not external to man but are inward. Man's very own heavens and earth within must be made new. Otherwise, he can neither be nor become a New Creature within.

Third consideration: Think about who might be the restorer and creator or maker of these New Heavens and New Earth. It is a virgin, the eternal virginal Wisdom of God. She is both the destroyer and the rebuilder. She, and no other, is the arm that pulls down, shatters and dissolves the old, and is the same arm of power that rebuilds everything in a new form and pattern. Know, therefore, that this office of breaking down and building up again is Wisdom's day

SOPHIA

and office. The day of the Father is over and the day of the Son has passed. Therefore, the Day of Wisdom must now also be revealed on the stage of the visible world and creation. It is absolutely certain that this eternal energy cannot exist without the presence of the persons of the Holy Trinity within it, and that the Holy Trinity, the Father, the Son and the Holy Spirit, secretly cooperate in this active and effectual energy, so that you may ascribe its working to whichever of the persons you will. Nevertheless, for the sake of right order and differentiation, it is truly ascribed to the Day of Wisdom. It is the good pleasure of the Holy Trinity to grant the honor and glory of this work of renewal to the eternal virgin, Wisdom.

Here one could raise an objection and say: Does this not diminish the work of Christ and [162] the spirit of Christ within our hearts? Does not Holy Scripture attribute this work to the spirit and person of Christ? Does it not state that He is the destroyer and restorer? Has it not been said that He shall destroy the works of the spirit of error and shall sweep the threshing floor of human nature with inextinguishable fire? Why was this work now withdrawn from the spirit of Christ, which works within us, and attributed to virginal Wisdom? Is this not to diminish the energy of the seed of Christ working within us? Answer: A great deal could be said in response to this objection, but a short, sufficient answer would be that the spirit of Christ and the spirit of Wisdom are one and the same. They are not two different spirits; rather, the spirit of Wisdom is the spirit of Christ and the spirit of Christ is the spirit of Wisdom. Thus, you may ascribe this revelation to whomever you wish. Yet, for

CHAPTER 21

the sake of differentiation, it is primarily attributed to Wisdom and not to Christ or to His spirit. Firstly, this is so because it is the Day of Wisdom, her day of resurrection, appearance and revelation. The day of Jesus, on the other hand, came with His first appearance in the world. His day was revealed to the entire world through His own teaching and that of His apostles. That day, however, has passed and gone. Now, after the revelation of the day of the Son, you must follow the order of the virgin of Wisdom. The day of the Son has passed and a new day has appeared which can now be ascribed neither to the Father nor to the Son, nor to Jesus Christ with regard to his first advent in the flesh, nor to the day of the Holy Spirit. It is not to be attributed to the Son's day or office, for although He effectually sowed a seed of grace and of eternal life in the heart of man during His day, that seed of immortality was, in and of itself, too weak in opposition to astrayness, anger and the wrath [163] of hell, and against the earthy nature wherein it had been sown. Thus, it was unable to free itself of all astrayness and selfness, or to overcome all weakness in human nature and in the heavens and earth of man. Instead, it inhabited and struggled within that nature, and battled with and against the world, the flesh and the devil. This seed was slain, killed and murdered within human nature, just as befell the just Abel at the hands of Cain the murderer. In the same way, Christ, in his first birth and appearance, was murdered in the innocent children by bloodthirsty King Herod. Since the day of the Son is passed and gone and this office has been completed, the Day of Wisdom has now come, to support the eternal seed that has been sown in the hearts of Christ's members and to avenge His death. For this reason, this day is explicitly ascribed to the office of Wisdom and not to those of the Father or the Son, that is, to previous revelations.

One may further object and ask why this day is not ascribed to Jesus in the spirit or to His Second Coming, or to the advent of the Holy Spirit, since these days will arrive in power and glory? To this we must answer "No!" and note that this cannot be the case, since the advent of Jesus in the spirit and the coming of the Holy Spirit cannot take place in tainted and unpure heavens and earth. Neither Jesus in the spirit nor the Holy Spirit can appear in such a place. This is the ground and cause why they have not descended into the heavens and earth of man, namely because of their unpureness. If man's heavens and earth were made new, then Jesus in the spirit, together with the Holy Spirit and Mount Zion, would immediately descend into them. It is necessary, therefore, that a new office should come after the death of Christ to make all things new, and to prepare the way for the advent of Jesus in the spirit and for the day of the Holy Spirit. [164] Therefore, this day must be ascribed to someone, and that someone is none other than the virgin of Wisdom of the Holy Trinity, which virgin is united corporeally with the Trinity in one body. This fact is absolutely no disadvantage for the advent of Jesus in the spirit or for the day of the Holy Spirit, nor does it diminish their work. The day and office of Wisdom must prepare the way and make straight the path and make all things new and holy, so that Jesus in the spirit and the day of the Holy Spirit might be

CHAPTER 21

revealed, arrive and appear. Otherwise, these things could never happen, in all eternity, because the pure cannot dwell with the unpure in unpure heavens and earth. Her day is, thus, a transitional day and her office a transitional office before Jesus in the spirit, before the Day of Pentecost, and before the descent of Mount Zion into the New Heavens and New Earth in man. Therefore, it is a preparatory day and unavoidably necessary for opening the way for the New Jerusalem. The teachings of the Old and New Testaments have declared and demonstrated, however, that her office is different from those of the Father and the Son. Because it is a different office from those of Jesus in the spirit, the advent of the Holy Spirit and the descent of Mount Zion, it is appropriately and rightly ascribed to the virgin of Wisdom.

Fourth consideration: Think about what might be the noblest instrument which Wisdom employs in her work. What is the instrument with which she destroys all things and then makes them new? I would answer that it is fire, and that this is the reason why her fiery office and her burning, fiery day are so called. Fire is her one and only instrument. She works through fire, destroys through fire, and through it she melts the old heavens and earth in man. [165] Through this selfsame fire, she restores all things and makes them new. If you desire to know what sort of fire this is, I shall answer: it is no earthy, visible, elemental kitchen fire, not the sort of fire that can burn down cities and villages and reduce them to ashes. No! It is a spiritual fire, philosophical, divine, supernatural and heavenly. It is a pure, virginal fire; it takes its cause and origin from the nature of Wisdom, and so

SOPHIA

it is Wisdom's love-fire. For the nature of Wisdom consists only of love; no anguished fire of hell and darkness, which is in the spirit of error, can exist in Wisdom's nature. It is a pure flame of the brightly shining love-fire, for this is its essential nature. It is the love-fire which goes forth from the love-fire within Wisdom and enters into man to dissolve and smelt around the old heavens and earth within him. Only she avenges the blood of those who have been slain, the righteous blood of Abel, who has been slain in all the members of Christ. She does this only out of flaming love toward man. Wisdom knows well that the old heavens and earth prevent the Holy Trinity from dwelling in man's nature, and hinder human nature from dwelling in God. The children of Wisdom know that it is her magic fire; for she accomplishes all of her works in man's heavens and earth in a magical fashion, and the instrument in her hands is fire. It is, thus, Wisdom's magic fire that possesses the proper activities of fire and the true effectual properties of fire, namely those of melting and smelting around, of refining and purifying, of separating and making new. Yet it is no visible, elemental fire but the magic fire of Wisdom. If you want to understand its activities and its effectual properties by experience, then you must wait for Wisdom's fiery office within you, and you must look for her and seek her, until she comes to make all things new within you. Then you will recognize, see, taste, smell, feel and experience what sort of nature the magical fire of Wisdom possesses. [166]

I must tell you that the magical love-fire of Wisdom has two different names, given to it by Holy Scripture

CHAPTER 21

in accordance with the two different effects which it accomplishes and evokes. This love-fire-essence is called anger-fire on account of its properties or because of the active effects of its dissolution, destruction and smelting around of the old heavens and earth and of the evil inhabitants who dwell therein. It is called thus although it contains not even a single tiny spark of anger-fire. You may read concerning this in the book of *Revelation*: "And the kings of the earth . . . said to the mountains and rocks: Fall on us, and hide us from the face of him that sitteth on the throne, and from the wrath of the Lamb. For the great day of His wrath is come."[140] This is the Day of Wisdom in its property of dissolution, destruction and smelting around. It is also referred to as the seven plagues and the seven bowls of the wrath of God which shall be poured out upon the earthy nature in the old heavens and earth of man.[141] This is the anger-fire which burns and rends the flesh of the whore of Babylon, that is, of the whorish Babylonian nature in man's old heavens and earth. This is the anger-fire that shall utterly burn Babylon with fire, devastate and destroy it,[142] for the Lord God is mighty. That is to say, the Holy Trinity is strong and mighty to judge Babylon, namely the city of Babylon which lies within man's old heavens and earth, to destroy it by the fire of Wisdom, and to let the smoke of its destruction rise up. It is called a wrathful fire, the fire of God's anger, despite the fact that it contains not even a spark of any sort of infernal, dark

---

[140] *Revelation* 6:15-17
[141] *Revelation* 16:1
[142] *Revelation* 18:8

or anguished fire. Rather, it is called thus because of its property of dissolution and destruction, and because all of the wicked inhabitants, all the seven wicked nations or abominable tribes, all of the infernal, earthy and astral spirits, which dwelled in [167] the old heavens and earth of man are effectually destroyed and tilled out by it. God's anger-fire does the same to Babylon, Babel and to all Babylonians, because it burns them to ashes and melts or spoils their heavens within man and makes their earth a desolate wilderness. For the heavens and earth of the eternal man, God's anger-fire is, in and of itself, no anger-fire or wrathfully devouring flame; for they are not consumed by it, but are spared, smelted around and purified. For them it is a joyful love-fire. Their heavens and earth rejoice to see their own Babylon and Babel standing engulfed in flames, after this has occurred. As it is written: "I heard a great voice of many people saying: Hallelujah! Salvation and glory, and honor, and power, unto the Lord, our God."[143]

This heavenly, divine fire is also multifarious, or to be differentiated, in its efficacious, active property, for there are various degrees within it. In its destructive property, it is no terror-fire but rather a mighty, strong and energetic fire, an irresistible fire, a devouring and consuming fire. It has been endowed by the Holy Trinity with sufficient and all-powerful energy, in order to accomplish that which it has been assigned and commanded to perform and to effect. It is, I say, a fire which nothing can resist, oppose or endure. It penetrates rocks and stone, and

[143] *Revelation* 19:1

CHAPTER 21

when it has penetrated, it devours and consumes, because it is stronger than any other thing. There is nothing that can resist it, and nothing that is too hard for it. There is nothing which it cannot effect, perform and accomplish. Everything must be subject to it, and for this reason it is called a strong and mighty fire. It is described as a burning, devouring and consuming fire. As we read in Scripture: "She shall be utterly burned with fire, for strong is the Lord God who judgeth her."[144] And again: "The day cometh, that shall burn like an oven."[145] In its refining and purifying property, however, it is a gentle, sweet, soft and benevolent fire, for it refines and purifies all things which must be refined and purified. [168] For this it needs no strong, devouring flames but only a soft, gentle fire for its work of refining and purifying. Here, too, there are degrees in Wisdom's magic fire. She is a wise, understanding spirit who knows how to order, moderate and temper the operation of her fire. She knows when it should destroy and consume, and when it should refine and purify. Moreover, there are also degrees of fire in the work of purification. At times it will be necessary to apply a stronger flame than at other times. Thus, on the day when Wisdom comes and reveals herself, she customarily reveals herself as a refiner who smelts and refines silver and gold. She alone creates a philosopher, for she is the most artful artist of all philosophers, and is also the most outstanding and excellent chymist. She must order all things in chymistry, and without her nothing can

---

[144] *Revelation* 18:8
[145] *Malachi* 4:1

be properly or faithfully accomplished. She knows precisely the degrees of her refining and purifying fire and how to order the handling of her fire with regard to her fiery oven, in order that her fire might never be extinguished, either by day or by night. She knows when the fire must burn strongly and fervently, when softly and gently, and when she must stoke the fire and maintain it steady at a constant temperature. She knows when she must separate, when she must sublimate, when to concoct and digest, and when she must ultimately coagulate. With her philosophical oven she is exceedingly accurate, precise and careful, even in the smallest matters. Otherwise, her stone of stones could never be formed or manifested in the oven of man.

You will reply to this and say: Who may abide the day of her fiery coming? And who shall stand when Wisdom appears in this way in a fiery region? I reply to this that even before the rocks and mountains of astrayness and selfness are destroyed and devoured by her consuming and devouring fire, [169] the old world of unrighteousness and disobedience, the wicked nations of evil spirits, the Dragon and the Beast, with all their godless powers or energies, shall not be able to endure her fiery day of judgment and condemnation. They cannot stand when she appears, for they shall be consumed by her irresistible flames and reduced to dust and ashes. The eternal heavens and earth of man, however, his spirit or intellect, will and senses, his sensory and rational energies and capacities, and his eternal soul with its affections and passions, shall endure the day of her coming. They shall remain steady and constant in their smelting

CHAPTER 21

around when she appears in her fiery dress or garment, since such fire is only a cleansing, refining and purifying fire for them. For the heavens and earth of man it is a fire possessing a benevolent, gentle, soft property that only refines and purifies. If you wish to know about this fire of separation and purification, read *Malachi* 3:2-3. It is referred to as a fire of testing and trying in *1 Peter* 1:7, and again at *1 Peter* 4:12-13 as a fire of trial and testing which heals and preserves even the heavens.

Fifth consideration: Fifthly, what are these New Heavens and New Earth within man, or what is this New Creation in man? I answer clearly and explicitly that man's New Heavens are nothing other than his eternal spirit, with his intellect, will and senses. His New Earth is nothing other than his eternal heart or soul, together with all of their various desiring affections and angry passions.

Sixth consideration: Sixthly, what does it mean to make new these heavens and earth within man? I answer that this is to inherit a new spirit, which is a new intellect, will and senses, as well as a new heart or soul, with new affections and passions. [170] When is it said that this work of renewal and regeneration of man's nature, of his heavens and earth, shall be completed? Answer: Man shall be said to possess New Heavens and a New Earth when nothing else but the righteous nature of the Godhead lives, moves and is active in man's heavens and earth; when only the virginal nature of Wisdom moves within; and when only the virginal nature of purity flows therein. Only then are man's heavens and earth new, and not before. Until then it is only a work in progress, not yet completed or manifest. It is merely in the process of renewal and not yet fully renewed. It is still weak and imperfect within, and has not yet achieved the full state of complete perfection. When man's heavens and earth have been made totally new, they must be made absolutely fixed or constant in utter perfection, with no taint or spot. Nothing but the pure, virginal nature of divine Wisdom and the pure nature of her Godhead must live, move and flow in all of the active properties of the nature of man, that is, in his eternal heavens and earth. If they naturally and constantly flow through his spirit, that is, his intellect, will and senses, and through his heart or soul, affections and passions, then man has become a new creature.[146] The work of restoration to the original, first state is then completed, and not before.

Seventh consideration: Seventhly, what are the final purposes of this work of restoration, renewal and purification? Why is such a work unavoidably necessary? Why must the inward, eternal man be regenerated and renewed, and his heavens and earth be made new in this fashion? [171] I reply that the necessity and ultimate purpose of the making new of man's heavens and earth is the following: This office of renewal and the creation of New Heavens and a New Earth in man's eternal nature is a preparatory office which must make preparation for the birth of Jesus in the spirit and the advent of the Holy Spirit. If all things were not made new, then Jesus in the spirit and the day of the Holy Spirit would never be revealed. The only impediment to their coming is that

---

[146] *2 Corinthians* 5:17; *Galatians* 6:15

CHAPTER 21

man's heavens and earth have not been prepared or renewed. If they were prepared and made new, Jesus and the Holy Spirit would no longer be delayed in their coming. This is, therefore, the first ultimate purpose of Wisdom's office, that she might prepare a people and make it fit and ready for the advent of Jesus and for the reappearance of the Day of Pentecost in this world. This purpose emerges clearly in *Revelation* 21:1. In a vision, John saw a new heaven and a new earth, which were prepared for the descent of the New Jerusalem, in place of the first one. After this the New Jerusalem immediately came down to dwell in the new heaven and earth. Therefore, it is unavoidably necessary that Wisdom create New Heavens and a New Earth through her office, in preparation for the descent of the New Jerusalem. Her office by fire is the true Elijah and the true John the Baptist, and is a forerunner, before the advent of Jesus in the spirit, before the day of the Holy Spirit, and before the arrival of the New Jerusalem. This is the first reason.

The following might be another cause: Jesus in the spirit, the day of the Holy Spirit and Mount Zion can never come down or reveal themselves for the purpose of living in human nature and dwelling in the unpure, tainted, unclean and sinful heavens of man. This is a matter which is absolutely clear. [172] Even if nations, tongues and languages have waited 1,600 years for their coming and were even to wait 6,000 years more, yet Jesus, the Holy Spirit and Mount Zion cannot arrive until the heavens and earth of man have been made new. Thus, it is unavoidably necessary for the office of Wisdom to make New Heavens and a New Earth, so that the world might be blessed with

SOPHIA

and inspired by these incomprehensible spiritual blessings. Otherwise, this visible world would be and would remain eternally deprived of these high graces. Therefore, it is necessary for the fiery office of Wisdom to come and root out wickedness and to melt around, refine, purify and transfigure man's heavens and earth; in this way Jesus in the spirit can come and visit the earth again, and can draw down with Him the day of the Holy Spirit, Mount Zion and the state of the New Jerusalem, seeing that these three shall arrive together. By the creation of New Heavens and a New Earth in man, the office of Wisdom might become a blessing for this world, and Christ in the spirit might come and appear in the power of the Holy Spirit in the New Jerusalem, to reign and to rule.

A third ultimate purpose and cause for why the advent of Wisdom in her fiery office must create New Heavens and a New Earth in human nature could be: Before this occurs, the heart of the Holy Trinity cannot be revealed to man. The flaming, burning heart of love cannot be revealed to man. Eternal love cannot flow freely, intimately or steady as a stream out of the flaming heart of love into the heavens and earth of man, or out of the heart and spirit of man back to the heart of the Holy Trinity again. This mutual inflow of love from the heart of God into the human heart and from man's heart back to God's heart can never occur until the heavens and earth of man, [173] that is, man's spirit and soul or heart, have been made new. To this purpose, the office of Wisdom must come and must make all things new and lay the foundation for the love of the highly glorified Trinity. Thus, love might flow freely and

CHAPTER 21

unimpeded into man's nature and through human nature back into the Godhead. This can only ever occur by means of pure vessels and through vessels which have been smelted around and well refined. The office of Wisdom must necessarily come to purify the heavens and earth in man, together with all the vessels that appertain to them. Otherwise, the highly praised Holy Trinity cannot come and dwell in the heavens and earth of man, have free access to them, or enjoy constant fellowship in and with human nature. Nor can man enjoy free fellowship with God until all things have been cleansed, purified and sanctified, made fragrant, and devoted wholly to the service of God. Therefore, it is unavoidably necessary that the fiery, purifying office of Wisdom appear beforehand, to make all things new and to create New Heavens and a New Earth, that is, a new spirit and soul in human nature. These particular circumstances and mysteries were presented to the spirit of my intellect as a number of general chief reasons and purposes, with regard to this work of restoration and renewal. [174]

CHAPTER 22

July 12th

On this day Wisdom visited me and said: I have brought you to my second gate of renewal and restoration, where all things are made new. This is my lovely, charming gate; it is the day of my lilies, on which my lilies shall bloom and blossom forth on the peak of the mountains, according to the prophecies of ancient days and of the former prophets. On that day I shall instruct you in studying and investigating them. I shall show you the New Creation, the new world within you, the *microcosm* or the small world, the new globe or sphere within you, which consists of heavens and earth. The old heavens and earth are dissolved and past, and their place shall be found no more. Know, therefore, that I am able to destroy the old heavens and earth in an instant and to build a new world and my New Heavens and New Earth within you, but for your sake I must do this from one degree to the next, slowly and gradually. I do this so that you might become a wise philosopher and see, recognize and learn how I establish a New Creation within you. On my day I shall do this so that you might come to understand the sayings of the ancient patriarchs, and the obscure words and prophecies of the prophets, and the explanations of the words of the wise, namely the teachings of Christ and the apostles in the letter of Holy Scripture, which have been sealed as in a locked book until the rising of my morning star. In the beginning, God the Father created first the heavens and then the earth. In my work of [175] creation in you, however, I shall begin with your New Earth, then proceed to your New Heavens, and then on to the New Adam who shall possess them.

Wisdom continued and said: "Behold your New Earth, as the first part of your new globe, your sphere within." Here she referred to the words of *2 Peter* 3:13. Nevertheless, according to the promise of Saint Peter, we look for a New Heaven and a New Earth; that is, despite the fact that the old heavens and earth have been dissolved or smelted around and are passed away, we look for New Heavens and a New Earth. I say now to your spirit: Behold this New Earth, your New Earth, the promised earth, the earth about which so many prophecies have been made. The New Earth, which you see before you with the eyes of your intellect or spirit, is the New Earth according to the promise which God made to Abraham and to his seed forever, as well as to Isaac and Jacob: "And the Lord appeared unto Abram, and said: Unto thy seed shall I give this land"[147] or earth, the land of Canaan that was a figure of this new land or earth, which I shall show you. Is this not an obscure expression and speech? Who can understand it? And again: "I am the Lord, who brought you out of Ur of the Chaldeans to give

---

[147] *Genesis* 12:7

thee this land to inherit it."[148] What land? It is the land of Canaan, a figurative land. I tell you, however: Behold your new land according to the promises which God made to Abraham and to his seed. In the days of the Father and the Son these were obscure sayings which I have come to reveal and explain to you. It is, namely, the same land to which my rising day points. This New Earth is the earth about which the prophets prophesied: "For, behold, I create new heavens and a new earth."[149] What sort of earth? [176] Concerning what sort of New Earth can the prophet be prophesying, if not about the New Earth within you, which you see placed before your eyes? Are these not obscure words and sayings? Who has understood them? The prophet is not prophesying about the visible earth of this out-birth outside of human nature but about a New Earth which has been created within man, not outside of him. We should no longer consider the former earth, and no thought of it should rise up in the intellect; that is, the old heavens and earth are passed away so completely that we need give them no further thought; rather, they should be forgotten. "But you, be glad and rejoice forever in that which I create,"[150] that is, in my New Heavens and New Earth, which I have created in the nature of man and not outside of him, as has been until now improperly understood and badly explained. The same prophet prophesies further concerning this New Earth: "For as the new heavens and new earth,

---

[148] *Genesis 15:7*
[149] *Isaiah 65:17*
[150] *Isaiah 65:18*

CHAPTER 22

which I will make, shall remain before me, saith the Lord, etc."[151] What sort of New Heavens and New Earth are they? I will create New Heavens and a New Earth within man's nature, not outside of him. This is the New Earth that your intellect beholds. This is the New Earth that was to be created by me, Wisdom, in the eternal nature of man on my day, as the prophet Isaiah foretold. Hereupon Wisdom pointed me to the book of *Revelation*: "And I saw a new heaven and a new earth."[152] In a vision of his intellect Saint John the apostle saw the new heaven and new earth and prophesied concerning them, foretelling my future day and the fact that I would create them. Yet are these not dark and obscure parables? Who among the learned has possessed the key to explain them? Have they not all looked outside themselves for the key? Have they not expected these New Heavens and New Earth not to arrive until after their deaths, [177] and after they have departed their bodies and this visible world or creation? Have they not imagined that it would be only when they stand before me in the heaven of heavens that I would create New Heavens and a New Earth within them, in which they would eternally dwell? Yet, truly, it is not there and then, in the heaven of heavens, in that same divine sphere of my creating that there is need of New Heavens and a New Earth. That is why I have risen up on my day to instruct you that my New Creation of New Heavens and a New Earth shall take place in human nature, because that nature still inhabits fleshly bodies and

---

[151] *Isaiah* 66:22
[152] *Revelation* 21:1

still finds itself in this visible, outward creation. And so I have entered into you to effectually create my New Heavens and New Earth within you, so that you might essentially have and possess this prophetic earth in your own nature. For the first heavens and the first earth are passed away; that is, the previous, old heavens and earth have been dissolved and melted by fire. This fire removes all unpureness from them and opens and prepares the way for my New Heavens and New Earth to enter you, so that you might inherit and possess them.

Behold your New Earth! I have not come to show you these things merely as a vision or as the revelation of a mystery on this my day, which is dawning and appearing. I have not descended to you to prophesy to you of these things as if they were future events. Rather, I have descended into you, into your own proper eternal nature, to bring about a New Creation, to create a New Earth within you. I have come to make a New Earth, to prepare, effect and perfect a New Earth within your eternal humanity; I have come to effectually present it, so that the ancient promises and prophecies might now be confirmed and fulfilled in it. Therefore, I say to you: Behold your New Earth. Examine it with your spirit. Contemplate it with the eye of your [178] rational intellect. See, it is your own New Earth and not the New Earth of another. See, it has been created by my creative *Fiat*. Where has it been created, if not in you? Not in another person outside of you. Turn the eye of your spirit inward, and do not look outward or outside of you for your New Heavens and New Earth. Do not gape any longer at the stars in the heavens or at the clouds of the

CHAPTER 22

external world, expecting the New Heavens and New Earth to come down from them. Instead, turn inward and look inside yourself. Behold, your New Earth has been made effectual and substantial within you by my creative word. It is a plant of my own planting, a work of my own hands. Therefore, examine it and consider its nature and properties!

These words awakened my spirit as if out of a deep sleep (for I was amazed at the sight of this New Earth) and impelled me to contemplate with my searching spirit what the nature of this New Earth might be, and to ask what were the qualities and properties of this New Earth?

After my spirit had so often been summoned and commanded to examine and contemplate it, Wisdom began to reveal to me the substantiality and autonomy of this New Earth, namely what it was in its original essence and substance. This was in accordance with her promise to make me a wise and understanding philosopher.

I recognized this New Earth within me to be a true, substantial, autonomous, solid and stable earth in its substantiality and autonomy. It was a dense ground; it was as solid to walk upon as dry land and soil. It was as dense and solid as the visible earth of this out-birth, yet it possessed a different nature. It was an invisible earth to the outward eye. It was not so grossly visible, not so grossly tasted or felt, and not so coarse, thick, and graspable an earth as the visible [179] earth of this visible creation, made up of the four elements as it is. Instead, it was a sort of visible, spiritual, substantial, autonomous, solid earth, in and of itself, which was to be understood spiritually, magically and philosophically. That is to say, this New Earth is a spiritual earth, far higher and purer, more sublimated or glorified and spiritualized than is the outward, coarse, visible and graspable earth of this visible creation. For this reason, it is called the philosophical earth, that is, the earth of the philosophers. It is a sort of spiritual, invisible and supernatural earth which cannot be seen by every common eye and every common spirit. It can neither be recognized nor understood by the man of outward reason, for it is an invisible earth to him and incomprehensible to his understanding. For the illuminated eye, and for the spirit of the inward man, the wise philosopher, it is a visible earth, which can be grasped and comprehended by his reason. This New Earth is a magical earth, that is, an earth that is coagulated, has flowed together or been made substantial. It is an earth which has been made new or formed new by my own divine magic. It is my earth, which has coagulated or been made substantial. It is formed out of my own four eternal elements, namely of fire, air, earth and water, since it is neither fire, air, water or earth, but rather a quintessential material, substance and essence, which takes its cause and origin from the mixture and coagulation or flowing together of the four eternal elements that stand in a relationship of equality, number, weight and mass at an equal temperature. For this reason it is called quintessential earth; after great reflection and out of a deep understanding, it is also referred to as magical earth, the earth which is formed instantaneously by the divine magic of Wisdom. This magical earth is truly a visible, material, substantial, autonomous

CHAPTER 22

earth, although it is an invisible, immaterial and spiritual earth with regard to the coarse, visible and material earth of this out-birth. Therefore, it is called an invisible, immaterial [180] and spiritual earth or territory.

Do not imagine that this is only an imaginary earth, an ideal earth or a mere shadow. Regard it, touch it and walk upon it. It is solid land, a dense ground, a substantial, autonomous earth, upon which a man can move and walk. It shall be called a magical earth on my day, because it is a substantial, true and autonomous solid earth. On account of its spirituality or subtle essentiality, however, it appears to be an invisible, immaterial earth. And yet, this magical earth is very appropriate and conformable to its nature for those inhabitants who are to dwell therein. Only eternal spirits, only the inward eternal man, with his intellect, will and senses, and with his soul and its affections, may dwell there. These are all invisible energies, however, and thus this magically created earth is an appropriate earth for them. In the same way that the outward, visible earth has been created for the outward, visible man, this inward New Earth has been created for the inward, invisible man, in order that he might live and move upon it. This New Earth has been just as appropriately conformed to the inward, eternal man as the outward world has been adapted to the outward man.

Secondly, this New Earth was presented to the eye of my intellect to be the lower part of the globe and to be in the likeness of a central-earth, like unto this outward earth of the visible creation, save that the New Earth, in its spirituality or spiritually subtle essentiality, fineness and clarity, was differentiated from the other yet was a fixed *centrum*. It appeared to be both within me and outside of me. It seemed to be able to contract and remain within me, yet, by the energy of its subtlety and spirituality, was able to spread throughout this whole visible earth, so that it could be neither excluded from any place within this earth nor limited or contained in a single place. Wherever my spirit [181] happened to be, I was within this new central-earth, for it was a universal earth which was everywhere, and was an earth which permeated this entire visible earth. It was a new-created earth within this earth inwardly, so that I could be nowhere in this visible earth or in any place without it being my new-created earth within me and ever present with me there. When I wished to turn inward into it with the spirit of my intellect, then I was truly and effectually within that earth, for it was in and through all places of this visible earth. Nevertheless, it was invisible, immaterial and incomprehensible to the outward man of reason. For the spirit of the inward, eternal man, however, it was a visible, material, corporeal, substantial, autonomous and comprehensible, magical earth.

In addition, this magical earth was so universal and omnipresent that the spirit-man had no need to be anywhere else but in the New Earth, no matter where the outward man might turn or whatever land of this out-birth it might be; for the New Earth was omnipresent, and nowhere excluded. It was present in and through every location of this visible earth if man desired to turn in his intellect, will and senses toward it. He could not depart from his own earth

CHAPTER 22

within him, unless his spirit turned around by an act of his own free will, in order to draw and lead into his land and realm his brother Esau, the outward reason-man. Otherwise, the inward man possesses just as great and broad a realm within his own earth as the outward man possesses in his.

After the nature and essence of this new-created earth had been revealed to me in such an effectual and lively fashion, I was shown that it not only dwelt within me but that I carried it around with me; that where I was, it was also; and that my spirit had no need to dwell outside of it. Moreover, I had also contemplated its size, width and breadth, its extent and furthest borders. Then Wisdom revealed to me the [182] nature of this new-created earth within me, in terms of its implanted qualities and properties.

The first property of this New Earth was that it was an eternal, imperishable and incorruptible earth, for it had been created from eternal material, namely from the mixture, coagulation and compaction of the four eternal elements. This earth was an immediate effect and concomitant that emerged from the same immixture and temperature of the four eternal elements. It is, therefore, emphatically and clearly referred to as the quintessential earth because it is an essence that is neither fire, air, earth nor water, but is a quintessence or fifth essence which is extracted from all four. For this reason it is called quintessential earth and also properly referred to as one-element earth, that is, the one, single, elemental earth. Although it has been created from all four eternal elements, it is, nonetheless, no fire-earth or water-earth or air-earth. Instead, it is an earth created and born from the immixture of the four eternal elements, achieving the state of being a one-element earth. Thus it is an eternal, imperishable and incorruptible earth, possessing an eternal, imperishable and incorruptible nature. Consequently, it is not subject to change, destruction, dissolution or annihilation. It is explicitly called the eternal earth because of the eternal material from which it takes its primal origin. The second property of this earth was that it was a substantial, autonomous earth. It is a solid, autonomous earth, for it has been created from substantial autonomies, namely from the four eternal elements of eternal nature. These four are, in and of themselves, eternal essences and eternal substantial autonomies, which have been generated and engendered directly out of God's eternal *Chaos*. Therefore, since the one-element earth [183] has been generated and engendered directly out of the same mixture from them, it must inherently and necessarily be a true, substantial and autonomous essence. To the extent that this is so, it must also necessarily be a true, substantial and autonomous earth. Thus, he who would deny that it is a true, solid and autonomously substantial earth must first deny that eternal nature and its four elements are not, in and of themselves, substantial and autonomous essences. If they are eternal essences *per se* then the earth which has been generated and engendered from them must necessarily be, of itself, an eternal and autonomous essence. Then again, it must inherently be either an *Ens* or a *non-Ens*.[153] It cannot

---

[153] A being/existent or a non-being/non-existent

be a non-existent, in and of itself, because it has been directly generated from eternal essences, as we have indicated. Thus, this earth is a created essence or substance and, consequently, a substantial earth, in the most intrinsic way possible. In addition, it must have been generated as a substantial and autonomous earth because it is, of itself, a created Principle. Consequently, it must necessarily be substantial and autonomous in its nature and essence, since God would never create a Principle that lacked substance and autonomy. A Principle that was unsubstantial and lacked autonomy would be an essence without essence, implying a contradiction in terms. Thus, it is necessarily a substantial or essential earth. If it were not a substantial earth, then God would not call it such, since God calls things what they are, not what they are not. God knows that the earth is intrinsically both an eternal Principle and an eternal essence. Hence, God names it such. Therefore, it is a true, substantial and autonomous earth in its essence, without any ambiguity. He calls it earth, and therefore it is an essential Principle *per se*.

The third property is that it is a material earth and consequently a substantial earth. [184] Now, if it is in its essence a material earth, then it cannot be an immaterial earth. If it is not immaterial, then it is a material substance or essence and thus a material earth. It is truly a material earth, but its material substance has been so greatly purified, sublimated or exalted, and spiritualized that we lack the words to express it and do not possess anything with which to compare it. If we were to compare it to the air, the fire, or the light and clouds of this visible world, which are the most subtle or finest bodies and the highest corporeal substances which we possess, or to the most spiritualized material substances and autonomies with which it might be compared, yet all these would still be material substances which are too coarse, thick and dense to be taken as descriptions or expressions of the spiritualized material essence of this New Earth. For this reason, some people have called it an immaterial earth, from lack of appropriate words or comparisons to describe it. It is not that it lacks material substance or corporeality, in and of itself, but that the material of this earth is so greatly purified, and made so subtle or fine, and spiritualized that it cannot be comprehended by any sort of thought or imagination. Yet now, in the appearance of the Day of Wisdom, she calls it the magical earth. Since she knows best of all the nature of this earth, she also knows best what name to give it and what it should be called. Hence, she has called it her magical earth because of the fine subtleness of its material and the subtlety of its parts, as well as because of its fluidity. It is a fluid, flowing material and a permeating material, which penetrates and flows through all things. She calls it the magical earth on account of the essential properties belonging to the material substance or essence of such an earth. Here you must not fall back on obscure reason and imagine that an earth existing [185] solely in the imagination was merely an idea or image of the earth, or a shadow of the earth lacking substantial and autonomous essence. No, not at all! Such an earth would be no true earth but a mere *non-Ens*, only an appearance without any substantial material. The word "magical" implies, secretly but not obscurely, a substantial, autonomous earth which, however, has been made so subtle and spiritual that it remains incomprehensible to stupid, blind reason (no matter how sharp it may otherwise be in its *centrum*). Here you may wish to object and reply: Who is capable of making any judgment concerning this magical earth as to whether it is immaterial or material? If reason is incapable of forming a judgment, how shall we tell if it is true, substantial autonomous earth or an earth that is false, invented, deceptive and existing only in mere imagination? My answer: The spirit of the inward man in union with the spirit of belief can judge this. That is to say, if he is illuminated by the light of faith and is thus provided with the eye and senses of faith, then it is he alone who can judge rightly concerning this earth. It is he alone who is able to perceive it, for it is only to the eternal spirit of the eternal intellect that the seeing eye is given, to perceive such things. The dull reason-eye, however, is incapable of making a true judgment.

The fourth property: Fourthly, this earth, about which I am writing, is a visible earth. Now if it is a visible earth then it is also a material earth, a substantial and autonomous earth. If it is a visible, palpable and graspable earth, however, the sort of subtilized earth that is compatible with the senses of the inward, eternal spirit-man, then it is easily recognized by his intellect and seen by his eyes. The fruits which this earth brings forth can be touched or grasped and its aromas can be smelled. It is a solid and firm [186] earth, a dense ground, upon which its inward man can go forth and walk. Now if it is a visible, palpable and graspable earth, upon which a person may go forth and walk, then it must also be a substantial, autonomous earth. Thus, this earth is compatible with all of the inward senses of the inward, eternal man, so that it can be seen, comprehended, touched, smelled and felt. And so this earth is a substantial, autonomous, visible, graspable and palpable earth. Furthermore, the inward, eternal man can just as easily see, feel, smell and touch this earth as the outward reason-man can see, touch and feel the outward earth of this visible world. You must consider, however, that this inward earth is not so crassly visible, palpable or graspable to the senses of the inward man as this visible world is to the senses of the outward corporeal man. Nevertheless, it is just as truly substantially and autonomously subject to the senses of the inward man as the visible earth is to all of the senses of the outward reason-man. To the extent that this earth, in its substance and essence, is a visible, palpable and graspable earth, it is not an invisible, immaterial or incorporeal earth. This earth is of such a condition that it can be seen, felt and touched by its inhabitants, namely by those for whom it was first created. For it was originally created solely for the eternal spirits of the inward, eternal man and absolutely not for the outward man. This is why it is visible for the spirit-man, and may be touched and experienced by him, but not by the outward reason-man. This outward man was born only for the outward, visible creation, and not for the inward, which remains invisible to his eye and immaterial and incorporeal to his grasp. Here one might ask: Why is this inward, magical earth called an

CHAPTER 22

invisible earth, [187] if it is visible in its essence and substance? Answer: Holy Scripture calls this magical earth an invisible earth and this inward creation an invisible creation. As we read in Saint Paul: "For by Him were all things made, that are in heaven, and that are in earth, visible and invisible,"[154] that is, all things that are in the invisible heavens or the visible heavens, in the invisible earth or in the visible earth of this external out-birth. Here we see that this inward earth is called an invisible earth because its nature has been made so subtle, so flowing or spreading out, so fluid in all of its working motions, so subtilized, fine and penetrating in all of its penetration of all things; its material substance is so transparent that one may look completely through it; its parts are so inseparable, indivisible and impenetrable that they cannot be separated out. Yet it is a dry, solid and dense earth, in and of itself, and, as such, it can be touched. It is such a solid earth that one may walk upon it and, at the same time, it appears as if it were an invisible earth—yet it should not be understood as invisible in its substantial autonomy. Wisdom calls this New Earth her magical earth on account of the properties of this substantial-solid earth.

Another ground and reason why this inward earth is called an invisible earth—although it is certainly a visible earth, in and of itself—might be because this inward New Creation is hidden within the visible creation. The inward, magical earth is hidden within this visible earth and cannot be seen, and thus it is properly called an invisible earth. Nevertheless, it

---

[154] *Colossians* 1:16

should not be understood that this magical, invisible earth is an invisible earth in its essentiality, although it is hidden within and clothes itself with this visible earth, just as the outward body covers itself in garments. [188]

The third ground and reason why this inward, magical earth is properly and appropriately called an invisible earth is that the outward reason-man and the rational spirit in the outward man cannot see it. Although this magical earth is omnipresent, and flows like water through all places of its realm, and is everywhere in its regions and dominions, yet not one single outward man of flesh and blood, not one single reason-man (even if he possesses all of the arts and sciences of the lower schools of this world), can either see or understand this invisible world. Despite the fact that it is omnipresent in the entire visible earth of this world, yet it can neither be perceived nor understood by the reason-man who dwells in the outward man of flesh and blood. Therefore, it may, in truth, be considered to be an invisible, magical earth, even though it is as truly visible in its essentiality as is the outward, visible earth of this world.

The fourth ground and reason why this magical earth is sufficiently visible in its own essence yet is called an invisible earth is that the spirit of the inward man, on account of whom it was originally created, cannot see it, even though the spirit is in it and it is in the spirit. For although it is present before his eyes in every place, above and through this entire visible earth, yet he can neither see, touch, nor recognize it. He has been so blinded, beguiled and bewitched by the spirit of this world and by the sensual life of this present outward world that even this earth, visible in and of itself, is invisible for him. It is called an invisible, magical earth because it cannot be seen by every common eye; it can be seen neither by the reason-spirit in the outward man nor by the blinded eye of the spirit of the eternal soul. Therefore, it is called an invisible earth and a magical earth. Nevertheless, this invisible, magical [189] earth is perceived as visible by a true Christian philosopher. It is also seen by the children of Wisdom, to whom Wisdom reveals it. This invisible, magical earth is perceived and recognized as visible by such persons. This invisible earth is visible to each and every true believer who possesses the spirit of faith, a gift from God the Father, and whose eyes have been illuminated by the light of faith. For everyone else, however, it remains invisible.

Finally, to the extent that this earth, in its substance or essence, is a visible earth, it is not an invisible earth, although it may be said to be invisible with regard to the delicate simplicity of its essence. To the extent that it is a visible, palpable and graspable earth, it is a comprehensible earth. If it is comprehensible, then, in its autonomy, it is a substantial and autonomous earth. I can prove that it is a comprehensible earth because it is a comprehensible Principle in its substantiality and autonomy. To whom is it comprehensible, however, and by whom can it be grasped? Answer: This earth-Principle is grasped by the inward man when his eye has been opened. It can be grasped or, better still, seized. It is seized by the eternal spirit of the eternal intellect. The eternal intellect of the eternal spirit is the eye which, in conjunction with the light of faith, seizes this forth-casting, this earth.

Thus it is seized and its measure comprehended by the inward, eternal man alone, and by no means by the outward reason-man. For the magical earth is a different Principle, sphere or earth than the globe of this out-birth, in which it moves and is contained. One might ask: What is it that is comprehended or seized by the opened eye of the spirit of the inward man, regarding this inward, magical earth? Answer: This Principle of the inward earth, of which we speak, is a universal Principle or is omnipresent and stretches forth or expands over this entire visible world. [190] There is no place from which it is excluded, but it is in and through each and every location. Thus the spirit of the intellect clearly comprehends and understands its width, breadth and length, and knows that it is just as broad and long as this visible, outward creation. It understands clearly that the boundaries of the outward Principle set the limits for this inward Principle, so that it is simultaneously confined and enclosed within the borders of the outward Principle. It is as though this out-birth contained and enclosed within its boundaries and borders an earth-Principle very different from it. Nevertheless, the spirit of the intellect, if it remains still, sees that this inward earth-Principle still extends and stretches out beyond the boundaries and the periphery of this visible world. Even if this earth-Principle had imposed limits and boundaries upon itself in that it allowed itself to be contained and restricted by the domain of the outward Principle, such that its extent should be as wide and broad as this visible world; even so, it now appears to the eternal spirit in its [full] expansion because it is inherently flowing and fluid. It extends

CHAPTER 22

beyond the confines of this visible out-birth and spreads out immeasurably, without limit or border, a domain that is unrestricted and without boundary. Know, however, that this inward earth-Principle cannot extent *in infinitum*[155] or endlessly, for its circumference is not limitless or borderless. God the Creator has established the domain, limits and boundaries of this Principle, and said: "Thus far shalt thou come and no farther."[156] God alone knows the boundaries of its circumference, and for Him it is not immeasurable or limitless. For the spirit of the inward, eternal man, however, and for his understanding and comprehension, it is an endless circumference. Its expansion and extension is limitless and boundless; that is, the spirit cannot grasp or comprehend the limits and bounds of such an inward earth-Principle. This principle reveals itself clearly to be a Principle or sphere that spreads so wide that this [191] outward earthly globe is contained within its circumference or domain.

Here the spirit of the intellect sees clearly and evidently that there are two different Principles, one within the other, and that the one is not the same as the other. Rather, each resides within its own discrete circumference, without confusion or immixture, yet each differentiated from the other. There is an inward Principle or world, inwardly hidden within a different world or Principle, which is the external world or the outward Principle. The inward world or Principle is a magical world, an incomparably higher,

---

[155] Infinitely, to infinity
[156] *Job* 38:11

purer, more transfigured and spiritualized, invisible world than is the external world, which is its casing or covering. This outward world is coarser, more compact or dense, harder, more visible, palpable and graspable. Thus, the inward dwells in the outward yet in two different Principles: one world in another world. Nevertheless, the one world is neither seen nor understood by the other; the one world is not intermingled with the other, for then there would be confusion. Instead, they retain their differences, or one remains differentiated from the other. The inner world resides in the outer and penetrates the outward world. The cause for this penetration is that the inward world possesses a fluid manner and nature. Let not the lower schools and academies of this visible world, with all of their academic degrees and grandeur, and with their berets and caps, by which they think to set reason upon their heads, let them not rise up and pour out their laughter and sarcasm upon these two differing worlds or Principles, where the one in the other is hidden, the inward in the outward, and the invisible in the visible. Instead, let them know that along with their reason-spirit they also possess an eternal spirit within, which is capable of recognizing and comprehending the inward, magical, and yet substantially autonomous world. You see, thus, that the inward world is a comprehensible world in its essentiality, and you also see what of [192] it can be grasped. You understand that since it is comprehensible in this way, it is also a substantial and autonomous Principle of the earth, and that the inward earth is just as substantial-autonomous as the outward earth, if not more so.

CHAPTER 22

The fifth property of this inward, magical earth. Fifthly, this inner earth is a created earth: "For, behold, I create new heavens and a new earth."[157] To the extent that it is a created earth, a created earth-Principle in its essence and substance, it is a substantial and autonomous earth in its eternal substantial autonomy. Now if it is a created Principle or earth, then it must be either fashioned or unfashioned. The text, however, says that it was fashioned, and I have demonstrated above the material or instrumental cause by which it was fashioned, namely from the same immixture of the four eternal elements in number, weight and measure, through the understanding, science and art of divine Wisdom. The ground from which these four eternal elements took their original cause, or flowed forth and were made by God the Creator Himself, was the eternal *Chaos*. You see the ground, therefore, from which this inward, eternal, magical Principle, world or earth was fashioned, namely from the blending and the flowing together of the four eternal elements into a single eternal element of like temperature. Out of this one eternal element, out of the union and harmony of the four, springs up and arises this single-element Principle or earth. Now if it is an essence and substance fashioned from substantial, autonomous material, then it necessarily must be a substantial, autonomous earth, in and of itself.

Another point. If it is a created substance, then it must either have created itself (according to Hobbes' philosophy) or it must have been created by someone

---

[157] *Isaiah* 65:17

or something else. The text states, however, that it did not create itself but had been created. The passage clearly [193] indicates its creator and fashioner in these words: "For, behold, I create new heavens and a new earth."[158] These words make clear who the cause is of this work, who the creator and maker is of this inward globe or inner world and Principle. According to Isaiah, it is none other than the spirit of eternity, who is the only true God, the Creator both of the visible world and of this invisible one. The Holy Trinity, the Father, the Son and the Holy Spirit in the Father, is the Creator of this New Heavens and New Earth, which together comprise a globe.

I would add that this points to God the Father, the Creator of this New Earth, whereof I speak. He created it in union with Sophia, who is His own Wisdom. For the Holy Trinity works and creates nothing without its eternal Wisdom, and Wisdom can also do nothing without the eternal Holy Trinity. Thus, the eternal Godhead does and creates nothing without Wisdom; and because the Godhead incorporates Wisdom, they work united with each other in an invisible manner—not variously or one without the other, but together and with one another, in perfect union and fellowship. The Holy Trinity works in and through Wisdom and Wisdom in and through the Holy Trinity. Here the Holy Trinity is the primary cause of the work and Sophia or Wisdom the outstanding instrumental cause of this inward created Principle.

If you desire to know the manner and way of this Principle's fashioned birth or how it was born and

---

[158] Ibid

CHAPTER 22

brought forth, I would reply that it is enough for our eternal spirits to know that the eternal Trinity, in cooperation with its eternal Wisdom, produced the eternal elements from its eternal *Chaos*. At an equal temperature with each other, it coagulated them or let them flow together into a single eternal element. Out of a single eternal ground this birth or fruit and effect, namely this [194] inward world, Principle or globe has arisen and been brought into being through the work of Wisdom. For Wisdom held the creative *Fiat* of omnipotence and all-sufficiency in her energy-hand, and in this creative energy or *Fiat* of omnipotence stood the speaking word which said: "Let there be! And it was so." Here you see the way and manner of its fashioning or birth. The Holy Trinity is the first working- or original cause, and divine Wisdom is the primary instrumental cause among them. The instrument in her hand is the creative word in the creative *Fiat* of omnipotence for the production of this inward world or Principle. She went to work according to the magical understanding and art within her, because she alone knew what weight, number and measure of fire, air and water to weigh in her scale. In addition, she knew how to coagulate them or make them flow together and how to mix them together such that they would be brought to eternal harmony and unity. After she had formed them in this way by the art of her divine magic and brought them into a single eternal element, she fashioned from it this inward globe or sphere. This globe is rightly and properly called the inward, eternal, magical world or Principle, on account of its manner of composition and structuring, achieved through the art of Wisdom and produced in her magical fashion. Thus, this eternal earth is called the magical earth because of the way and manner of its fashioning, composition, and mixture of the four eternal elements by the magical art of Wisdom. What eternal searching spirit would not gladly rest and be content with this ground or manner of formation and fashioning of this magical earth, but would instead obscure and darken itself within by words, and place itself in a labyrinth or maze of confusion? [195]

Lastly, regarding the final cause of the creation of this inward, eternal, magical earth, such a wide, broad and spacious place would not have been fashioned without cause or uselessly. That would be as if God and Wisdom had created it for nothing. Thus, it was created for a single goal and purpose: that it might be possessed and populated by inhabitants, as no one will doubt. One might well ask: Who were these inhabitants, for whom it was created? Answer: No one should doubt that this inner world was created by God and Wisdom for the first Adamic Man and for his descendants. This was the final purpose and intention of the Creator, that the first man, Adam, in his angelic form, along with all his seed and royal descendants in that same first-created form, should be the inhabitants of that magical ground and earth and should live and move upon it. Therefore, only the inward man, the eternal man, the spirit-man, with his eternal energies and capacities, namely his intellect, will and senses, as well as with his soul or heart and its affections and cravings and desires, was to be the inhabitant and possessor of that world and earth. This outward, coarse, visible Principle

CHAPTER 22

and *Centrum* has been created for the outward man. The inward, eternal, invisible spirit-man is born to possess and enjoy the inward, eternal, invisible world. The outward, visible, mortal reason-man, however, is born to inhabit the outward, visible, temporal, ephemeral world.

Thus, you see which inhabitants belong to each world or Principle, as well as the final purpose of their creation. There are inhabitants in each of them, and each is to possess its own Principle. To the inward spirit-man the inward Principle pertains, which, with its spiritualized nature, made [196] subtle or pure and delicate, corresponds to him. This Principle is also provided with fruits, trees, herbs and plants, meadows and pastures, promenades and gardens, which are appropriate to its nature, just as the outward world is furnished with trees, herbs, plants, flowers and fruits that are appropriate to and correspond to the nature of the outward, visible, mortal reason-man, who consists of a coarse, fleshly body. Consider the Wisdom of the Creator of these two different Principles or worlds. Be amazed at the art and the understanding of divine Wisdom! Each world corresponds to the nature, condition, qualities and active properties of each inhabitant—the inward with the inward eternal man and the outward with the outward reason-man.

Here you have all four causes of this inner world. The first cause is God the Father in union with Wisdom. The material or instrumental cause is the four eternal elements, which have been drawn forth from the eternal *Chaos* of eternal nature. The formal cause which endows it with form and frame

SOPHIA

is Wisdom's immixture and coagulation of the four eternal elements into a single element. The inward world is nothing other than an extract that has been formed into an eternal ground by her magical art. The final cause or the ultimate purpose of its creation is that it might be possessed and dwelt in by eternal inhabitants who are compatible with its nature. These eternal men are pure spirits consisting of body, soul and spirit, which are compatible with this eternal Principle and are able to dwell therein, just as the outward, rational, mortal man is compatible with and for the outward Principle.

Now you will ask, however: When was this inward world created? Where is it located? In what place may we find it? Regarding the question of the time when it was created [197] and where, I would reply that time and place are two different factors which both come into being together with all created essences and substances. Since the inward world is a created essence, there must be a time for and a beginning of its existence, as well as a place and location where it came into being. It is certain that time and place are not created essences but rather essences that accompany creation, essences that depend upon the things which have been created and which arise simultaneously with the things or essences that were created. Despite the fact that they possess no complete essence, yet they possess an essence in relation to the created things themselves. Accordingly, in answer to the first question, regarding the time when this inward world was created and had its beginning, as well as where it had its beginning, took on time and dressed itself in time as in a garment, I would answer: The way

CHAPTER 22

and means to discover the beginning of this inward creation is to consider and meditate inwardly upon the creations which have previously been generated and brought forth by God and Wisdom. The spirit of eternity itself has produced many mansions, resting places or habitations from the active properties of eternal nature in the house of immeasurable eternity. Jesus clearly understood this and declared it explicitly when He said: "In my Father's house are many mansions."[159] God the Father is to be understood as the spirit of eternity, the one, sole, true, eternal God, the creator and fashioner of all the worlds and Principles. The Father's house is to be understood as eternal nature with all its active properties, which is great, immeasurable, incomprehensible eternity. Within this Principle of immeasurable eternity there are many mansions; that is, there are many different dwellings, different Principles, and different globes and circumferences, without confusion and [198] immixture among themselves. They are all included within this infinite, incomprehensible, boundless circle of eternity. Each remains within its own circumference, which encloses it. None is mixed with another; none flows into another. Instead, each remains a constant world within its own sphere.

These many and various, differing and discrete habitations of eternity within immeasurable eternity have not been meditated upon by men. If men had done so, they would not have limited these various habitations to only two, namely to heaven and hell, to the world of darkness and the world of light. They

[159] *John* 14:2

claim that all eternal spirits which depart from this body and from the visible world must necessarily enter either heaven or hell. They neither confess nor permit any other habitation but only these two Principles, namely the world of darkness and the world of light. They conclude that every sinner who dies in unholiness and wickedness, without repentance or faith, immediately goes to hell. Similarly, every believing, repentant sinner departs from this outward Principle immediately into heaven. Thus, they reduce these many habitations to just two and wish neither to hear of nor permit anyone to speak of any other resting place, habitation or anteroom. For them there is no other place that eternal spirits might enter when they depart this life than heaven or hell. They stop their ears to whatever someone might speak or say concerning any other habitation, beyond the aforementioned heaven and hell. They cry and shout "Heresy and blasphemy," and do not consider Christ's own words, which speak explicitly of many mansions. "Many" doubtless means more than just two. They also do not consider that no spirit can immediately rise up to the state of glorification, upon departing the body, but those which have been fully perfected, are free from all astrayness and selfness, and are [199] without stain or blemish. In addition, they do not consider their own precepts: no one in this life, in this fleshly body, is utterly without sin and free from all original sin; all men must die in a mixed state, in a state that consists of good and evil, light and darkness, flesh and spirit; all men must die in a state of weakness and imperfection, because the perfected state of complete perfection is unattainable

CHAPTER 22

in this world—according to their precepts. Yet Holy Scripture clearly and explicitly testifies that no unpure spirit, nor anything that is defiled, may enter into the state of the New Jerusalem.[160] Scripture states further: Make no mistake or do not deceive yourselves. "No fornicator, nor unclean person, nor covetous man, who is an idolater (understood spiritually), hath any inheritance in the Kingdom of Christ and of God."[161] Instead, who among all of us can say that his spirit, intellect, will and senses, his heart and affections, have not gone whoring after creatures, not been covetous and not bowed down before such things? Yet all who die in such an unpure state can enjoy no inheritance in the Kingdom of Christ and of God, but are outside it and excluded.[162] According to the precepts and teachings of men, where must all of these eternal spirits go, which die in a state of unpureness, weakness and imperfection? Holy Scripture excludes them from the glorified state in the kingdom of heaven, and since these men do not wish to permit any other habitation for the state of purification of those spirits, they then condemn them all to enter hell, according to the words of their own mouths. O what a cruel sect! This doctrine is, at one and the same time, the teaching concerning the election to grace and predestination and the declaration of those spirits' reprobation. Yet Christ Himself was a Good Samaritan, a gentle and merciful latitudinarian, and instructed his [200] disciples

---

[160] *Revelation 21:27*
[161] *Ephesians 5:5*
[162] *Revelation 22:15*

that there were many mansions in the house of immeasurable eternity which belonged to God His Father.

To return to the question, however, let us consider how many habitations were created, or rather generated and engendered, before the dwelling of this inward, eternal world. We read of high eternity and of the highest eternity, which is the eternal world that, for the sake of differentiation, is called quiet eternity. Above and beyond this is unknown eternity, the unknowable Godhead, about which nothing other than itself knows anything. Out of this unknown Principle of highest eternity, however, quiet eternity was generated and engendered, directly out of this Principle, through that Principle's inherent energy which it is, in and of itself. This quiet eternity has been directly generated and engendered from that Principle's divine substance or essence, which it itself is. This quiet eternity is above eternal nature and existed before eternal nature was created. This is the first or primary Principle and the first habitation of which we read. The second habitation or eternal Principle that was generated out of this eternal world was God's eternal *Chaos*, the deep abyss of His eternal nothingness, out of which was created eternal nature with all seven of its active, effectual properties. This is the second eternal Principle or eternal habitation and is called the immeasurable, incomprehensible and infinite eternity. Out of its unfathomable depths and immeasurable circumference or domain many eternal dwellings in this house of God the Father have been subsumed and fashioned from its bowels. This is the other eternal world that was generated

CHAPTER 22

and fashioned from God's eternal nature and from its active properties. Many different habitations were fashioned from this immeasurable eternity, among which was the first domicile or resting place and differentiated world of the angelic sphere, the angelic Principle or [201] circumference, which was the angelic world. In this sphere the angels, in their glorified state, contemplate the countenance of God in the splendor of His majesty: "When the morning stars sang together, and all the sons of God shouted for joy."[163] Everyone understands this to be the angelic hierarchy, which thanks God unceasingly with praise, singing and psalms, and which serves and worships Him in harmony and in the unity of love. As far as any one knows—for Holy Scripture says nothing about this—God could have ceased the work of His creation here and created no further Principles. God and the angels could have lived together eternally in divine joy, in the play of divine love and in highest fellowship. The fall of Lucifer and his angelic throne from his dwelling and habitation, however, which rent the eternal unity and the unanimous bond of triumphal love beneath the high angelic throne, gave God cause to continue in the work of His creation. By his fall and ruination, Lucifer formed and fashioned his own hell, which is expressly termed the dark world and the dark fire-world. It is his own eternal Principle of eternal darkness and is his own groundless chasm or abyss, his lake of fire and sulfur. His own hands have formed and fashioned it, for the merciful, exalted and blessed God did not create

---

[163] Job 38:7

this dark, anguished fire-world for the torment of eternal spirits. The demons themselves formed and fashioned it in their own fall. In their fall they broke the bond of eternal nature, and the Principle of fire (which also desired to become creaturely) formed itself into a Principle of dark, anguished fire. At the same time they themselves made for themselves their own god, who took their will-spirits captive and bound them with the chains of the four first fiery figures of eternal nature. Out from the fiery [202] *centrum* of the darkness a dark, wrathful, bitter, thorny, sulfuric, nitrous, poisonous spirit emerged—their god—whom Holy Scripture refers to as the Dragon with seven heads and ten horns and many diadems upon his head.[164] His seven heads are his active properties in the dark abyss of hell; his ten horns are the dark constellations which hold dominion in the *centrum* of eternal darkness; the many diadems represent his victory, conquest and rule over the fallen angels. This Dragon is no created angel or a dragon in form, with heads and horns and crowns. It is no such formless creature; it is a mere spirit, a mere dark energy which has arisen within himself out of his own *centrum* and become a venomous, torturing, anguish-inducing, consuming and devouring spirit. This is the angel of the bottomless abyss and lake; this is the spirit of error, Lucifer's god, the Dragon, the angry, wrathful and fiery spirit. Before this spirit the demons must bow and worship and can do nothing to help themselves. For their own dark god has dominion over them, and is stronger than they,

---

[164] *Revelation* 12:3

and is yet the work of their own hands. This is how the fallen angels made themselves into devils by their fall and rebellion. They extinguished the gentle light within themselves, the light-fire became a dark-fire, and they burned up the gentle, mild oil which allowed their light-fire to burn gently and pleasingly with a joyful property. Thereupon, their fire immediately turned into a property of hellish wrath, burning darkly, wrathfully, intensely, and full of anguish, while they themselves became devils. They created for themselves their own hellish Principle, wherein they now live and dwell with their own Dragon and infernal energy, which now rules over them as if it were a god, although it is no god. Because of His merciful and blessed nature, God did not fashion hell; He never created devils [203] and never created a hellish Dragon or energy. To be sure, a hell was formed and fashioned here; here a hellish, wrathful, anguished, angry Principle was brought into being. This is undeniable. It is a wicked spring or source in its eternal essentiality. The devils themselves are the wicked inhabitants who dwell therein and possess it. Here is located the ruling energy of darkness that has raised itself up to godhood and which would gladly reign and rule over God in the power of this anger-fire. In its *centrum* it truly behaves and displays itself like God, as if there were no one above or beside it, and yet it is no god. Instead, it is merely the energy of anger and anguish, formed and fashioned by the devils in their state of apostasy.

Although it is absolutely certain that this infernal, anguished Principle has a place and location in immeasurable eternity, and possesses a particular

Principle differing from others in its own sphere and circumference and a habitation different from all others in its anguished active property, I shall, nevertheless, not reckon it among the many and varied habitations of God's creation, because it was not created by God. Although it is included among the many habitations, the only true God is above it, rules over it and holds it captive, so that it must stand under His dominion and be subject to Him. This hellish Principle of anguished anger-fire existed before the inward, eternal world was formed or created. It may, for this reason, be called the first Principle, because it was formed immediately after the fall and ruin of the angels who were expelled from the heavens and from the heavenly spheres.

After their fall had taken place and their sphere stood empty, and a dark world of agony, pain and anguish had been erected and fortified, God was moved to undertake a further creation. By the active, effectual properties of His eternal nature, He was impelled to create [204] another Principle, a Light-Principle or Light-World, as some call it. It was a Love-World in which God desired to reveal and manifest His goodness, love and mercy toward all men: "Give thanks unto the Father, who hath made us fit to be partakers of the inheritance of the saints in light. Who hath delivered us from the power of darkness (into which we had fallen because of Adam's fall), and hath translated us into the kingdom of his dear Son."[165] To this end He created the paradisal Principle, a light-dwelling established directly in opposition to the

---

[165] *Colossians* 1:12-13

CHAPTER 22

infernal and devilish world. Just as Satan had formed a hellish world and Principle of darkness, God formed and created a Light-Principle. Just as Satan's dark world existed in anger and anguish, so God's world, which He called Paradise and the paradisal world, exists as a world of love and joy.

Here you see how many habitations were created before the inward eternal world. The time and beginning of its creation was, in the order of things, immediately after the fall of the angels from the light and after they had become devils. The beginning of its birth and creation took place immediately after the formation of the dark world, when the Holy Trinity, in union with divine Wisdom, effectually created, revealed and brought to light this inward light- and Paradise-world, *centrum* or Principle. Yet it already existed as an idea in the eye of eternity, like a shimmer in a mirror. It existed as a potential but not real world lies in the eye of eternity, before it is effectually brought forth and made substantial, as you have previously heard, concerning the manner and fashion of its creation. Then this inward, invisible Light- or Paradise-Creation clothed itself in time. Then, and not before, it experienced its beginning. When this Principle of light, love and joy was effectually fashioned, made substantial and revealed, its time and beginning, which had [205] come into being with it, were co-created circumstances and concomitants. Holy Scripture calls it Paradise, the paradisal world, the paradisal Principle or the paradisal habitation. Hereupon God, through Wisdom, created the first Adamic man and in him all his descendants, that they might be the inheritors and possessors of His new-created Principle, world or habitation. God established him in that place, as in a Garden of Eden, of pleasure and of joy. Thus, this inward, created Paradise-world was fashioned and had its beginning (as no man may doubt), before this outward, visible world was revealed. Otherwise, how could this visible world or creation be an out-birth of the inward, paradisal world? In addition, although Moses describes the creation of this visible world, we know that it was hidden within the inward world, just as the inward world is hidden within the outward one today. We also know that the temporal world was hidden within the Paradise-world, yet the Paradise-world flowed through and permeated the temporal world, living and moving within it. Although this temporal world effectually saw Adam as he truly was (and, in accordance with this recognition, yearned that he might bring it into effectual and creaturely substance and reveal it), yet this world might have eternally remained invisible, unperceived, unrevealed and hidden within the paradisal world. But Adam brought it forth by his own lusting, desirous will and revealed it, just as it is to this present day. Thus, you see the origin and beginning of this inward, eternal Principle: that it had its birth and beginning after the birth or original state of the dark world and before the birth and revelation of this outward world.

Who can say how many created Principles or spheres and circumferences the Creator formed and fashioned out of the properties of His eternal nature after the loss and desolation of this paradisal Principle, and after the birth of this outward [206] world, which was the Principle that followed immediately after the Light- and Paradise-world? Who can tell how many and varied they are? We read about Mount Zion as of a different Principle, which was revealed after this outward Principle. Likewise, we read of Mount Zion and the New Jerusalem as of another different Principle, which was not revealed until after the ascension of Christ. Where is the wise man? Where is the scribe, the scholar or the disputant of this world, who could tell us how many and variously fashioned habitations God, in His infinite Wisdom and goodness in His immeasurable eternity, has formed and fashioned, since the revelation of this fallen world, for poor lost and imperfect sinners, so that they might enter in after they have departed this outward, fallen Principle? The words of Christ, given above, point to this and instruct us. What are we to think about the eternal spirits with eternal souls who died during the Father's day of purification, and about all of our predecessors who died still in a mixed state during the day of the Son and, consequently, can enter neither into the inward, paradisal state nor into the transfigured state of Mount Zion? Where have they all gone? How are they doing? Have they all had to enter directly into the dark world, together with the spirit of error and his angels, to be tormented under the rule and might of the Dragon? God forbid! If that were true, why would then Christ, the true latitudinarian, wish to console us with the words that in His Father's house, that is, in immeasurable eternity, there were many and variously fashioned mansions? The spirits departing this outward world and their bodies would enter into these eternal habitations, together with their eternal souls. The

SOPHIA

eternal spirits would inhabit these various dwelling places, according to the measure and degree of their purification, so that they might come [207] to rest in Paradise and enjoy it at the proper time.

These various habitations have not been contemplated by us since the fallen state of this world, for there need to be more than two, namely more than heaven and hell, or the kingdom of God's love for His children and the kingdom of God's wrath and anger-fire against evil, astrayness and against disobedient sinners.

The passage which here follows, indicated by dots, was illegible in the manuscript. It was written in cipher, and we lack the key to translate it.

1 ....
2 ....
3 ....

The *limbus*[166] or the rampart of the fathers was a figure and fore-image of it.

These many and various habitations were created after the fallen state of this outward visible creation, which had originally been created good, even very good. When, however, God withdrew the paradisal world from it, it came under the curse, for its blessing had consisted in the fact that the paradisal virtues, energies and power essentially and effectually flowed through it. After Adam became disobedient, however, God draw Paradise back into its own sphere and circumference, such that it remained a discrete, differing Principle in its own essentiality,

---

[166] The border, edge

CHAPTER 22

and was hidden, enclosed and covered over by the outward Principle of this world. Thus it has remained concealed in this visible world to this day. It shall doubtless thus remain until the Day of Wisdom appears for its restoration. On that day this inner paradisal world shall become outward and visible. The outward, visible world, on the other hand, shall be swallowed up again and invisible, [208] as it was in the beginning. Then the kingdoms of this visible world shall again become the Kingdoms of God and of His Christ. This shall be the triumphant Day of Wisdom.

After Paradise had drawn back, to live hidden in itself, the curse was revealed and broke forth over this visible earth, that is, the curse of aridity and infertility, for it bore nothing but thistles and thorns. Compared to what it had been previously, it was now an infertile desert and a wilderness covered with brush and scrub. Now followed trouble, sorrow, toil and work, for tilling or plowing, digging, sowing and planting were now necessary. Otherwise, the soil would bring forth nothing, because its fruitful energy lay in the fact that Paradise penetrated it and flowed through it, as we read in Scripture: "And unto Adam God said: Because thou hast hearkened unto the voice of thy wife, and has eaten of the tree, of which I commanded thee, saying, Thou shalt not eat of it: cursed is the ground for thy sake; in sorrow shalt thou eat of it all the days of thy life. Thorns also and thistles shall it bring forth to thee."[167] Here God curses the field and the earth of this outward Principle because of man's

---

[167] *Genesis* 3:17-18

SOPHIA

disobedience. God, however, who is pure goodness, cannot curse. Curse and blessing do not both come out of His mouth. He only blesses and does not curse. He could not plant any seeds of evil in the earth or infuse with the form or condition of infertility soil that was previously fruitful. Instead, God warned Adam that He was going to withdraw Paradise into its own Principle because of Adam's disobedience. He, God, would abstract it from the outward Principle and separate it out, such that it would henceforth be a hidden Principle, concealed within this outward Principle. God said that after the original ground of its paradisal fertility had been withdrawn, infertility would ensue. This would be the curse which would cleave to it until it was finally released and returned to its previous state. God establishes the final objective of this threat when He says: "In the sweat of thy face shalt thou eat bread,"[168] that is, with toil, labor, trouble and unrest. You shall work diligently for nourishment and clothing so that you might maintain your outward man until death, until you return to the dust. Your outward man is of dust, and you must return to the dust of mortality. And so your labor in some calling or other shall come to an end. In the midst of this God comforts sick Adam and says to him: "Until you are able to lead your inward Paradise-man back into Paradise, into the paradisal ground and earth, for your inward, paradisal man was formed from that same ground. Then the inward shall be able to nourish and maintain the outward without labor and effort, and will hearken unto this

---

[168] *Genesis 3:19*

decree regarding how he can again attain to his primal, lost, paradisal state.

In addition, Paradise had not withdrawn so quickly from the outward Principle of this world but that the spirit of error and its angels had obtained the power to enter and to depart this outward Principle, and to prowl in its domain and circumference, roaring like lions and seeking their prey. It thus became a mystical Babylon, as you may read in the book of *Revelation*: "Babylon the great is fallen, and is become the habitation of demons, and the hold of every foul spirit, and a cage of every unclean and hateful bird."[169] As long as Paradise penetrated and permeated this outward Principle, it was good; it was very good within. As soon as Paradise withdrew itself, however, it became an evil Principle, the habitation of the spirit of error. This was a part of the curse which was contained within the threat that God uttered against Adam, and which would come upon the earth and upon the fields of this outward Principle because of Adam's disobedience. This was [210] by no means all, for the threatened curse went further. On account of the nature of this outward, fallen Principle, the spirit of error and the fallen angels gained free access to human nature and a dwelling place within man's inner nature, namely in the property of the anguished fire-torment of the spirit of error. They sowed the seeds of evil within man in order to let their wicked tares grew forth from him, namely wrath, anger, envy, jealousy, and other such evil growths and plants. Thereby, evil established its infernal dominion within

---

[169] *Revelation* 18:2

man and impressed its Mirror-Image upon the souls and hearts of Adam's descendants. Thus it happened that the fallen seed of Adam and Eve came to possess the mystical Babylon, both inwardly and outwardly, both in the eternal nature within and in the eternal Principle of this world without. This is explicitly referred to in the book of *Revelation*: "And the great dragon was cast out, that old serpent, called the Devil and Satan, who deceiveth the whole world; he was cast out into the earth, and his angels were cast out with him."[170] Into what sort of earth? I answer: into this outward, fallen earth, into the earthy Principle of this out-birth, which has fallen away from God's Paradise and has been separated out. In this way they entered into the inward ground or earth of man and possessed it. At *Revelation* 12:12, note the menace and the sufferings which come down upon the inhabitants of the earth: "For the devil is come down unto you," that is, he is come down into this outward Principle, in order to dwell through it in your eternal natures, "having great wrath because he knoweth that he hath but a short time"[171] in this external world. The spirit of error knows that it is merely a temporal or ephemeral Principle.

From this you will perceive that God is the author neither of human misery nor of atrayness. Regarding the question of the beginning of this new creation of Paradise, we have made an [211] extended digression. We have discovered that it was born after the original state of the dark world and before the creation of the

---

[170] *Revelation* 12:9
[171] *Revelation* 12:12

first Adamic man. How could he otherwise have been placed in Paradise, unless Paradise, his habitation, had not been present before him in existence and essence, and had not been created before his fall and the descent of the curse upon him? For this world had been created good and hidden in the *centrum* of Paradise. It was Adam's disobedience that corrupted and made evil the paradise that preceded him. Paradise and this world were created together, and the one created within the other. The paradisal principle was originally the outward, however, and this visible creation the inward.

If you have eyes to see, you will have easily discerned in the aforementioned hypothesis or principle who the author of astrayness and evil must be. You will perceive where the evil primal source and the active energy of astrayness derive their origin. They must come from the spirit of error. The hellish and evil nature of the fallen angels, and not God, is the author or originator, the primal beginning and active cause of all astrayness and evil. For we never heard anything of astrayness or evil until after the apostasy of the fallen angels, and until hell was formed and created by them and by their active disobedience. Then broke forth the source of evil, astrayness, misery and anguish. You tell us that hell is the lowest world, a horrible, unpure and frightening place of punishment intended for angels and human beings. You maintain this as if God, of His eternal goodness, had already created hell, that is, a place of never-ending, unbearable and awful pain and torment, and a fiery lake, in which to torment the fallen angels and wicked, disobedient humans, even before transgressing angels and disobedient humans had come into existence or taken on essence. We deny this categorically and maintain that God is not the author or creator [212] of any such hellish Principle or *centrum* which might potentially have been created from eternal nature through His will or energy. You cannot adduce a single true or clear proof from Scripture to support your claim. It is not our intention to deny the existence of hell, nor are we of the opinion that there is no hell, seeing that Scripture frequently and copiously maintains and depicts it. Rather, we deny your claim that hell is restricted to a particular place, established and determined by God, which you maintain is somewhere in the air, on the earth or under the earth. We confess rather, in accordance with the testimony of Scripture, that there is truly a hell and a dark Principle, which has enclosed itself in a round circle and circumference, and which, in the eyes of God and His saints, is a place of all evil, wickedness, unpureness and astrayness. It is a place that stands in its eternal essentiality in enmity and contrariety to the pure nature of the eternal Godhead. It is a place of eternal anguish and utterly unimaginable misery. It is also a large, deep and broad place which the Dragon inhabits, together with the entire dark hierarchy of the fallen angels, in eternal darkness and misery. We maintain further that this dark, hellish Principle possesses its own locality, its own particular place and site, which is its own enclosure, circle and circumference. This dark world's enclosure, we maintain, flows through the entire visible world, such that it is present everywhere, above and through all its regions, and is, thus, nowhere excluded. And yet it is confined within

CHAPTER 22

its own circumference (as none may doubt), and this circle is its own particular locality. Therefore, we deny your fantasy, which attributes to hell a particular spatial location, although you are unable to demonstrate where that might be. We affirm with you that this hellish Principle (as Holy Scripture testifies it to be) [213] is a deep and fathomless pit, a dark cave, the unpure, shameful and terrible prison of the Dragon's maw and *centrum*, or the terrible, fearful palace of the Dragon. You, however, do not tell us its particular location, or place and site, nor where it is stably and constantly centered or placed. We do, however, reject and deny that this dark, hellish Principle was created by God. He did not create it, nor was He its author or originator. Furthermore, we deny that God created it before the angelic world or before the angelic thrones were fashioned. Where do you find the least shadow of proof by which you could support your delusion?

We further reject your claim that a gracious and merciful God could ever have entertained the intention and final purpose of creating a hell for angels and men who had yet to be created or to transgress, before they had come into existence or taken on essence, and before angels and men had ever actually transgressed or sinned. What can such ideas be but your own dreams and fantasies, which you are unable to support from Holy Scripture. The idea that God created hell as a dark prison, in order to torture transgressing angels and men in unending eternity in anguished torment, cannot be reconciled with God's holy nature (that of purest love in its divine essence in still eternity), goodness and mercy. For this reason, we abhor this blasphemous opinion. Does not the opinion that God had purposely created a spatial hell in which to torment transgressing angels and sinning men before they had actually taken on essence, and before they had, in fact, become sinners—does not this opinion turn Him into a merciless God? Would this not be as if He had foreseen and foreknown the fall of the angels and their transgression, as well as the fall [214] and transgression of Adam and his descendants? This is an incorrect and highly debatable conclusion. Let us assume, however, (and we will concede this) that in the eye of eternity, the all-seeing and all-foreseeing eye, God's crystalline mirror, in which He see all things past, present and future, He had foreseen and foreknown that Lucifer and his angels, by an act of their own will, would fall into transgression. Let us assume that God had foreseen and foreknown that they would turn themselves into devils by extinguishing their gentle light, their gentle fire and their gentle oil—that they would become creaturely through their dark, anguished fire-torment, that is, that they would reveal themselves and turn themselves into the hellish Principle which, with you, we call hell. Is it not possible that the eternal God, the spirit of eternity, could both foresee and foreknow this by His all-seeing eye, and by His consent allow hell to come into being, without His eternal will-spirit either commanding or desiring it to take place and without His being its author, creator or originator? We reject your groundless opinion and maintain, upon the basis of truth, that God did not create hell, nor did He ever command or will hell, dark hell, to be created, although He did consent and permit the fearful fire-torment, in its own disclosure and in its self-production, to become creaturely.

Secondly, we maintain, upon the basis of truth, that God did not create or fashion hell—neither purposely nor with forethought, nor by an act of His own will-spirit of eternity. Much less did ever He intend to eternally damn eternal creatures or eternal angels or eternal human-spirits to endless anguish, despite the fact that there is such a hellish Principle in effectual essence.

Thirdly, upon the basis of truth, we say that God has never, in all eternity, willingly or purposely created eternal creatures, namely eternal angels or eternal human-spirits, in order that they [215] should be tortured and tormented in the fearful flames of eternal darkness. It is not reconcilable with the most merciful goodness of God that it should have created eternal creatures, angels and men, in order that they should be eternally tortured in the fearful torment of the hellish Principle. In particular, it is unthinkable that the most-gracious and most-merciful God should have commanded this, according to his eternal purpose, even before they had attained existence and essence, and before they had ever actively transgressed or sinned. Such an opinion would make God the author and cause of misery, not of blessing. Therefore, we abhor such thoughts and, on the basis of truth, instead maintain that God never fashioned eternal creatures for the purpose of dwelling in the fearful fire and ceaseless flames of hell or the dark world as eternal inhabitants.

On the contrary, we say and maintain that God has never sent or relegated to hell a single eternal spirit, as a sinner, or as a punishment for astrayness, to be an eternal inhabitant of that place. That is to say, He has never, by virtue of His absolute and highest royal prerogative, said to a single eternal spirit: You are an abominable sinner; you have been an exceedingly sinful transgressor. Therefore I shall throw you into hell, to be tormented together with the devils. God does not wish to show so much favor to the Dragon or to his Principle as to send him a single eternal spirit, in order that that spirit might be punished for its transgression. Such a thing would be a diminution of God's majesty. In virtue of His merciful nature, God is powerful enough to forgive every sin and every punishment which sins and transgressions deserve. It is His good pleasure to forgive sins and transgressions, because He takes pleasure in mercy. It is His good pleasure, and it accords better with His divine essence, graciously to forgive, [216] rather than to consign the works of His hands, by the path of avenging punishment, to the Dragon in the dark world, in order that God might punish them for their offenses against His majesty. Where would God's all-sufficiency be? And where would be His omnipotence, if He were not able to punish sinners Himself but must send them to another power for punishment? Therefore I say that God did not create hell, nor did He create any eternal spirit to be an eternal inhabitant of that hellish Principle. He has never sent any eternal spirit to hell, nor has He, by the royal prerogative of His own eternal will, ever commanded anyone to go there.

Now you will object and say: If God does not send them to hell or consign them to Satan and the Dragon to be tormented, how do so many eternal spirits of sinners and transgressors still enter there? To this I reply that it is sufficiently certain that one group after another and one host after the other enters hell. Yet God did not create them for such a place, nor did He send them there. The question here is about the way in which such a great host comes to enter therein. Accordingly, you must know that after the angels had made themselves into devils and the Dragon had formed his own anguished Principle and *centrum* for himself, hell was a large and spacious empty room and a place without inhabitants. No other inhabitants dwelled therein but the fallen angels, who knew well that God would create no other inhabitants there, nor would He ever send anyone to them, for they were the enemies of God and were in a state of hostility toward Him. Thus, the dark world possessed no other inhabitants, not even a single eternal spirit; nor would it receive any others except those it drew to itself. For the *centrum* in the dark world is a dark magical fire that is an energy which almost irresistibly attracts. It is this energy which draws and devours those eternal spirits which give their will over to it [217] and become one nature with it, just as those who allow themselves to be magically drawn and sucked into it effectually become one nature and one spirit with the hellish Principle. Such spirits, and none other, become inhabitants therein. Without this inward, strong, magical fire that draws spirits into it, it would have been and eternally remained alone and devoid of inhabitants. Thus, this dark, magical *centrum* possesses not a single inhabitant except those whom it draws in. The devils know all too well that their smoke hole and dark Principle would remain without inhabitants. Therefore, Scripture testifies of them that they prowl around like roaring lions, seeking prey to catch and devour. What sort of prey do they seek to catch? Answer: They do not care about the mortal spirit of outward men but rather seek after their eternal, immortal spirits. Why, and to what purpose? Simply that they wish to make them inhabitants of their anguished Principle, along with themselves. How do they accomplish this? By ceaseless prowling around and going back and forth—by courting man's free will, by tempting him and drawing him to themselves—so that he might turn to them, or might surrender his will to them, in order that he become one intellect, spirit and will with them. In this way, they might dwell in him with their wicked natures, intimately join or incorporate their natures with his, and he might permit his nature to be impregnated by their evil seed. Thus, men might become devils incarnate in their spirits, and the evil spirits might make men comformed inhabitants with and beside themselves in their anguished torment. This is how it comes about that the dark world receives a countless host of inhabitants.

Insofar as the devils shared your attitudes and opinions, [218] they would no longer need to prowl about like roaring lions, seeking to devour human beings. All they would need to do would be to sit still. There would be enough sinners for God to send to the dark prison and jail in their hour of death, in order to be tormented there for their sins and transgressions. Instead, the devils know God's merciful nature better than this. Their practice demonstrates sufficiently

CHAPTER 22

that they do not believe that sinners will be sent to them by God to be tormented there. So they fearlessly go forth to tempt all men and try to entrap as many as they can. In fact, they do effectually deceive and overcome all those who surrender their wills to the devils' wills and become a single will and a single nature with them. Otherwise, they have neither ways nor means of winning eternal spirits, in order that those spirits might become comrades and fellow inhabitants in the realm of the Dragon. Moreover, they see and know from experience that they can never be certain of their prey until it is present with them in their *centrum*, seeing that many who have walked for many years with them in their wills nevertheless turn away through faith and repentance. Thus, their prey and booty is torn from their hands. Of those spirits which are not completely within the devils' *centrum*, there is not one which dies without a mighty battle and struggle for the eternal spirit. Thus, the hopes of the devils are disappointed. The devils have come to know that God is infinitely merciful in His forgiveness, and that if the eternal will breaks with the will of the devil and turns to the will God, they cannot make it an inhabitant of the eternal darkness. Therefore, the devils work very hard to make everything solid and secure in their *centrum*. They work in vain, however, and their hopes are disappointed. They know all too well that God never willingly gives up or surrenders a single spirit but only consents that [219] those who completely surrender and consign their will-spirits to the devils should also be one with them, both here and afterwards. Only such spirits do they receive and possess, those spirits which are like unto them and which they have pulled from the fire and drawn after themselves by their craft, deception and invention.

Thus you may see how many and various eternal spirits wish to become inhabitants of the anguished Principle by the misuse of their own wills, in that they consign those wills to the devilish nature and thus become one will and one nature with the devils. It is not that God ordered them there, or desired to have them there, or Himself sent or relegated them there. Why do we want to make God the origin and cause of the eternal misery and damnation of mankind? What necessity is there for us to do that? Why not, rather, attribute it to the Dragon, the spirit of error and the act of our own free will, which turns away from God's will and toward the will of the Dragon and the will of the spirit of error? I am absolutely certain and convinced of the fact that this conforms to the teaching of the Old and New Testaments.

Here ends this Treatise

CHAPTER 22

REGISTER OF WORDS AND CONCEPTS

Contained in this Treatise

A

Adam (Adam). After his fall and before he is regenerated, Adam consists of pure noxious herbs of anger, wrath, evil, etc. (35) / No one knows anymore what Adam was in his first state as the image of God (73) / The newly re-created Adam in us is our eternal spirit, which is to reign and rule in the renewed paradise within us (6) / That spirit must first be tempted, tested and proven. It must endure the forty days of temptation better than the first Adam was able to do. It must ever keep its eye upon Christ, its pattern and fore-image (6)

Affekten (Affections). The affections or lusts and cravings of human beings, and how those affections are entirely corrupted (33/34/35/36/37) / Affections are mankind's animals and beasts of burden (22/23/26) /Affections are housed in the hearts or souls of man, not in their spirits or intellects (16) / The affections are renewed along with the heart or soul (38) / Renewed affections are heavenly and are like the feet of the soul (45/46) / The affections remain constant during the melting of the heart or soul. They are simply purified and renewed (54/73) / The animal affections and passions in man must be eradicated (63) / The affections are perfectly renewed when nothing other than the divine nature works through them (79/80)

Ägypten (Egypt). In the intellect and heart of man Egypt must be destroyed (67)

Allerheiligste (Holy of Holies). In the fallen spirit of the inward man the holy of holies is polluted and has become a synagogue of Satan (33) / It has been raised up as the dwelling of the Holy Trinity within the heaven or spirit, intellect, will and senses of man; through man's falling away it has been turned into a den of murderers, the lair of the Dragon, of the Antichrist, of the Beast, of the Whore and of the False Prophet (37) / The promise that Wisdom will renew it on the day that is now dawning for it (37) / It will be opened in the spirit in its renewed state, so that God can again take up His habitation there (47) / When this Holy of Holies is opened in the heaven and earth, or spirit and soul, of man, along with the holy place, then it will grace Mount Zion and the New Jerusalem again (47) / After departing the body, no one may immediately enter this holy of holies, Zion or the New Jerusalem except he who has successfully ended the war against the Dragon, the Beast and all other enemies, and has gained the victory (52) / The holy of holies, or the highest office of our spirit, intellect, will and senses, must also be devastated and destroyed, according to the ancient outward figure of the temple (67) / That the holy of holies must be established in the spirit and intellect of man, and the holy place in the heart and soul (69)

Altar (Altar). The altar in the holy place of the heart has been devastated and trampled underfoot by the heathen (37)

Alten vor Gott (Elders before God). These are the patriarchs and prophets in the office and days of the Father (67)

Ältesten und Väter (Elders and Fathers). These have attained holy divine understanding, and they enter into Zion and Jerusalem when they depart the body (52/55)

Apostel Christi (Apostles of Christ). The inward-eternal spirits, souls and bodies of the patriarchs and prophets are in heaven and are inseparably joined together in joy (18/19)

Ärgernisse (Stumbling Blocks). The false idols in the spirits and souls of men are the stumbling blocks of which the prophets speak (63)

Artist (Artist). The philosophical artist is the indwelling eternal spirit in man. If it is to achieve anything, however, it must be united with the spirit of Wisdom (24)

Atem (Breath). The breath of the regenerated man is a pure, love-flaming, penetrating, tincturing and energetic breath (43)

WORDS AND CONCEPTS A

Augen (Eyes). How tremendously did the eyes of the inward eternal man darken after his fall? (29) / His regenerated eyes, however, are bright, pure and clear eyes (87/88)

Autor (Author). How earnestly the author has used his abilities and powers to work toward Wisdom (1) / Even after Wisdom has appeared to him, he hovers between hope and fear and does not know what has happened to him, because he does not know Wisdom (2) / A numberless host of infernal and earthy spirits attempts to convince him that the New Earth that has been revealed to him will dissolve again and he will again fall back into his fear (8) / He can hardly believe (because he has spent so many years in a state of penance) that his heavens and earth, or spirit and soul, are still unrenewed, as Wisdom demonstrates to him (49/56) / When he hears that he is still unpure, he is worried about where his soul would end up if he died in that state. Wisdom reassures and comforts him (51) / Wisdom explains to him why he has not progressed further in those many years; namely because he abandoned Wisdom and with his spirit and will he turned to the spirit of the outward world (56/57) / His new inward earth is shown to him by Wisdom (81/82)

B

Baals Übrige und die Chemarim (Remnant of Baal and the Chemarim). The prophet Zephaniah speaks about who and what they are (63/64) / On the Day of Wisdom all of the priests of Baal will be eradicated from the soul and the spirit (64)

Babel/Babylon (Babylon). All worship in Babylon, which is a stubborn self-willed worship, must be destroyed and rooted out (64) / Babylon cannot be banished from the spirit and soul of man unless, at the same time, all the worship and the stone temples of the outward man in the world fall and are also annihilated (67) / The secret place in human nature where the Devil and satanic spirits operate, and where all unpure beasts and crawling things circulate in their lusts and cravings (70) / Once Babylon has been demolished in the human spirit, it should never be rebuilt (71) / Babylon must be devastated and destroyed by the fiery office of Wisdom (71) / Outside of us Babylon is the external, visible world with which we should have no contact. The fire of Wisdom does not destroy this visible external world but rather destroys Babylon, or the earthy nature, within us (71/72) / The devastation of Babylon points to the destruction of all mixed Babylonian worship in our wills and hearts (72) / Babylon has established churches of the Antichrist upon earth. These churches blaspheme and libel each other most despicably (75) / Through the fire of Wisdom (which is a fire of wrath for Babylon) it is destroyed in the spirits and souls of men (78) / How our inward Babylon has become a dwelling place of the Devil and the habitation of all unpure spirits (97/98)

Blumen (Flowers). The virtues are the flowers of our regenerated, paradisal earth (11/20) / The sorts of shameful flowers that grow in the fallen, corrupted earth within us (35)

Bote (Messenger). According to *Malachi* 3:1, the messenger which the heart will send out to prepare the way before it. This messenger is the Wisdom of whom John the Baptist is the forerunner (65)

C

Canaan (Canaan). The true spiritual Canaan is the renewed earth of the inward man, that is, his heart or soul (44/82) / Why the seven abominable nations in the days before Solomon cannot be driven out of the fore-image Canaan (59) / That the Israelites who did not enter into Canaan died in their immature childhood (60)

Chaos (Chaos). The divinity in humankind is shown to the author inwardly within himself, because he describes what it is (3) / Chaos is the ground out of which the four eternal elements flow (90) / God's eternal chaos has been generated out of still eternity, and eternal nature born from God's chaos as the second eternal world (93)

Chemarim (Chemarim). The prophet *Zephaniah*, at 1:4, mentions what these are (63)

Christ [Falscher] (Christian [False]). A false Christian is one who insists upon only the letter of Scripture or upon its mystical sense and understanding, yet lacks the real essence of Christianity (35/36) /

There are three grades of Christians: 1. children, 2. adolescents or strong men, and 3. elders or fathers (51/52)

Christus (Christ [Jesus]). Christ cannot appear again in spirit and power in the heaven and earth of humankind until they have been utterly purified from all sin and impurity through the fire of Wisdom (80)

Chymicus (Chymist). What are the abilities of the truly spiritual chymist? (21) / Reason ought to be a true chymist in the external realm (21)

Creatur (Creature). Wisdom must transform our spirit and soul into a new creature (8) / This is the inwardly renewed eternal man (38) / The new creature results when our spirit and soul are returned to the primal state in which they were originally created (53) / If our spirit, intellect, will and senses, our heart or soul and all affections and passions are re-created, then we become new creatures, according to 2 *Corinthians* 5:17 and *Galatians* 6:5 (75) / When the pure virginal nature of divine Wisdom fully permeates our spirit, intellect, will, senses, heart or soul, affections and passions, then we become perfectly new creatures (79/80)

D

Demut (Humility). Humility is a fruit of paradise and the food of the inwardly renewed human being (5/11/46)

Dienst (Office/Service). The fiery office of Wisdom is not the great day of the Last Judgment, but it prepares the way for the arrival of Jesus Christ in the spirit through the divinization of the spirit by the Holy Trinity (55/56) / That the office of Jesus in the spirit is a higher office than the office of Wisdom (60/65) / That the fiery office of Wisdom is an office that mightily tests, disempowers and destroys all false service (64) / That it is an office that prepares us for the arrival of Jesus in the spirit; it is different from the office of Jesus in the spirit and the office of the Holy Spirit (65/66/69/ 76/77/80/81) / This fiery office of Wisdom convicts man of the impurity of his old heaven and earth, or spirit and soul, and then ordains them to be melted and refined (68) / This office of Wisdom prepares the spirit and soul of man for the birth of Jesus in the spirit, for the day of the Holy Spirit, for the marriage feast of the Lamb, for the descent of Mount Zion and the New Jerusalem, in order that these should dwell essentially in man's intellect, spirit and heart as longings and desires (69/71) / This fiery office renews heaven and earth within man after their destruction (69) / If we would experience the fiery office of Wisdom in our spirit and soul, then we must wait eagerly for them and remain alert and attentive (77)

Drache (Dragon). The infernal Dragon whom all adore and worship after their fall if they have not been renewed, and who bear his image and mark upon them (27) / The Dragon is worshipped in fallen man (31) / The labor or office of the Father rescues the souls of those who died in His days from the anguish-realm of the Dragon (51) / During the office of the Father and the Son the Dragon has been still too strong to be utterly cast out (54/55) / What its seven heads and ten horns represent, and that it is Lucifer's and the devils' god (94) / It rules as a god, but it is no god (94) / According to *Revelation* 12:9, that great Dragon and old serpent was cast out into our external fallen earth and continues to battle against us day and night (98)

E

Ebenbild Gottes (Mirror-Image of God). The Day of Wisdom shall return this image to us, along with paradise and everything else that was lost in Adam's fall (20/45)

Eden (Eden). The lost garden of Paradise blooms again in our renewed earth or heart and soul (20) / It was planted in the fallen earth or in our hearts or souls, and was a garden of pleasure and joy (35) / A garden of pleasure and joy (95)

Ehebrecher (Adulterer). Spiritual adulterers are those who, in their intellects, will, senses, hearts, desires and cravings, commit adultery with the creatures of this world (65)

Eichen (Oaks). The strong oaks of Bashan, in *Isaiah* 2:13, are the great and mighty spirits in reason-Wisdom (61)

Eigen Vermögen und Kräfte (One's Own Abilities and Powers). These are far too weak to overcome the enemies of man's soul. Therefore, they must remain still and await the advent of a higher power from above (1/2)

Elemente (Elements). There are four eternal elements (4) / How they are conjoined and coagulated into a quintessence by the Spirit of God that moved over the *Chaos* (6/7) / The elements that are mentioned in *2 Peter* 3:7 are the earthy properties which adhere to the intellect, the will and the senses (13/14) / The soul of man was created as a quintessence from the four elements (17/18) / The elements will melt away on account of the great heat on the Judgment Day of Wisdom (53) / The four elements have flown forth from the eternal *Chaos* (89/90)

Elias (Elijah). Elijah was a model of the fiery office of Wisdom (65/80)

Engel (Angels). In the angelic world all praise God unceasingly and serve Him in harmony and unity (93/94)

Erdbeben (Earthquake). The earthquake mentioned in *Revelation* 6:12-16 refers to the godless earth, heart or soul of man (69)

Erde (Earth). In this treatise earth stands for the heart of man with its affections and passions. Wisdom desires to renew that earth within the author (3/4/16/24/25) / Wisdom dwells upon the earth in us if it has been renewed (4) / A central fire has been implanted in us for the preservation of that earth (4) / According to *Genesis* 2:10, there is a stream of the water of life that flows around this earth to water it and make it fruitful (4) / What sort of fruit it brings forth (5) / The tincture, strength and life within it is Wisdom itself (5) / Wisdom wishes to deal intimately with us in the renewed earth of our hearts and nowhere else (6) / The new heaven and earth within us must live together in sweet harmony if they wish to be fruitful. Otherwise there will be nothing within us but sterility and hunger (9/10) / Our inward earth cannot be fully renewed until all sin and impurity has been melted out of it by the fire of Wisdom (10/11) / The lost Tabernacle, the Holy Temple, Mount Zion and the New Jerusalem will be established again upon this renewed earth (12) / The new earth of man is his heart and soul (19/32/43/45/47/53/68) / The outward external earth is a pattern for the inward eternal earth (20) / The lost Paradise blossoms forth from the renewed eternal earth within us (20) / The wondrous harmony of the inward earth with the external (20) / The central fire planted in our inward earth by Wisdom causes vegetable life to be verdant and grow forth when that fire is ignited by the light of Wisdom (21) / There is an animal life that includes good and bad animals on and in the external earth as well as on and in the inward earth (22/23) / The comparison of external and inward earth in terms of the mineral realm, according to *Genesis* 1:11-13 and 25-27, as well as *Genesis* 2:11-12 (23/24) / The new earth is magical (24/25) / The old earth is the corrupted heart or soul with its affections and passions, so that in its degeneracy it brings forth nothing but thistles, thorns and weeds, and is forlorn (32) / The prophets cried out to this corrupted earth that it should harken to the voice of the Lord (32) / This corrupted earth is filled with unpure spirits, desires and cravings (33) / This earth of mankind is utterly fallen. When will it be renewed? (36/37/38) / What Scripture testifies concerning the renewed earth (43) / The inward earth is the true Canaan or the spotless heart and soul, freed from all sin, selfness and evil (43) / The mineral goldseed grows into the Philosophers Stone out of this renewed earth (44/45) / This new earth or the holy place of man is the renewed, eternal, pure, and holy heart and soul (45) / The lost Paradise is planted in the renewed earth, in which no weed, no thistle, nor thorn can grow (46) / All of the prophets have given testimony and prophecy to this renewed heaven and earth, or spirit and soul (47) / It is not enough that we know and recognize that our heaven and earth, our spirit and soul, are corrupted. We must plead day and night with Wisdom until she renews them (48) / The heaven and earth of humankind are subject to the dispensation or office of the Father and the Son, and have been truly renewed. Yet it has remained a mixture of good and evil and has not been perfectly purified (50) / Our earth or heart and soul are the matter of renewal (52/53) / Earth's ancient, evil, and persisting characteristics are to be destroyed, not the earth itself (53) / Its destruction, not as formerly by water but by fire, is inevitably necessary, according to Holy Scripture (53) / From the melting down of the old we await a new heaven and earth, according to the testimony of Peter (53) / Wisdom alone is commanded to renew our heaven and earth, because no angel is able to do so (57) / In *Isaiah* chapter 24 the prophet speaks of the utter destruction and eradication of the seven abominable nations and of the unpure spirits (61) / The earth which God promised once again to move, as in *Hebrews* 12:28, is primarily the godless earth in the heart and spiritual nature of man (67/68) / Heaven and earth, or spirit and soul, will firstly be convicted of their sinful impurity on the Day of Wisdom and then be condemned to refining, as in *2 Peter* 3:7 and 3:12 (145) / The complete renewal of the earth or of the soul and heart consists in the eradication of all their unpure properties, sins, selfness and all evil spirits. Earth or soul and heart will, however, remain in their essences (68) / The earth and soul will be purified and cleansed by the fire of Wisdom, but will not be destroyed (79) / The remaking of heaven and earth in man is a renewed spirit, intellect, will and senses; also the inheritance of a new heart or soul and new desires (79) / The earth or heart and soul in man is perfectly renewed when nothing other than the divine nature lives and moves within it (79/80) / The causes and ultimate purposes of why the earth of man must of necessity be renewed (80) / The new earth of which all the prophets have spoken is demonstrated to the author to be essentially within himself (82) / All the learned have expected this new earth to come into being only after their deaths (82) / What the properties and nature of this new earth are within man (83/84) / It is a spiritual, magic, philosophical and essential earth (84/85/86) / It is a quintessence formed and coagulated from the four eternal elements (84/85/90) / The new earth was created only for the inward eternal man, so that he might live upon it and inhabit it (84) / It extends over the entire external earth (84/85) / It is eternally unchanging and has been immediately generated from the eternal Chaos (85) / Its properties (87/88) / Why is it called a magical earth? (88/89/90/91) / Who can see and know it? (88) / This inward earth permeates the entire external earth and is, at the same time, covered by the outward earth (88/89) / Its creator is the Spirit of Eternity who is the one true God, the Holy Trinity in union with Wisdom (90) / This inward new earth has been made one essence out of the four eternal elements (90/91) / This inward earth or world was created as a habitation for the first man in his purity (91)

Erkenntnis (Understanding/Insight). Literal understanding and even mystical understanding simply produce proud hypocrites and deceivers if there is no essential grounding (35/36) / If, however, understanding penetrates to the essence, then it has achieved its goal (48) / All historical, learned knowledge and even mystical insight that have been achieved in the dispensation of the Father and the Son must be humbled on the fiery Day of Wisdom (61)

Erlösung (Redemption). Full redemption is effected by Wisdom in our patient, quiet spirits (9)

Erneuerung (Renewal). Wisdom can easily effect the renewal of the spirit and soul, although this appears impossible to the reason-spirit operative in our flesh and blood (9) / No renewal of our earth or heart can occur unless they are tested, refined and purified by the cleansing fire of Wisdom (11) / How and by what means the renewal occurs, and concerning the conviction that we desperately need this to happen within us (49) / Renewal begins within us in the office of the Father, continues in the office of the Son, and is completed in the fiery office of Wisdom, in order that the Holy Spirit should descend upon us and enable us to participate in the Spirit (49/50) / Destruction and refining must precede the renewal of our heaven and earth or spirit and soul (53) / Our heaven and earth or spirit and soul are the matter to be renewed within us (53) / Complete renewal can occur neither in the Father's office nor in office of the Son, because in both of them selfness and sin have not yet been completely destroyed and eradicated (56) / In order to fully accomplish renewal in us, Wisdom demands of us a patient and resigned will (57) / This renewal is possible, despite the fact that false prophets try to convince our reason otherwise (57/74) / Wherein the full renewal of our heaven and earth or spirit and soul consists (73/74)

Evangelium (Gospel). The eternal Gospel is the renewal of all things in the heaven and earth of man, or of his spirit, intellect, will and senses; also his heart or soul, desires and longings (69) / The Day of Wisdom reveals this Eternal Gospel, toward which the office of the patriarchs and prophets in the days of the Father and the office of Christ and the apostles in Christ's days have pointed (72) / If this Gospel is to be realized in the holy of holies or in our fully renewed spirits, then all human offices and statutes must cease (72)

Ewigkeit (Eternity). The great or still eternity that has been generated from the divine essence is the first and highest world. It is above and prior to eternal nature (93)

F

Fall/Abfall (Fall). The fall of man from God is a separation or alienation from the life of God and the resulting loss of inward, intimate communion with God (37) / The fall of Lucifer occasioned God to create other worlds (94) / Did God desire the fall of angels and human beings? (99/100)

Fegefeuer (Purgatory). There is no intermediate state or purgatory between the light-world and the world of darkness. Yet, for those in the lower stages of the light-world or heavenly world who are not yet fully purified, there are habitations prepared (51)

Feuer (Fire). A central fire has been implanted for fruitfulness in the new earth (4) / Wisdom's fire for melting and purification serves to refine and purify our old heaven and earth or spirit and soul (10/11) / The fire of Wisdom is demonstrated to the author (24) / It is through the love-fire of Wisdom that the old evil properties in our heaven and earth or spirit and soul are melted away, and not through the fire of wrath (53) / The love-fire is a strong and mighty fire; nothing else could destroy and eradicate the vanity, evil, sin and selfness within us (53/54) / In its own nature the love-fire is gentle and mild; therefore, it can be compared to a melting fire that destroys and devours only what is unpure (54/55) / Wisdom's fire for melting and purification prepares the way for Jesus' advent in the spirit and for the presence of the Holy Spirit in our soul and spirit (55) / The fire of Wisdom is a destroying fire that consumes and devours everything earthy in its children (57) / The fire and smelting furnace of purity must be established in the heart and experienced (58) / According to Scripture, the magical fire of Wisdom is a love-fire for one person and a wrath-fire for another in its effects (77/78) / This magical fire is mighty and devouring (78) / The fire of Wisdom within us can never be allowed to go out and must burn gently and fiercely in turn (78/79)

Fiat (Fiat). The fiat of omnipotence or the creative power of Wisdom, through which everything is renewed in man (73)

Finsternis (Darkness). In the days of the Father and the Son light and darkness struggled against each other for superiority within us; light cannot fully overcome darkness before the appearance of the Day of Wisdom (74/76) / God did not create hell or the world of darkness (94)

Fische (Fish). The fish of the sea, spoken of in *Zephaniah*, chapter 1, are a metaphor for the inconstant thoughts of man that waver and rush from place to place (63)

Fluch (Curse). What is the curse? (96/97) / Who is freed from the curse: "In the sweat of thy brow shalt thou eat bread"? Namely those who have gone down into the dust of the paradisal ground (97) / How very far that curse extends in us (97/98)

Friede (Peace). Peace is a fruit of paradise and the food of the inward new man (5)

Früchte (Fruits). The fruits of Paradise (the nourishment of the renewed man) are peace, love, gentleness, and other similar virtues (5/18/19)

Fürst (Prince). In *Zephaniah* 1:8, the prince is the Eternal Spirit, the King of Kings within man (64)

G

Gebet (Prayer). Prayer and pleading by one's own power are too weak to open the gates of Paradise (8)

Gefässe (Vessels). The golden vessels of our inner temple, which have been polluted and desecrated, are a metaphor for the sensory, rational powers and capacities of the inward eternal man (37)

Geist (Spirit). What is the spirit of Wisdom? (3/4/8) / It is the mother of our eternal soul, just as the Spirit of Eternity is the father of our eternal man (18) / The spirit of Wisdom must be united with the spirit of the eternal inward man if the Philosophers Stone within us is to be brought to full perfection (24) / The spirit of understanding departed so completely from man at the time of the fall that he eats husks with the swine and does not realize it (31) / What is the spirit of man, and how is it differentiated from the soul? (16/17) / Man's abstract spirit, which is separated from the soul, is not a person. It resides in the head (14/16/17/18) / Our spirit cannot rise up again into Paradise or into the light-world until Wisdom descends into our spirit with that same light-world and makes it a new creature (8) / Spirit and soul are two different essences, but when they are joined, the spirit has dominion over the soul and is accountable to God for its actions; for this reason the spirit should not allow the spirit of reason to have dominion and power over it (16/17/18) / The spirit is a seed that has been generated and has flown forth immediately from God, the Spirit of Eternity. It is higher in its degree than the soul; this is because the soul does not come directly from God's essence but is derived immediately from the four eternal elements, which themselves have been derived from the divine *Chaos* (17) / The father of man's eternal spirit is the Spirit of Eternity, the one true God (18) / The spirit, soul and body of the inward eternal man remain eternally inseparable, whether in heaven or in hell (18/19) / The eternal spirit of man has descended into such a state of ignorance through the fall that it no longer knows the path nor can find the door to gain its sustenance (21/22) / The spirit of man must rule over the heart's affections and passions and not be ruled by them (22/23) / Our spirit should eat flowers and herbs, not the flesh of beasts (understood in a spiritual sense) (23) / The spirit of man must be tinctured into pure gold (24) / The spirit of the eternal man is magical;

therefore, everything pertaining to it is magical (24) / The spirit is God's heavenly *Magus* and ambassador, a ministering spirit and a noble flame of fire (25) / This realm of the inward eternal man or world is as unpure in its fallen condition as he itself is (27) / This corrupted spirit is bound with chains and bonds and in the power of darkness. It is preserved in this condition until the great Day of Judgment in order to convince it that it is in darkness and not in the light (28) / In its decadence it eats only noxious herbs that grow from the corrupted earth of its heart. By eating such things, it develops a wrathful, fiery and angry nature (35) / In its fallen state the soul-spirit can only rise so high in its religious obligations as its Principle allows. Even in religion it acts only out of selfness (36) When the soul-spirit is renewed within us, everything else is renewed along with it. Then it becomes a new creature, a newly created man in true holiness and righteousness, the second Adam, a life-giving spirit (38) / When it rises again from death and the grave, the spirit of the inward man is a blessed spirit, for he lives again essentially in the life of God and in Paradise (43) / Although great struggle and anguish has accompanied the planting of the good seed in our spirit and soul for renewal, the work is by no means accomplished. We must guard carefully that the seed of astrayness does not still gain the upper hand (50) / Our eternal spirit, intellect, will and senses shall not be destroyed on the fiery judgment Day of Wisdom, but rather be refined, renewed and converted into a new creature (53) / Our eternal spirit will not be destroyed by wrath-fire on the Day of Wisdom (as long as evil, astrayness, selfness, and the outward, shallow appearance of religion are eradicated), but shall be purified and renewed by love-fire (53/54) / The spirit of Jesus and the spirit of Wisdom are one spirit (59/60) / Everything that the spirit of Wisdom accomplishes may be ascribed to the Father, Son and Holy Spirit (60) / All thoughts that tell us that we can truly be a spirit with the world, and that we must not always pray, seek God and wait upon Him in our inward holy place; all such thoughts will be eradicated from our spirit on the Day of Wisdom (64) / The eternal spirit, intellect, will and senses will be regenerated on the Day of Wisdom by the eradication of all sins and evil spirits (73) / The Holy Spirit cannot appear in our spirit and soul until Wisdom has prepared the path for it by the eradication of all sins, vanity and selfness (80) / The spirit of the eternal inward man may only be judged by his spiritual actions if he has been united to the spirit of faith (86)

Geister (Spirits). How the spirits of fear, unbelief and mistrust attempt to compromise our faith (1/7/8) / How our own spirit of reason attempts to do the same thing (9) / How numberless spirits, namely those that are unpure, shall be excluded from the New Jerusalem (27) / All earthy and satanic spirits, and those that derive from the influence of the stars and planets, must be eradicated in us on the fiery Day of Wisdom (58/61/62/64) / In the destruction of the kingdoms, Holy Scripture depicts the eradication of savage spirits in us (65) / On the Day of Wisdom all evil spirits will be devoured and burned out of our spirit and soul by fire (73) / The spirits that have departed their bodies must be perfect if they wish to enter into the glory of Mount Zion and the New Jerusalem (92)

Gelehrten ([The] Learned). The learned lacked the key to explain the obscure parables of Holy Scripture concerning heaven and earth. Therefore, they expected that the renewal of heaven and earth would take place after death (80/82)

Gemein[d]e (Congregation). The congregation of the first-born is the church of Mount Zion, which shall be established upon earth to make preparation for the office of and Day of Wisdom (67)

Gemüt (Intellect). Intellect is the first part of the spirit and is the matter to be renewed in us (8) / The intellect is the upper firmament of the heaven of the inward eternal man. Wisdom must be sun, moon and stars for the intellect, in order to drive from it the darkness of the senses cause by the fall (19/28) / The intellect must not cease to plead with Wisdom until Wisdom has perfectly renewed the temple of God within it (37/38) / The renewed intellect is an enlightened, illuminated, heavenly intellect (39) / Intellect, will and senses are the horses and chariot of the savage spirits within man (65) / Intellect, will and senses shall be refined, purified and made anew in the love-fire of Wisdom (73)

Gerichtstag der Weisheit (Judgment Day of Wisdom). This is the conviction that our spirit and soul are still unpure (27/28)

Geruch (Scent). This is the scent of the inward eternal man, which demonstrates how utterly corrupt he is (29) / What his condition is after he has been renewed (41)

Geschmack (Taste). What the taste is of the inward eternal man in his corruption (63) / What his taste is, on the contrary, after his renewal (41/42)

Gestirne (Heavenly Bodies). The divine heavenly bodies in our renewed heaven, or spirit, intellect, will and senses must influence, rule over and make fruitful the affections and passions of our new earth, or heart and soul (9/19)

Glaube (Faith). Faith is opposed, weakened and cast down within us by the evil spirits (8) / Faith is a fruit of the renewed paradise in our inner earth (11/46/47) / The strong men who, in the office and the days of the Son, fought in fierce battle against the flesh, the world and the devil, and who died in the faith of the Gospel, will enter the habitations of the valiant heroes (52)

Glorie (Glory/Splendor). No one can enter into the highest glory after his departure from the body unless he has been fully purified (51) / There will be various degrees of glory or glorification (51/52)

Goldsame (Gold seed). The Philosophers Stone is formed from the gold seed that grows in the earth of our renewed heart (44)

Gott (God). How may God be recognized within oneself? (14) / When God and man are reunited into one spirit (47) / When the highest and most essential unity and communion of God and man shall again occur (47) / God alone shall be exalted in man on the Day of Wisdom (61) / After all godless powers, authorities and spirits that dwell in the soul and spirit of man have been eradicated, then the eternal God, the Lord of Hosts, shall rule and reign in man (62/63) / The one true God and creator of the inward eternal world is the Spirit of Eternity, the Holy Trinity (90/92) / The merciful, gracious God did not created Hell or the dark world as a punishment for the eternal spirits. It was the devils themselves who did this as a punishment for their fall (94) / God was occasioned to create other worlds by the fall of Lucifer (94/95) / Does God curse? What does it mean when Holy Scripture speaks of cursing? (97) / God is the author neither of human misery nor of sin (98/99/100) / It is a completely false claim that God sends sinners to the Dragon for punishment in Hell (100/101) / God does not completely abandon or desert any sinner unless that sinner utterly breaks in his will with God (101/102)

Gottesdienst (Service of Worship). To the extent that this is performed out of selfness, it is always rejected by God (35/36) / It must always be performed in obedience to God's will if it is to be pleasing to Him (36) / All false and self-chosen service of worship must be eradicated by fire on the day of Wisdom (63/64/68)

Gottlosen (Wicked [The]). The wicked, of whom the prophets speak, are the earthy spirits and dark powers in the heart of man, and also in the affections and passions (63)

Götzen (Idols). These are images that have been impressed within us, which shall be destroyed and eradicated by fire on the Day of Wisdom. According to *Isaiah* 2:22, the idols shall then quit the man whose breath is in his nostrils (61)

Greuel (Abomination). This is called the abomination of desolation because it is set up within the office of our spirit and soul. On this account, the entire temple, including the holy of holies, the holy place and our entire service to Babylon must be destroyed and converted (67)

H

Heer des Himmels (Host of Heaven). The Host of Heaven is worshipped on the roofs of the houses (as the prophet Zephaniah said) and is the spirit of this world. He who serves this spirit also worships the influences of the stars and allows them to work, rule and reign within his spirit (64)

Heiden (Heathen). The heathen and the unbelievers of whom the prophets speak are the earthy spirits (64) / The destruction and eradication of their kingdoms is a metaphor for the destruction of the kingdom and eradication of the wicked spirits in man (65)

Heilige (Holy Place). The holy place in the temple was established by God. The holy place in our unpure heart has been trampled underfoot by the savage or evil spirits (32/33/37) / Our heart ought to be the holy place of the temple, but it has been utterly destroyed and devastated by our enemies; it has now become inhabited by evil spirits and has become a false church (37) / Wisdom desires to rebuild and re-establish this pure holy place in our heart (37/74) / How it is reopened in its renewed state in the heart (47) / When the holy of holies and the holy place are reopened in the heaven and earth, or spirit and soul of man, then he participates again in Mount Zion and the New Jerusalem (47) / When the tabernacle and the booth of holy place and the holy of holies shall descend again (47) / The holy place will be established in the heart or soul of man and the holy of holies in his spirit and intellect (69/74)

Heiligkeit (Holiness). Outward assumed holiness without inner essence is hypocrisy (35/36) / Wisdom must make an end of all self-assumed, outward holiness und destroy it in our spirit and soul, before we can enter Zion and Jerusalem (56)

Heiligtum (Sanctuary). How the sanctuary of God has been destroyed and devastated in man's heart, and when it is to be rebuilt (5)

Heiligung (Sanctification). Full sanctification will be effected in patient stillness by Wisdom in the heart of man (9)

Herbarius (Botanist). What are the abilities of a proper spiritual botanist? (21)

Herz (Heart). The heart or soul of man is his earth (16/20) / The condition of the heart in the fallen state (33/35) / The heart ought to be the holy place of God's temple but is instead a habitation of unpure spirits in the fallen state (37/38) / The renewed heart is the true Canaan (43) / The lost paradise and the Garden of Eden bloom again in the renewed heart (44) / From which heart has the covering been removed? (45) / When does the heart enjoy the blessing of the new heaven? (47) / The holy place will be established in the heart, as the holy of holies and the altar for sacrifice will be established in the intellect (47/69) / The heart of the Holy Trinity cannot be revealed to man until his spirit and soul have been fully purified by the melting fire of Wisdom (80/81)

Hieroglyphica (Hieroglyphics). These are symbols and images by which Holy Scripture points to the fiery Day of Wisdom and to the destruction of our heaven and earth (58/69/70) / The throwing down and destruction of Sodom, Egypt and Babylon are directed toward the destruction and eradication of evil in the human nature or spirit and soul, because evil has crucified and killed the divine life within them (70)

Himmel (Heaven). Wisdom desires to remake the heaven of the author (3) / The harmony of the New Heaven and New Earth within us produces fruitfulness (9) / The old heaven is the spirit, intellect, will and senses within man which, according to *2 Peter* 3:7 and 12, must be utterly refined by the fire of Wisdom on the Day of Wisdom (13/60) / Wisdom cannot move within the unpure, stained heaven and powers of man (13) / The heaven of the inward man is his spirit, intellect, will and senses (16) / The external heaven with its sun, moon and stars is merely the outward image of the eternal heaven of our inward man (19/24) / The new inward heaven is a magical heaven (24/25) / The ancient prophets cried out to the unpure, sinful heaven of the inward eternal man that it should pay heed (27/28/38) / The heaven of the fallen man is his spirit, intellect, will and senses (28) / The old heaven of the eternal man must be destroyed and refined before its renewal (28/32) / The heaven of the inward man is utterly fallen (36/37) / What Scripture says and testifies about the renewed heaven (38) / After the eternal spirit of man has been renewed, his heaven and earth or intellect, will and senses, as well as his heart, soul, affections and passions, are also renewed (38) / God's glory inhabits the New Heaven. Its light is the light of glory and of the Lamb (39) / The renewed heaven of man consists of his renewed spirit, intellect, will and senses (39) / All of the prophets prophesied concerning the renewal of the heaven and earth or spirit and soul of man (47) / The heaven and earth or spirit and soul of man were truly renewed during the office of the Father and the Son. They will remain in a mixed state of good and evil, however, and not be fully perfected or purified until the fiery Day of Wisdom (50/79) / Those who practiced true penitence in the office of the Father and the Son, and those who are still locked in battle against sin shall, when they depart the body, enter heaven but not high glory (51) / Heaven is also the heavenly or eternal world, which Christ called his Father's house (in which there are many mansions) (51/52) / On the fiery Judgment Day of Wisdom the old evil properties that intimately adhere to the heaven of man shall be melted away, but the heaven itself shall remain and shall be renewed (53/54) / After the old sinful properties of our heaven and earth or spirit and soul have been melted away by the fire of Wisdom, the new properties will reveal themselves (53) / Holy Scripture testifies to the inevitable necessity of the destruction of our old heaven and earth (53) / According to Peter's testimony, we await the new heaven and earth out of the refining of the old (53) / Our old heaven and earth, along with the earthy and dark, infernal spirits that dwell within them, were judged during the office and days of the Father and the Son but have not been melted down or destroyed. On the day of Wisdom, however, they will be refined and eradicated (58) / Our heaven and earth or spirit and soul must be refined and renewed by the fire of Wisdom before Jesus can inhabit them in spirit, along with the Holy Spirit, and before Jesus can bring down Mount Zion upon them (60) / When *Hebrews* 12:28 and *2 Peter* 3:7, 12 speak of the heaven and earth that are to be moved and melted away, they are primarily referring to the old, unpure heaven and earth in the spirit and soul of man (67/68) / The fiery office of Wisdom first convicts the old heaven and earth or spirit and soul of their impurity and then orders them to be refined (68) / The evangelical office of Wisdom is to establish the new heaven and earth as the place of descent of the New Jerusalem; the new heaven and earth must, however, first be dissolved and refined on the fiery Day of Wisdom (69) / Heaven and earth or spirit and soul (as in and of themselves eternal essences) shall not be destroyed on the Day of Wisdom; astrayness and selfness, impurities and all evil spirits shall be melted out of them; they themselves will remain (72/73) / Wisdom has commanded that the old heaven within us should be destroyed and then remade. Yet this command may also be attributed to the Father, Son and Holy Spirit (75) / The old heaven and earth within us must be melted away by the fire of Wisdom and must be renewed (77) / Our heaven and earth or spirit and soul are only purified in the fire of Wisdom, not devoured (79) / Reasons why the heaven in man must necessarily and inevitably be destroyed and renewed (80) / Until now people have not understood the renewal of spirit and soul, and have expected this to occur after death; yet this renewal must occur in human nature during life in this body (82/83) / The new heaven and earth is the Spirit of Eternity, who is the only true God, the Holy Trinity in union with Wisdom (90)

Hoffnung (Hope). Hope is a fruit of Paradise in our renewed inward earth (5/20/46/47)

Hölle (Hell). The work, day or office of the Son of God, by sowing the divine seed in the souls of believers, frees them from going to hell if they die in the faith (51) / Hell was not created by God but was fashioned by the devils themselves after their fall (94) / God did not create hell, although Babylon teaches this (98/100/101) / Where is hell? What is hell? (99) / How do sinners come to hell? (100/101)

Hunger und Durst (Hunger and Thirst). The author's hunger and thirst for Wisdom (1) / What causes this hunger and thirst? (8/10) / There is no more hunger or thirst in our renewed earth or soul and heart (46)

Hure (Whore). According to *Revelation* 17:16, the whore is the corrupted, depraved, lusting, whorish intellect in its evil nature and being that strays from God, finds its company with the creatures of this earthy world and commits promiscuity with them (70) / The destruction and eradication of this whore occurs when Wisdom brings destruction upon her with its fire. That fire consumes her flesh or burns out and devours her earthy cravings (70)

J

Jerusalem (Jerusalem). All unpure spirits will be excluded from the New Jerusalem (27) / When the New Jerusalem will be revealed in the spirit of man (47) / Wisdom prepares its children for the state of the New Jerusalem through its purifying fire (56) / When the Principle of the New Jerusalem will be created or revealed (96) / When the holy of holies in the spirit and the holy place in the soul are again revealed, man will possess and enjoy Mount Zion and the New Jerusalem (47) / He who would enter Zion and Jerusalem must enter through all four gates of Wisdom (48/49) / The New Jerusalem is the house and habitation of the fathers, elders and those who were perfected in Christ, after they departed their bodies (52) / The destruction of Jerusalem and of the temple with its holy of holies and holy place points toward all of the false churches of God and false temple service that have been established in the earthy nature of man (72) / The New Jerusalem cannot descend to us until Wisdom has fully purified the heaven and earth of man through its fire (56/80) / No unpure spirit can enter the New Jerusalem (92) / The world of the New Jerusalem (96)

Jesus (Jesus). Jesus cannot appear in spirit and glory in the unpure heaven and earth of man; they must therefore first be refined and purified (80)

Johannes der Täufer (John the Baptist). John the Baptist is the model of the fiery office of Wisdom. Just as he was the forerunner and prepared the way for the coming of Jesus in the flesh, Wisdom shall make preparation for Jesus' arrival in the spirit (55/60/65/80)

K

Kampf und Streit (Battle and Strife). The mighty battle and strife of many mortals. What does this signify? (101) See "Strife"

Kaufleute (Merchants). According to *Revelation* 18:11, the merchants of the earth who weep over the downfall of earthy nature are the inconstant senses of our intellect (71)

Kinder (Children). After their departure from the body, children who die in Christ enter a low level of the light-world (51/52)

Kirche Christi (Church of Christ). On the Day of Wisdom the true Church of Christ, which has not existed since the days of Christ and the apostles, must be established (74) / When it is equipped with everything necessary, it shall be called the House of Wisdom (74) / The horrible dissent and dispute in Babylon, where every sect claims to be the true Church of Christ (74/75) / All churches of the Antichrist are founded upon lies, with regard to Wisdom (74/75) / The true Church of Christ must be established in our spirit and soul (75)

Kleid (Clothing). The foreign clothing of which the prophet Zephaniah speaks is the foreign nature that opposes divine nature (64) / Foreign clothing cannot survive in the fire of Wisdom which melts and purifies (64)

Könige (Kings). According to *Revelation* 18:9, the kings who have committed harlotry with great Babylon or with corrupted, promiscuous human nature are the royal capacities and powers of our own eternal spirit which lament the destruction of earthy nature when they see the fire (70/71)

Königreiche der Heiden (Kingdoms of the Heathen). The kingdoms of the heathen, which the prophets threatened with destruction, are the dominant evil spirits in man (65)

Königskinder (Royal Offspring). In the prophet Zephaniah, royal offspring are the kingly powers and capacities, the eternal intellect, will and senses in man (64)

Kraft (Power/Energy). Man's own power is far too weak to overcome his spiritual enemies and must simply keep still (2) / Running around and searching, relying upon one's own powers and capacities, will not bring us to the center or Principle of Wisdom (2) / The attempt to attain Wisdom by the efforts of our own power only leads to anxious hunger, thirst and despair within us (8) / Our own power considers itself rich and happy, but it is poor, miserable, naked and wretched before God (36/37)

Kräuter (Herbs). The paradisal herbs, which grow out of the new earth or our hearts, are gentleness, good nature, friendliness, spiritual loveliness (20) / Man could live from such paradisal herbs if his lack of knowledge of his eternal spirit were not so great (21) The evil herbs that presently grow out of the corrupted earth within us (35)

Kriege (Wars). The wars of the nations arise from the confusion of light and darkness, of flesh and spirit (60) / The souls which are still involved in war and struggle will not enter into the highest level of glory when they die but will still enter the light-world (51/52)

L

Leben (Life). All life that separates us from the heavenly life must be eradicated from us by the love-fire (54) / Out of the spirit of faith the life of faith, not the life of reason, shall rule and reign on Mount Zion and in the New Jerusalem on the Day of Wisdom (62) / Sensory, rational life and also animal life must be destroyed in man (63) / All self-righteousness and all life in worship of God that is merely external or merely literal and according to the letter of Scripture must be eradicated from man on the Day of Wisdom (63)

Lehre (Teaching/Doctrine). The teaching of Christ and the apostles concerning the fiery Day of Wisdom and how it accords with the teachings of the prophets (66)

Licht (Light). During the days of the Father and the Son the divine light that is reignited in the spirit and soul battles against the darkness but cannot completely overcome it until the Day of Wisdom (74) / When did God create the Light-World or paradise? (95)

Liebe (Love). Love is a fruit of paradise and the nourishment of the new inward man (5/11/46) / When was the love-world or paradise created by God? (95)

Liebesfeuer der Weisheit (Love-Fire of Wisdom). This love-fire refines the old heaven and earth or spirit and soul in man and eradicates from them all evil spirits (58) / In the saints it is a love-fire, and in the wicked it is a wrath-fire, because all evil spirits are devoured and eradicated from man. The love-fire purifies and renews the soul and spirit of man, causing man to rejoice greatly when this work is accomplished (77/78)

Lilien (Lilies). The lilies are the divine virtues in the renewed inward earth of the heart or Eden (11)

Lippen (Lips). The lips of the inward eternal man are utterly corrupted (30) / Their condition in the renewed state (42)

Luzifer (Lucifer). In his fall from God Lucifer himself created hell or the dark world (93/94)

M

Männer (Men). Men whose souls have grown strongly in Christ do not enter immediately into the Holy of Holies or the New Jerusalem or the highest glory when their souls depart the body (52)

Maul-Christ (Lukewarm Christian). Who is the Christian who is neither hot nor cold? (36)

Medicus (Physician). Who is the spiritual physician and what is his art? (21)

Mensch (Man/Human Being). The human being must remain patient in his own capacity until Wisdom works within him, reconciles him again to God, makes him righteous and holy, and ultimately perfects him in full salvation and glorification (9) / It is not within the power of man to take the keys of Wisdom and use them (15) / Man's heaven is his spirit, intellect, will and senses (15) / His earth is his soul or heart, with his affections and passions (15) / The invisible eternal man is hidden within the outward visible man (16) / The inward man is a globe consisting of heaven and earth (16) / Man's rational powers and capacities, his spirit, intellect, will and senses are located in his head and not in his heart (16) / What man's spirit and soul actually are, and how they differ from each other (17) / The father of his eternal spirit is the Spirit of Eternity, the one true God, and its mother is eternal Wisdom (18) / The spirit and soul of man are two different essences but, together with the body, make up one person (18) / In pure nature the eternal spirit, soul and body of man make up an inward eternal, invisible human being that can inherit beatitude (18) / The inward eternal spirit, soul and body of man are eternally inseparable, whether in heaven or in hell (18) / What is the vegetable realm in the new man? (20/21) / The tremendous ignorance of the eternal spirit of man in his fallen state causes him to seek his nourishment and medicine outside of himself, although he could find them within (21) / Man's cattle, beasts of burden and other animals are his affections and passions (22/23) / His spirit must rule the animal affections and passions and not be dominated by them (22/23) / The spirit of man should not eat flesh (understood spiritually) but rather flowers and plants (23) / The mineral realm of man is located in the inward earth of his heart (23/24) /

The spirit-man must be transformed into utterly pure gold and become completely perfect if he is to enter Zion and Jerusalem (24) / The invisible eternal spirit of man is magical (24/25) / How to distinguish the inward man from the external one (25) / Whatever the condition in which a man stands (in that of the fall or of resurrection) that will be the condition of his heaven and earth also (26) / What Scripture says about who he is in his fallen state (26/27) / The man who bows down before the desires of his own will as before Baal-Peor makes himself into a god, worships the Dragon and the Beast, and bears their mark and image (27) / The fallen, unpure heaven and lights of the eternal man are his spirit, intellect, will and senses (27/28) / The inward spirit-man, in his fallen state, is dead to the divine and paradisal life (31) / The spirit of understanding departed so completely from man at the time of the fall that he eats husks with the swine and does not realize it (31) / He remains in this state as long as he continues to eat from the tree of death (31) / If the spirit of the inward eternal man eats of the fiery-wrathful plants that spring forth from the corrupted earth of his heart, he will become a similarly fiery nature (35) / How does the inner eternal man become a merely outward, sham believer and lukewarm Christian, who is neither hot nor cold? (36) / This inward eternal man becomes the new creature when he is renewed (36) / The renewed inner spirit is the spiritual man who judges all things and is judged by none (38) / This inward man is a sphere consisting of heaven and earth or spirit and soul, or a sort of small globe (48) / He lives in a state of sin and misery because he still stands under the dispensation or office of the Father and the Son (50) / The Third Day, that of the Holy Spirit, which appears within him, completely banishes, and utterly frees him of, sin (50/51) / The eradication of man, of which the prophets speak, refers to his sensual, rational life; the destruction of cattle refers to his earthy, animal life (63) / How greatly the man will lament when he see how the flame of Wisdom burns and devours within him the spiritual riches and gifts, the historical knowledge of the Scriptures, the mysteries, visions, revelations and prophecies that he commands and possesses (64) / Adam was created in the image of God to be a holy man without sin in paradise (73) / During the office of the Father and the Son men became so blinded that they decided that they could be neither freed from astrayness and selfness nor saved (73/74) / Why must the inward eternal man be regenerated and renewed? (79/80) / The illuminated eye of the inward eternal man sees and recognizes the magical earth in itself (83/84/87) / Only the spirit of the inward eternal man, illuminated by and united with the light and spirit of faith, is capable of judging spiritual matters, because it is only to him that the seeing eye is given (85) / How and in what way does man come to Hell? (100/101)

Mond (Moon). The old unpure heaven within us must be refined by the melting fire of Wisdom (13/28) / The heavenly divine moon must be placed again in the firmament of the inward man by Wisdom, in order to illuminate his intellect (19) / The moon, representative for the earthy life of the senses, must become red with shame on the Day of Wisdom (62)

/ On the fiery Day of Wisdom the moon will lose its glow within man (66) / The moon that appears as hideous as blood in *Revelation* 6:12 is the life of the senses in the earthy Principle (69)

Morgenstern (Morning Star). The bright morning star that shines in the new heaven within us is the Wisdom or spirit of God (9/19)

Mund (Mouth). What the mouth of the inward eternal man is in his corrupt state and also in his renewed state (30/31/42/43)

N

Natur (Nature). The nature of the inward man consists of heaven and earth, that is, of spirit, intellect, will and senses and soul or heart, with their affections and passions (14) / His nature will be determined by the types of nourishment, whether good or bad, that the spirit of man consumes through imagination (35) / Wisdom calls us to depart with full will from the wicked nature of our spirit and heart because they are the secret or mystical Babylon that must be consumed by fire (70) / After the downfall of the godless earthy nature in the heaven and earth of man there is great rejoicing, although men experience suffering when they see that downfall (71) / It imposes pure sorrow, worry and misery upon the inward man (71) / When it is destroyed, spirit and soul, along with the prophets and apostles, praise and magnify Wisdom (71) / The evil, earthy and satanic nature in human selfness kills the divine life and the holy blood of the prophets, as recorded in *Revelation* 18:21-24 (72) / God is highly praised for condemning the godless, earthy nature, according to *Revelation* 19:1, because it has corrupted the spirit and soul of man, has spilled the blood of the seed of life during the office of the Father and the Son, and has slain the Lamb (72) / When the earthy spirit and nature in man's intellect and heart are destroyed, then God, the Lord, the Almighty, will take up His kingdom and begin to rule therein (72) / The corrupted, evil nature will be destroyed by the fire of Wisdom, because it is Babylon within us (72/73) / The eternal nature created out of the eternal *Chaos* is the other eternal world, the immeasurable eternity and the Father's house. In this house there are many mansions prepared for the souls departed from the body, according to the witness of Christ (93) / How has the spirit of error gained such great access to our corrupted nature? (98)

O

Offenbarung (Revelation). We should not content ourselves with revelations alone because they are only exhortations that encourage us to reach out for the true essences of these revelations (25) / All revelations, visions and intuitions come to an end when we attain to their substance (48/58)

Ohren (Ears). The condition of the ears of the inward eternal man in their corrupted state and after their renewal (29/40/41)

Öl (Oil). The oil of Wisdom salves and soothes the intense fire of the inward eternal spirit (1/2) / What are the powers and virtues of this oil and how do they differ from the powers of its wine? (12) The spiritual vegetable energy-oil expels all weaknesses and diseases of the soul and takes away all complaints, troubles and sadness from the eternal spirit (21)

P

Paradies (Paradise). The inward renewed man lives from the fruits of Paradise, which are peace, love, gentleness, etc. (5) / The Paradise in man becomes verdant again by virtue of the tincture of the oil of Wisdom (5) / None of the fruits of vice grow in the renewed Paradise within man (5) / The prayer and pleading of our own powers and capacities are far too weak to open the gates of Paradise (8) / How and when the lost Paradise will again spring forth from the renewed earth or heart of the inward eternal man (20) / We must not be content to long for the renewed Paradise but must be intent upon attaining its essence (45) / When and how was Paradise created? (95/96) / The withdrawal of Paradise from the external world was the Curse (96) / When the Day of Wisdom appears, Paradise will again become visible, and the external world will be swallowed up in it (96/97)

Passionen (Passions). The strong inclinations of the heart within man are his cattle and beasts of burden (22/23/26) / How completely are they corrupted? (33/34/35/36/37) / They will be renewed along with the heart (38) / The renewed passions are heavenly and are also the feet of the soul, by which the soul may move (45/46/47) / In and of themselves, the passions shall not be destroyed on the fiery Day of Wisdom but will be refined and renewed (54/73) / The beastly and animal affections and passions should and must be eradicated from man (63) / When are the passions fully renewed? (79/80)

Patriarchen (Patriarchs). The eternal inward spirits, souls and bodies of the patriarchs, prophets and apostles of Christ remain eternally inseparable in joy (18/19)

Pfingsttag (Day of Pentecost). The perfect Day of Pentecost is yet to come. The original Pentecost brought merely the first fruits (56) / The office of Wisdom must make preparation for this perfect Day of Pentecost (77)

Philosophus (Philosopher). To be a true philosopher is to know God, Wisdom, Wisdom's Depth, and its keys in one's own self (14) / A true philosopher must know that the spirit and soul in man, in terms of their birth and origin, are two separate essences, although they comprise a single person (17/18) A true philosopher must know not only the animal and mineral realms but also the vegetable realm within himself (21) / He possesses a threefold oven for the boiling of his stone (23/24) / The true philosopher is the eternal spirit of the inward man (23) / Those who confuse Wisdom with the Holy Trinity are foolish philosophers (57)

Physicus (Natural Scientist). What does a natural scientist or a true spiritual nature expert have to know? (21)

Prophet (Prophet). The inward eternal spirits, souls and bodies of the patriarchs, prophets and apostles of Christ remain eternally inseparable in joy (18/19) All of the prophets have prophesied concerning the renewal of the heaven and earth of man or spirit and soul (47) / Their allusive way of speaking about the destruction of the heathen kingdoms points to the dominion of the evil spirits and their eradication (65) / The teaching of the prophets agrees with that of the apostles in this respect (66) / The obscure language of the prophets and apostles in Scripture must be revealed and explained by the fiery Day of Wisdom, so that man may understand it (81)

Prophezeiung (Prophecy). All of the prophecies and promises of the entirety of Holy Scripture are fulfilled when man has taken possession of Mount Zion and the New Jerusalem (47) / Prophecy is the illumination and vision of that which will take place or of what man will have or be. However, it is not the essence or possession of those things themselves (57)

Q

Quacker-Gemeinde (Quakers). On the Day of Wisdom the Quakers, like the others, will be convicted of their shortcomings (67/75)

R

Reich (Kingdom). When will the kingdom of this world become the Kingdom of God and of His Christ? (96/97)

Religion (Religion). External religion is merely a self-created balm for the guilty conscience, by which the Dragon and the Beast are worshipped (27) / Outward religion is utter hypocrisy (35/36) / That all self-constructed religious service and forms of Christianity must be destroyed and eradicated from man on the Day of Wisdom by Wisdom's fiery office (63/64) / Without the pure, just nature of Wisdom, external religion is merely an unpure garment before God (64)

Richten (Judge). No one should judge another because this is a wicked act (52)

Rosen (Roses). The roses in the renewed earth of our heart are the divine virtues (11)

S

Salbung (Anointment). The anointment with the oil of Wisdom causes all disbelief, doubt, mistrust and suspicious thoughts to flee from the soul-spirit (5) / The anointment with this oil is experienced initially as a subtle, pure, penetrating power, which permeates all of the sensory, rational powers and capacities of our spirit and soul (5)

Salomon (Solomon). The day of Solomon is a figure for the day on which Jesus will return in spirit and power (50) / Solomon's temple is a figure for all temple worship in the external man and in this world (66/67)

Same (Seed). In man the seed of grace and righteousness and the seed of sin battle and wrestle with each other for victory and superiority (50) / The Son of God sowed the divine seed in man in His days. That seed has also battled and striven within man's heaven and earth against his enemies. Because the divine was weakened by the flesh, however, and the Dragon and the Beast were still too strong, it could not completely conquer them nor completely free itself from them (55) / If we and our will persevere in the melting- and purification fire of Wisdom, it will fully destroy and eradicate the seed of the Dragon and the Beast within us (57) / Through the eradication of sin and evil the love-seed of Wisdom tramples upon the head of the serpent within us (58) / During the office and days of Christ, a seed of grace and life from God was sown in the heart of man, but it was too weak to be able to fully conquer sin, the anger and wrath of hell, or earthy nature (76) / Because this seed of eternal life was smothered and killed in the days of the Father and the Son, Wisdom has now appeared to avenge it (76)

Sanftmut (Gentleness). Gentleness is a fruit of paradise and the nourishment of the inwardly renewed man (5/20/46/47)

Schiffe (Ships). The ships of Tarshish in *Isaiah* 2:16 represent the inconstant, fleeting thoughts, imaginings and desires that will be destroyed on the Day of Wisdom (61)

Schlangen (Serpents). When and how the head of the old serpent will be trampled upon by Wisdom (47) / According to *Revelation* 12:9, the old serpent has been cast out into the external, fallen earth, where it now tempts and afflicts us day and night (98)

Schlüssel (Keys). The keys of Wisdom are the essential touches of its power within us, with which it can open all bronze doors and iron bars (14/15)

Schmelz- und Läuterungsfeuer der Weisheit (Wisdom's Fire of Melting and Purification). Wisdom's fire of melting and purification burns all astrayness and unpurity from the spirits and hearts of those who persevere in it with constancy (10/11) / This fire must refine heaven and earth, the sun, the moon and all stars within us (13/65)

Schöpfung (Creation). The creation of the new foundation and ground within us (3) / For our sake, Wisdom can bring forth this new foundation within us not all at once but gradually, from one stage to another (6) / Why is the fashioning of a new heaven and earth in human nature called a creation? (73)

Schrift (Scripture). When shall the Scriptures, beginning with *Genesis* and finishing with the *Revelation* of John, be fulfilled within us? (47/48)

Seele (Soul). Only Wisdom can break through the bronze doors and iron bars of the soul (3) / Our soul is located in the heart, and the spirit is located in the head (14/16/17/18) / The soul of man is his earth (16) / The soul and the spirit are two diverse essences (16/17) / What the nature of our eternal soul is (17) / The eternal soul is subordinated to and obedient to the spirit (17/18) / The soul is at a lower level than the spirit because it did not derive immediately from the essence of God, as did the spirit, but was born immediately from the eternal elements (17/18) / Therefore, our soul is a quintessence formed from the four eternal elements (18) / The spirit of Wisdom is the mother of our eternal soul (18) / Soul and spirit are two diverse essences yet compose a single person (18/19) / The eternal spirit, soul and body are eternal inseparable, whether in heaven or in hell (18/9) / The eternal soul is not Paradise itself; rather the lost Paradise, the Garden of Eden, blossoms forth again in it (20) / The renewed soul of man is his earth or holy place (45) / What does Scripture say about the renewed soul? (45/46) / The Holy of Holies (wherein God might again dwell) shall be established and re-opened in the renewed state of the spirit of the soul (47) / Where shall the soul, which is still engaged in struggle with its enemies, go after it departs the body? (51) / The souls that are still under the dispensation of the Father and the Son shall be saved from the Dragon's kingdom of hell and shall enter into the realm of light when they depart the body, although they will not immediately attain exalted glory nor join Christ and the greatest saints (51) / Which habitations shall the souls of children, adolescents and fathers enter when they depart the body? (52) / That the eternal souls of those who died in the office of the Father and the Son shall judge is a wicked teaching (52) / The souls, with their affections and passions, shall be refined on the Day of Wisdom by its fiery office, but they shall remain intact and shall be renewed (53/54) / They shall be purified by love-fire and not by wrath-fire (53) / All evil, vanity, sin and selfness, also self-appointed holiness and the assumed appearance of religion, must be burned out of the soul by the purifying fire of Wisdom (54) / Nothing has so hindered the coming of Jesus in spirit and power, and the appearance of the Holy Spirit, Mount Zion and the New Jerusalem, as the fact that the soul of man has not yet been purified from sin by the fiery office of Wisdom (80) / Have all the souls that departed this life during the time of the Father and the Son entered the dark world? (96) / How poor fallen souls have become a Babylon and a dwelling place for the spirit of error and all unpure spirits (97/98)

Segen (Blessings). The blessing of the world before the fall was that it was penetrated and permeated by the power of Paradise (96/97)

Selbheit/Eigenheit (Selfness). Selfness desires to serve God, but with all of its service still cannot attain Him (16/17) / Everything that arise from selfness or own-ness is displeasing to God (17)

Sichel (Sickle). The stroke of the angel's sickle in *Revelation* 14:16 and the harvesting of the earth point to the fiery destructive office of Wisdom (70)

Sinne (Senses). The senses of the inward eternal man are the matter which needs to be renewed within us (8) / These must be renewed by the Principle of Wisdom that [con]descends to us (8/9) / Wisdom cannot enter into unpure sensual powers (13) / The senses of our inward eternal man must be illuminated again by the lights which Wisdom has placed in our intellect-heaven (19) / How utterly corrupt are the senses of our eternal man? (28) / In such a corrupted state they become a man's own prison (31) / In the renewed state they become man's own freedom (43) / As long as the senses continue to eat from the forbidden Tree of Death, man is deaf, mute and dead to the life of God (31) / When the spirit is renewed, the senses of the inward eternal man are also renewed (38) / The renewed senses are the third part of the heaven of the inward man (40) / The renewed sensory life is a very valuable life in man, because he sees how Paradise has bloomed again in the spirit of his intellect and also sees Mount Zion and the New Jerusalem (43) / The entirety of corrupted sensory life shall be refined in man's spirit on the fiery Day of Wisdom (61) / These senses are the merchants of the earth mentioned in *Revelation* 18:11 (71) / The eternal intellect, will and senses will be remade on the Day of Wisdom (73)

Sion (Zion). Man possesses and enjoys this Zion when the holy place and the holy of holies are opened in his soul and spirit (47) / Whoever desires to enter into Zion and Jerusalem must enter through all four gates of Wisdom (48) / Zion and Jerusalem are the habitation of the elders, the fathers and of the perfect men in Christ, after they have departed this body (51,52, 56) / The state of Zion and Jerusalem cannot be attained without having endured the purification-flames of Wisdom (56/57/79) / The Day of Zion is the Day of Wisdom (59) / The new creation or the glory of Zion and the New Jerusalem follows upon the eradication of all sin and selfness (60) / The Day of Wisdom makes preparation for Mount Zion and for the congregation of the firstborn (67) / Mount Zion would soon descend to us if our spirit and soul were purified of all sin and selfness (76) / The world of Mount Zion and Jerusalem (96)

Sisera (Sisera). Among the spirits of this world a mighty general leading the Canaanite men at arms (59)

Sodom (Sodom). Sodom in the spirit and soul of man must be destroyed (70)

Sohn (Son). The dispensation, day or office of the Son of God saves souls from entering hell after they depart the body by sowing His wheat kernel or mustard seed within them (51) / The Son is the strongpoint around which men of might and valor rally in Christianity. Those who depart this outward life have their special habitation in the heavenly world (52) / In the days of the Son the seed of grace sown in the hearts of many saints struggled mightily with the seed of sin; that is, this was the struggle between death and life, between light and darkness. The seed of grace was not strong enough to fully overcome sin, and the saints died in this state (73/74/76) / The day and office of the Son has come to an end, and the Day of Wisdom has begun (54/55/56)

Sonne (Sun). The sun of the old unpure heaven within us must be refined by the melting fire of Wisdom (13/28) / The sun placed inwardly by Wisdom in our renewed intellect-heaven illuminates us from within (19) / The sun of which the prophets speak points to the earthy life of reason. On the Day of Wisdom it will be covered with shame (62) / It will lose its luster and light in man on the Day of Wisdom (66) / The sun which became darkened and black in the heaven of man, according to *Revelation* 6:12, is the light and life of reason (68/69)

Sophia (Sophia). Sophia, which is essential Wisdom, appears to the author, slakes his painful thirst, melts his spirit and dissolves it (1) / Its healing oil calms the spirit and alleviates and moderates the fire of the overheated soul-spirit (1/2) / He who wishes to find Wisdom must turn inward, not outward (2) See "Weisheit" (Wisdom)

Stand (State). The state of the inward eternal man in his fallen condition is miserable and lamentable (27) / All who live in this fallen state worship the Dragon and the Beast, and bear their mark and image (27) / The souls who live during the office or day of the Father and the Son depart this life in a state of grace. Although they do not enter into the full state of glory, they have still been saved and freed from the kingdom of the Dragon and from hell (51) / No one in the office of the Father or the Son can know Adam's primal sinless state (73/74)

Starken (Strong in Faith). Who are the strong in faith and where do they go after departing this life? (52)

Stein (Stone). The Philosophers Stone, or divine Wisdom, must be sought in the field and earth of the heart (23/24) / Constant, ongoing earnestness and diligence are needed for this search (24)

Sterben (Dying). The souls that depart this body during the office and days of the Father and the Son die in their immaturity as the fathers of the children of Israel died in the desert and did not enter Canaan (51/52) / All those who departed this body in doubt during the office and days of the Father and the Son died in their immaturity (73/74)

Sterne (Stars). The stars of our old unpure heaven must be refined by the fire of Wisdom (13/14) / The stars in the inward intellect-firmament of the new heaven of the eternal man are the pure effects of his imagination, thoughts and desires (19) / The stars of heaven (in man) which fell to earth, according to *Revelation* 6:13, are his imagination and thoughts (68/69)

Stille (Stillness). Our spirit must wait for Wisdom in patient stillness (24)

Streit (Strife). The battle and strife of the two seeds within man. There will be no resolution or victory until the coming of Jesus in the spirit and of the Holy Spirit (50/51) / Into what sort of habitations will the souls who have battled and struggled enter after they die? (51/52/73/74) See "Kampf" (Battle)

Sünde (Astrayness/Sin). As long as one lives in a state of astrayness and selfness, he is cut off from inward-intimate communion with God (49) / Astrayness has established itself so thoroughly in our spirit and soul that it could be completely driven out during the days and office of neither the Father nor the Son. Its final judgment will take place on the Day of Wisdom (50/54/55) / Astrayness and selfness must be completely conquered in the souls of those who desire to enter the Holy of Holies, or Zion and Jerusalem, after they depart this body (51/52) / Astrayness and all selfness must be completely driven out before the full renewal of our spirit and soul can take place (52) / On the Judgment Day of Wisdom both original sin and actual personal sin must be utterly eradicated from our soul and spirit. Nothing of them must remain, as they remained in the days of the Father and the Son (55) / All astrayness and selfness, along with all of the evil spirits that inhabit man, must be thoroughly eradicated on the Day of Wisdom by its melting fire. Then man's soul and spirit will praise God in the fire (62/65) / Astrayness and selfness are the tinder and fuel of the fire of Wisdom in man's eternal nature, which consists of heaven and earth or spirit and soul (73) / During the offices of both the Father and the Son human beings were so utterly blinded that they decided that it was impossible that man could ever be freed or saved from astrayness and selfness in this life (73/74) / Those who claim to be perfect before the Day of Wisdom, which will truly be revealed in them, appears shall be convicted of being liars on that Day of Judgment (74/75) / The melting fire of Wisdom shall utterly devour and eradicate from us all astrayness and selfness, along with all evil spirits, the Dragon and the Beast. Our soul and spirit, however, will remain intact and will be purified by this process (79) / A spirit and soul that desires to immediately enter glory after departing the outward body must be completely without sin, and without spot or blemish (92/93) / The spirit of error is the sole cause of all astrayness and evil (98) / It is God's good pleasure to forgive the astrayness of poor sinners (100)

T

Tag (Day). The Day of Wisdom, which, according to *Malachi* 4:1, will burn like an oven, must refine the old heaven and earth within us (10/11) / The conviction of the Judgment Day of Wisdom is different from the convictions and days of judgment that took place during the office of the Father and the Son (27/28) / The day of the coming of Jesus in the spirit and the advent of the Holy Spirit (for which this fiery Day of Wisdom prepares the way) cannot appear in man until all astrayness and selfness are utterly eradicated (56/65/76/77) / The final Day of Judgment of the old heaven and earth within man is the fiery office of Wisdom and the day of consumption by fire (58)

/ This fiery Day of Wisdom destroys and eradicates all earthy, satanic and infernal spirits from the heart of man, because it is only Wisdom which can achieve this (61/62/63) / On the Day of Wisdom the life of faith out of the spirit of faith will reign upon Mount Zion and in Jerusalem (62/63) / This fiery Day of Wisdom, in the refining of the spirit and soul, is a day of preparation and service for the coming of Jesus in the spirit, the advent of the Holy Spirit, and the appearance of Mount Zion and the New Jerusalem (62) / Which of the prophets prophesied concerning this Day of Wisdom? (62/63) / On the Day of Wisdom all thoughts that man is one spirit with the world and does not have to pray constantly must be eradicated (64) / The Day of Wisdom is near to those who have persevered through the days of the Father and the Son, and who are children of knowledge of the mystery (64) / The day of Wisdom will be a day of wrath, sorrow and fear, according to *Joel* 2:1, for all who will be suddenly robbed of their former spirits, powers and lives (63/64/65) / *1 Corinthians* 3:13 and *Hebrews* 12:22 also refer to the Day of Wisdom that is now being revealed (67/76) / The day of Wisdom, which must destroy all that came before, shall now arrive and be revealed (68) / The days of the Father and of the Son have already appeared (75/76) / The day of Wisdom shall make right again everything that Adam neglected (74)

Tempel (Temple). God has no temple in the unpure heart (32) / The eternal spirit and soul of the inward man is the polluted temple, in which the Dragon, the Beast, the Whore and the False Prophet are worshipped (37) / The temple of Solomon is a figure for all temple and church service in the outward man and also the Principle of this visible, external world (66/67) Solomon's temple cannot be destroyed without its holy place and holy of holies; the same is true of the mystical temple of man (67)

Teufel (Devils). In their fall the devils themselves created hell or the dark world and created their own god, the Dragon with seven heads and ten horns, who then captured their will-spirits. He holds them captive because he is stronger than they, even though he is their handiwork (93/94) / They made themselves into devils by extinguishing their gentle light and burning up their oil of love (94/99/100) / The devils can never be sure of their prey, namely wicked human beings, until they hold them fast in their dark *centrum* (101)

Thopheth (Topeth). This is the Valley of Ben-Hinnom. What does it secretly signify? (59)

Thronen oder Thron-Prinzen (Thrones or Throne Princes). These are the great throne princes who have their place within the Holy of Holies. No one may directly approach them after death except those perfect conquerors who have been fully purified and have ended their war with victory (51/52) / The thrones, powers and principalities that belong to the realm of the Dragon and the Beast shall be thrown into the pit and consumed on the fiery Day of Wisdom (62)

Tiefe (Depths). It is in the oil lamp of Wisdom that eternal Wisdom comes down into the spirit and soul of man (15)

Tier (Beast). All who have not been renewed after their fall worship the Beast and bear its mark (27/37/38) / Wisdom will destroy and eradicate the seed of the Beast, as long as we persevere in Wisdom's circulating fire (57) / The bestial life and beastly, animal affections and passions should and must be eradicated from the soul (63)

Tor (Gate). The first gate of Wisdom is the Gate of Conviction, in which man is convinced that his spirit and soul are still unpure (32/48) / Whoever desires to enter Zion and the city of New Jerusalem must pass through all four gates of Wisdom (48) / How necessary it is for us to open the Gate of Conviction, so that we can recognize that we still live in astrayness and selfness (58/95) / The second gate of Wisdom is the Gate of Renewal, which is opened by refining the spirit and soul and by eradicating all of the astrayness and selfness that adhere to them (52/53) / The third gate of Wisdom is that of further renewal and return to our original state, after we have been refined and purified (57/58) / The fourth gate of Wisdom is the pleasing and beautiful gate where full and perfect renewal takes place (72/73/81)

Trinität (Trinity). Because the Holy Trinity is prevented from dwelling within our unpure spirit and soul, they must be cleansed by the fire of Wisdom (77) / The Holy Trinity's flaming heart of love cannot be revealed to man until his soul and spirit have been perfectly cleansed by the fire of Wisdom (80/81)

Tugend (Virtue). The divine virtues are fruits of the Paradise that has been renewed within us and the nourishment of the inward new man (5) / These virtues spring forth from the renewed earth or heart within us (20)

U

Überwinder (Overcomers/Conquerors). The conquerors are those who have been perfected, who have overcome all sin, selfness, all of the seven abominable nations and all of the evil spirits in their heaven and earth. When these conquerors depart the body, they enter into the high glory of Christ, the patriarchs and the apostles (51) / The perfect conquerors and triumphant heroes who have fully ended their battles enter into the Holy of Holies when they depart this life (52)

Überzeugung (Conviction). What is Wisdom's Gate of Conviction? (31/32/48/49) / How absolutely necessary is the conviction that we are still in a sinful, unpure state? (48/49) / Each of the offices, that of the Father, of the Son, and of Wisdom, effects a different conviction within us (49) / The convictions of the Father and the Son are only preparations within us for the conviction of Wisdom (49)

Unfruchtbarkeit (Infertility). Spiritual infertility arises from the disharmony between the inner heaven and earth of the eternal man (10)

Unglaube (Unbelief). How intensely and powerfully is the soul-spirit of the one seeking God afflicted by unbelief? (1/8)

Unkraut (Tares/Weeds). The weeds that grow in our accursed, corrupted earth are the vices (11/12) / Our earth or soul must be utterly cleared of these weeds by the melting love-fire of Wisdom (11/12) / Such weeds do not grow in the renewed earth (46) / They must be utterly uprooted by the melting fire of Wisdom (53/54)

Unmündigkeit (Immaturity/Minority). All who died in the days of the Father and the Son remain in immaturity or minority (51/73/74)

Unrein (Unpure/Impure). Separating the unpure from the pure and discovering the Philosophers Stone requires steady, persistent diligence (24)

V

Vater (Father). The fathers or elders in Christ are those perfected in Him who have attained divine understanding (51/52) / The dispensation, day or office of the Father is the childhood state of a Christian. Those who die in this state have their own special habitations in the heavenly world (54/55) / Neither the day of the Father nor the day of the Son was able to completely eradicate astrayness and selfness. For this purpose the coming of Christ in the spirit and the advent of the Holy Spirit are expected (56) / The act of preparatory refining for this eradication may be attributed to the Father, Son and Holy Spirit, as well as to Wisdom (58) / The divine seed that was sown in the hearts of the saints as the beginning of regeneration in the day of the Father was not able to completely overcome and drive out the seed of sin (73/74) / Eternal nature is the house of the Father, in which there are many mansions, according to *John* 14:2 (92)

Verdammten (Damned). Their inward eternal spirit, soul and body remain eternally inseparable in the anguish of hell (16/18/19)

Vereinigung (Unification). When will the great essential unification of man with God or the wedding feast of the Lamb occur? (47) / The entirety of Holy Scripture points toward this unification, and the revelations of the prophets and apostles find their fulfillment in it (47/48)

Verherrlichung (Glorification). Glorification is achieved in patient stillness in the spirit of man (9/55)

Vermögen (Abilities). See "Eigen Vermögen und Kräfte

Vernunft (Reason). The idea of the full renewal of the inward eternal man seems impossible to the spirit of reason, and thus it tries to prevent belief in renewal. Wisdom can easily overcome this, however (9/57) / If the spirit of reason wishes to be a good chymist, it must learn to separate the toxic properties of minerals from the good ones (49) / The life of reason must be eradicated on the Day of Wisdom (54) / Reason is a false prophet who always tries to convince us that our perfect renewal is impossible (57) / Reason understands everything in Scripture wrongly. What it should understand as the eradication of sin within us it, instead, interprets as the devastation of lands and nations (56/65) / The life of reason, which is the sun for earthy man, will be disgraced on the Day of Wisdom and will no longer reign within us (62/63) / Reason interprets all of the prophecies concerning the eradication of the realm of sin and of the evil spirits who rule there as pertaining to the kingdoms and peoples of the external world (66) / The new magical earth remains unknown to the man of reason (83/84/85/87) / The man of reason is Esau (85) / One does not have to consult reason in spiritual matters. Its eye is too dim to discern these things clearly (86/87) / The man of reason cannot see the invisible earth (88)

Versuchung (Temptation). We must endure and resist temptation uprightly, as the Second Adam did (not as the First Adam), and always keep the Second Adam before our eyes as our pattern and fore-image (6) / We must earnestly implore Wisdom to be our help in resisting temptation (6)

Verzweiflung (Despair). The author's despair and terrible thoughts on account of the absence of Wisdom and the long delay in its appearance (1) / This despair is finally alleviated by anointment through Wisdom (3) / What causes such despair? (8)

Vögel (Birds). The prophets mention the birds of the air. In man these birds symbolize the fluttering, inconstant thoughts, desires and imaginings of his intellect, will and senses (63)

Vollkommenheit (Perfection). What is perfection in man? (47/48) / Perfection is the ultimate goal of all the prophets and apostles (47/48)

Vorhof (Outer Court). The outer court of the Temple is the outward man (38) / This outer court must be destroyed (67) / The inner court or the holy place signifies the heart and its service. All service that goes forth from the heart but is performed without the spirit of God must be destroyed (67)

W

Weiber (Women). All of the famous women in Scripture were simply figures for virginal Wisdom (59)

Wein (Wine). What is the wine of Wisdom? What sorts of powers and virtues does it possess? (12) / How does the wine of Wisdom differ in its ineffable powers from the properties of the oil of Wisdom? (12)

Weisheit (Wisdom). What is Wisdom? (4/8/10/11/15) / Its inward presence melts the spirit (1) / The Depth of Wisdom and the gate to it are inaccessible to a too intense fire or to a greedy spirit (2) / Whoever wishes to find Wisdom must sink down within himself in deepest humility and await its advent in the spirit (2/8) / Wisdom is not attained by climbing upward but by sinking down (2) / In the beginning, the author felt its power but did not know it, nor from whence it came (2) / It alone can break down the bronze doors and iron bars or hard shell of the soul (3) / It dwells within us only in the renewed earth of the heart (4) / Wisdom must first descend into our spirit and renew us before we are able to attain it (8/9) / Wisdom's Principle, descending to us, is the matter which must transform our spirit and soul (8) / Wisdom is such a subtle, penetrating spirit that it can break through all of the gates and doors in our spirit, then enter in to dwell and work therein (9/57/69) / Wisdom's fiery love-Principle burns out all astrayness, selfness and impurity in our spirit and soul, by means of the smelting furnace that it has established within us. Wisdom achieves this by demanding nothing less than the full acquiescence and agreement of our will (9) / Wisdom is the bright morning star in our renewed heaven (9) / According to *Malachi* 4:1, the Day of Wisdom will burn up everything from our old heaven and earth like a smelting furnace, as long as we remain constant and persevere in it to the end (11) / What the wine of Wisdom is, and how it indescribably strengthens our spirit, heart, soul and senses (12) / What it means to recognize Wisdom and its depths within oneself (14) / Wisdom's keys are its essential touches. How to recognize these keys within oneself (15) / It is not within man's power to take these keys and make use of them (15) / Wisdom acts upon eternal spirits and souls out of pity and sympathy (15) / It is superior to the spirits of men and of angels (15) / Wisdom acts with its keys in the man in whom it finds calm and serenity of spirit (15) / Wisdom is the mother of all who are marked with the divine signature, of those who seek it with earnestness and diligence and who consent to its discipline. To these it reveals itself (15) / Wisdom must be fervently implored by the soul-spirit to help it locate the Philosophers Stone (16) / Wisdom will re-establish the booth of David, the tabernacle and the sanctuary in the heart of man (38) / Man must importune Wisdom with prayers and pleading, and not rest until it has effectually found him (38) / Whoever hopes to enter Zion and Jerusalem must go through all four of Wisdom's gates (48/49) / The Judgment Day of Wisdom will utterly eradicate all evil and all seven abominable nations from the spirit and soul (55) / Its melting and purifying fire only prepares the way for the coming of Jesus in the spirit and the Day of Pentecost of the Holy Spirit (55) / Its melting and purifying Day is only an office of preparation for the great last day of the Holy Spirit. The Day of Wisdom prepares its children for Mount Zion, for the state of Jerusalem and for glorification (56) / Wisdom promises the author that he will feel and experience its fire of purification within him until all astrayness and selfness have been eradicated from him (56/57) / Wisdom courts us inwardly through its love-flame, in order to lead us up Mount Zion. Our spirit and desires turn toward the spirit of this world, however, and force Wisdom to abandon us (57) / Wisdom demands that we possess a patient, yielded will for the accomplishment of our complete renewal (57) / Wisdom alone is commanded to create a New Heaven and New Earth in us because no angel is capable of doing this (57) / Wisdom must not be confused with the Holy Trinity because it is a power that is different from the Holy Trinity yet one with it; for Wisdom can do nothing unless the Holy Trinity accomplishes the work through it (57) / It is a spirit that burns thoroughly and refines, which destroys and then renews everything (58/59) / Wisdom is pure Godhead and is one with the Holy Trinity (59/68) / Wisdom can do nothing without the Holy Trinity and the Trinity nothing without it (59/69) / Wisdom's office points to the coming of Jesus in the spirit and to Mount Zion (60) / Wisdom, with its fiery smelting oven, enters the heart and spirit of the author's intellect in order to fully refine and purify him (61/62) / In its office and days Wisdom appears in the power and zeal of Elijah against all the priests of Baal, whatever their names may be (64) / The virginal nature of Wisdom and its pure divinity; we must put this nature on, or we will not endure the melting fire of Wisdom (64) / Wisdom is the true Elijah. When Scripture speaks of Elijah and John the Baptist, these are simply figures for Wisdom's fiery destructive office (65/66) / On its Day Wisdom tears down all worship that has been created by man and not by Wisdom itself, because the worship of man is a pure Babylonian service (67/68) / Wisdom's office prepares for a new temple, priesthood and service pleasing to God (68) / In its office Wisdom is the angel of *Revelation* 14:6, who flies through the heavens or through the intellect of man (69) / It is a rapid, penetrating power (69) / Wisdom is not an angel but is rather a pure angelic power (71) / The fourth gate of Wisdom is the sweet, gracious and beautiful gate of full renewal (73) / On Wisdom's Day of destruction, when everything is restored, it will make liars of all the Babylonian churches of the Antichrist (75) / The refining and renewal of the heaven and earth within us is the day and office of Wisdom (76) / The spirit of Wisdom and the spirit of Christ are one and the same (76) / The divine-magical love-fire is the agency of Wisdom by which our spirit and soul are refined and renewed (77/78) / If we wish to experience the action of the nature of this magical fire within us, we must gather the forces within us and wait upon it (78) / In Holy Scripture the fire of Wisdom bears two different names, according to its twofold activities and effects. Depending upon the subject, it may be called love-fire or wrath-fire (78) / Wisdom is the most creative artist and the most excellent chymist (79)

Welt (World). The heavenly eternal world is the house of the Father, where there are many mansions for those who die in the savage affections and passions (51/52) / What Scripture says concerning the ultimate destruction of the old world of sin and selfness (60/61) / This external, visible world is Babylon, the forbidden tree, and the Abomination of Desolation outside of us. It must be destroyed by the fire of Wisdom (72) / The old world within man must, for his own sake, be renewed one stage after the other and not quickly (82) / There is an eternal magical world hidden in the external, visible one (89/91) / The four causes of the inner world (92) / The first and highest world is still eternity; the second is eternal nature; the third is the angelic world (93/94) / The dark, anguished world of wrath was not created by God but rather by the spirit of error in his fall (95) / The light-love-world or the paradise-world was created by God after the fall of the spirit of error (95) / The external, visible world is a birthing forth of Paradise that was created after Adam's fall (96) / Is it credible that all souls which departed the body during the office of the Father and the Son entered the dark world? (96) / Before the fall this external world was hidden within the paradise-world (98/99) / How do human beings come to hell and the dark world? Does God send them to the spirit of error? (101)

Wiedererneuerung (Restoration). The restoration of all things in the spirit and soul of man must take place before the state of Mount Zion and the New Jerusalem come into being (69/70)

Wiedergeburt (Regeneration). Our regeneration began in the days of the Father, continued during the days of the Son, and will be brought to completion during the day of the Holy Spirit (56)

Wille (Will). Our will is the matter that must be renewed within us (8) / If Wisdom is to fully renew and sanctify us, it must have the full repentance and surrender of our will (9) / The will must surrender completely to the fiery smelting oven of Wisdom and persevere within it until all astrayness, selfness and impurity have been melted out of it (11) / How completely has the will been ruined by the fall? (28) / The will shall be renewed when the spirit is renewed (38) / The renewed will is pure, holy and immaculate (40) / No unpure person may enter the holy of holies (40) / The renewed will is the throne of God and Christ from which the Dragon, the Beast, the Whore and the False Prophet have been expelled (40) / The intellect, will and senses of man are the horses and chariot of the savage spirits (65) / When the will-spirit is sufficiently overcome in the work of regeneration that the work takes hold, the greater part of the process has already been accomplished (24) / If our will-spirit perseveres with constancy in the circulating fire of Wisdom, then Wisdom will utterly destroy and eradicate the seed of the Dragon and the Beast within us (57)

Wissen (Knowledge). The historical and mystical knowledge that was useful during the days and office of the Father and the Son must perish in the devouring fire on the Day of Wisdom, because this knowledge is chiefly the property of hypocrites as long as it remains without essence (35/36/48/61) See "Erkenntnis" (Understanding/Insight)

Wohnungen (Habitations). There are many habitations in the heavenly eternal world prepared for those who died before the work of regeneration was fully accomplished in them (51) / Such habitations exist in certain levels of grace and glory (51/52) / Most people assume that there are only two possible habitations for those spirits which depart the body: either heaven or hell. This happens because they do not understand the words of Christ in *John* 14: "In my Father's house are many mansions" (92/93) / The hellish Principle cannot be reckoned among the many habitations in the Father's house because God did not create that Principle (97) / The spirits which departed the body during the days of the Father and the Son enter the eternal habitations, each according to the state and degree of its purification (96/97) / When these various habitations were created (97)

Wolken (Clouds). Clouds are the upper springs of water in the firmament of the New Heaven within us (19/20)

Worte (Words). How unpure and corrupted are the words of the inward eternal man in his fallen state? (31) / How lovely and charming, on the other hand, are the words of the renewed man? (43)

Würmer (Worms). The worms that crawl through our inward eternal earth are the earthy lusts and cravings that move in our inward parts (22)

Wurzeln (Roots). The roots of bitterness in our inward corrupted earth are the fruits of the Curse, as are all vices (12)

Z

Zauberer (Witch). Those who are bewitched by the wine and spirit of the external visible Principle, and who themselves bewitch (65) / The Witch of Endor is the external visible world, the Babylon outside of us, with which we should have no further contact (72)

Zedern (Cedars). The cedars are the trees that grow on the heights of Lebanon, as mentioned in *Isaiah*

2:12. They are the spirits that are exalted in their service of God (61)

Zentralfeuer (Central Fire). Central fire is planted in the new earth, maintains it and makes it fruitful (4) / It must be nourished by a powerful life-oil to keep it from going out (4)

Zerstörung (Destruction). The destruction or dissolution of our spirit and soul must take place before renewal can occur (53) / According to Scripture, this destruction is unavoidably necessary (53) / This destruction is not brought about by elemental or infernal fire but by the love-fire that devours only evil, sin and selfness, and which expels evil spirits (53/54) / This office of destruction occurs through John the Baptist who came to prepare the way for the birth of Jesus or for his re-appearance in the spirit (55) / The work of destruction by the Holy Trinity is attributed to Wisdom alone (59) / Although this work is attributed to the name of Jesus in the New Testament, yet the spirit of Jesus and the spirit of Wisdom are one spirit (60) / Wisdom's fiery office of destruction is an office of preparation for the coming of Jesus in spirit, as were the offices of Elijah or John the Baptist before Jesus' coming in the flesh (60/63) / Wisdom's day of destruction involves the complete eradication of all earthy, satanic and infernal spirits within man (62/65/66) / On Wisdom's day of destruction everything in man that is not built by the spirit of Wisdom upon the foundation of Jesus must be devoured by fire, according to *1 Corinthians* 3:13 (68)

Ziel (Goal). We should strive for the goal of our high calling and push forward and judge no one (52)

Zukunft (Coming [of Jesus]). The coming of Jesus in the flesh occurred in weakness; His second coming will occur in the spirit and in power (55) / What the signs of His coming in the flesh are (66/67) / Because the coming of Jesus in the spirit and of the Holy Spirit cannot take place in our unpure spirit and soul, the Day of Wisdom must precede them to purify spirit and soul, and must prepare the way (77)

Zunge (Tongue). What is the state of the tongue of the inward eternal man in its fallen and in its renewed state? What sorts of fruit does each of them bear? (29/30)

REGISTER OF SCRIPTURAL PASSAGES

Cited in this Treatise

OLD TESTAMENT

Book	Treatise Chapter	Page Number
Genesis 1:2	19	202
Genesis 2:17	13	122
Genesis 3:15	19	195
Genesis 3:17-18	22	292
Genesis 3:19	22	293
Genesis 6:5	13	127
Genesis 12:7	22	254
Genesis 15:7	22	255
Genesis 27:28	16	158
Leviticus 26:19	13	125
Deuteronomy 32:1	13	114
Judges 4:21	19	198
2 Kings 19:21	19	196

Reference	Ch	Page
Job 19:25	16	158
Job 38:7	22	284
Job 38:11	22	272
Psalm 45:9	19	197
Psalm 45:13-14	19	197
Psalm 51:10	13	136
Psalm 115:5	13	116
Psalm 115:6	13	117
Ecclesiastes 11:3	17	177
Isaiah 1:11-16	13	134
Isaiah 2:3	19	199
Isaiah 2:4	19	199
Isaiah 2:5-8	19	200
Isaiah 2:10-18	19	200/201
Isaiah 2:22	19	202
Isaiah 4:4	19	195
Isaiah 13:6-16	19	206
Isaiah 24:1-6	19	202/203
Isaiah 24:13	19	204
Isaiah 24:15	19	204
Isaiah 24:19-20	19	204
Isaiah 24:22-23	19	205
Isaiah 35:1-2, 6-7, 10	16	166
Isaiah 37:22	19	196
Isaiah 49:13	15	144
Isaiah 65:17	22	255
Isaiah 65:17	22	274
Isaiah 65:18	22	255
Isaiah 66:22	22	256

SCRIPTURAL PASSAGES

Jeremiah 22:29 .... 13 125
Jeremiah 24:10 .... 13 126
Jeremiah 31:11-14 .... 16 163
Jeremiah 31:13 .... 19 197

Hosea 2:21-22 .... 3 58

Joel 2:10-11, 31-32 .... 19 206
Joel 3:1-2, 9-17 .... 19 206

Zephaniah 1:2-3 .... 19 206
Zephaniah 1:4-5 .... 19 208
Zephaniah 1:8 .... 19 208
Zephaniah 1:11-12 .... 19 209
Zephaniah 1:15 .... 19 210

Haggai 2:21-22 .... 19 210
Haggai 2:23 .... 19 211

Zechariah 7:5 .... 13 135

Malachi 3:1-3 .... 4 62
Malachi 3:1 .... 19 211
Malachi 3:2 .... 18 183
Malachi 3:2-3 .... 18 183
Malachi 3:5 .... 19 212
Malachi 4:1 .... 4 61
Malachi 4:1 .... 18 185
Malachi 4:1 .... 21 246
Malachi 4:5 .... 19 212

SCRIPTURAL PASSAGES

NEW TESTAMENT

Book	Treatise Chapter	Page Number
Matthew 12:34	13	127
Matthew 24:2	20	216
Matthew 24:3-4	20	215
Matthew 24:4	20	216
Matthew 24:29	20	216
Matthew 24:30-31	20	216
Luke 1:46	7	80
John 1:13	15	147
John 14:2	22	280
Romans 1:26	13	128
Romans 1:29	13	128
Romans 3:13	13	121
Romans 9:16	2	37
1 Corinthians 3:13	20	218
2 Corinthians 5:17	21	249
Galatians 4:1	21	234
Galatians 5:19-21	13	128
Galatians 5:24	13	129
Galatians 6:15	21	249

SCRIPTURAL PASSAGES

Ephesians 2:2	13	110
Ephesians 4:22	13	110
Ephesians 5:5	22	282
Philippians 2:6	18	186
Colossians 1:12-13	22	287
Colossians 1:16	22	268
Colossians 3:5	13	129
Colossians 3:9	13	110
1 Thessalonians 5:23	7	81
2 Thessalonians 2:11-12	13	111
Hebrews 4:12	7	81
Hebrews 12:22	20	219
Hebrews 12:26	20	219
Hebrews 12:26-27	18	181
1 Peter 1:7	21	248
1 Peter 4:12-13	21	248
2 Peter 2:14	13	116
2 Peter 3:7-10	18	181
2 Peter 3:7-10, 12	18	185
2 Peter 3:7	20	219
2 Peter 3:10	18	180
2 Peter 3:10	20	220
2 Peter 3:12	6	69
2 Peter 3:12	18	181
2 Peter 3:12	20	220

2 Peter 3:13	2	41
2 Peter 3:13	22	254
Revelation 6:12	20	221
Revelation 6:13	20	221
Revelation 6:15-17	21	244
Revelation 11:1-2	14	140
Revelation 11:8	20	224
Revelation 12:3	22	285
Revelation 12:9	22	295
Revelation 12:12	15	145
Revelation 12:12	22	295
Revelation 14:6	20	222
Revelation 14:8	20	225
Revelation 14:16	20	225
Revelation 16:1	21	244
Revelation 17:9	15	146
Revelation 18:2	20	225
Revelation 18:2	22	294
Revelation 18:8	21	244
Revelation 18:8	21	246
Revelation 18:9	20	226
Revelation 18:11	20	227
Revelation 18:17	20	227
Revelation 18:20	20	227
Revelation 18:22-24	20	227/228
Revelation 19:1	21	245
Revelation 19:1-6	20	228
Revelation 21:1	18	180
Revelation 21:1	20	223
Revelation 21:1	21	250
Revelation 21:1	22	256
Revelation 21:23	15	144

Revelation 21:27 .... 13 112
Revelation 21:27 .... 22 282
Revelation 22:5 .... 15 144
Revelation 22:15 .... 13 112
Revelation 22:15 .... 22 282

SCRIPTURAL PASSAGES

www.ingramcontent.com/pod-product-compliance
Lightning Source LLC
Chambersburg PA
CBHW021815300426
44114CB00009BA/186